HEBREWS AND THE GENERAL EPISTLES

READING AND INTERPRETING THE BIBLE SERIES

HEBREWS AND THE GENERAL EPISTLES

KEVIN L. ANDERSON

THE FOUNDRY
PUBLISHING®

Copyright © 2023 by Kevin L. Anderson

The Foundry Publishing®
PO Box 419527
Kansas City, MO 64141
thefoundrypublishing.com

ISBN 978-0-8341-4171-1

Cover design: Caines Design
Interior design: Jody Langley

Unless otherwise indicated, all Scripture quotations are from the Holy Bible, New International Version® (NIV®). Copyright © 1973, 1978, 1984, 2011 by Biblica, Inc.™ Used by permission of Zondervan. All rights reserved worldwide. www.zondervan .com. The "NIV" and "New International Version" are trademarks registered in the United States Patent and Trademark Office by Biblica, Inc.™

Scripture quotations marked AT are the author's translations.

The following version of Scripture is in the public domain:
The King James Version (KJV)

The following copyrighted versions of Scripture are used by permission:
The Common English Bible (CEB). © Copyright 2011 Common English Bible. All rights reserved.

The Christian Standard Bible (CSB). Copyright © 2017 by Holman Bible Publishers. Christian Standard Bible® and CSB® are federally registered trademarks of Holman Bible Publishers. All rights reserved.

The ESV® Bible (The Holy Bible, English Standard Version®), copyright © 2001 by Crossway, a publishing ministry of Good News Publishers. All rights reserved.

GOD'S WORD® (GW). Copyright © 1995, 2003, 2013, 2014, 2019, 2020 by God's Word to the Nations Mission Society. Used by permission of Baker Publishing Group. All rights reserved.

The Lexham English Bible (LEB). Copyright 2012 Logos Bible Software. Lexham is a registered trademark of Logos Bible Software.

The New American Bible, revised edition (NABRE). Copyright © 2010, 1991, 1986, 1970 Confraternity of Christian Doctrine, Washington, D.C. and are used by permission of the copyright owner. All rights reserved. No part of the New American Bible may be reproduced in any form without permission in writing from the copyright owner.

The New American Standard Bible® (NASB®), Copyright © 1960, 1971, 1977, 1995, 2020 by The Lockman Foundation. All rights reserved.

New American Standard Bible® (NASB1995), Copyright © 1960, 1971, 1977, 1995 by The Lockman Foundation. All rights reserved.

The NET Bible® (NET) copyright © 1996, 2019 by Biblical Studies Press, L.L.C. http://netbible.com. All rights reserved.

The New Jerusalem Bible (NJB), published and copyright © 1985 by Darton, Longman & Todd, Ltd., and Les Editions du Cerf.

The New King James Version® (NKJV). Copyright © 1982 Thomas Nelson. All rights reserved.

The Holy Bible, New Living Translation (NLT), copyright 1996, 2004, 2015 by Tyndale House Foundation. Used by permission of Tyndale House Publishers, Carol Stream, IL 60188. All rights reserved.

The New Revised Standard Version Updated Edition (NRSVUE). Copyright © 2021 National Council of the Churches of Christ in the United States of America. All rights reserved worldwide.

The Revised English Bible (REB), copyright © Cambridge University Press and Oxford University Press 1989. All rights reserved.

The Revised Standard Version (RSV) of the Bible, copyright 1946, 1952, 1971 by the Division of Christian Education of the National Council of the Churches of Christ in the United States of America. All rights reserved.

Library of Congress Cataloging-in-Publication Data

A complete catalog record for this book is available from the Library of Congress.

The internet addresses, email addresses, and phone numbers in this book are accurate at the time of publication. They are provided as a resource. The Foundry Publishing® does not endorse them or vouch for their content or permanence.

Contents

Abbreviations[1]

General

//	used to denote parallel passages (e.g., 2 Pet. 1:17 // Matt. 17:5)
ANE	Ancient Near East
ANF	*Ante-Nicene Fathers.* Edited by Alexander Roberts and James Donaldson. 1885-87. 10 vols. Christian Classics Ethereal Library. http://www.ccel.org/fathers.html.
AT	author's translation
BDAG	*A Greek-English Lexicon of the New Testament and Other Early Christian Literature* (see Danker)
c.	century
ca.	circa
CE	Catholic Epistles
ch(s).	chapter(s)
d.	died
esp.	especially
fl.	Latin, *floruit,* "flourished"
Ger.	German
Gk.	Greek
Hebr.	Hebrew
LCL	Loeb Classical Library
LW	*Luther's Works.* American Edition. 55 vols. Edited by Jaroslav Pelikan and Helmut T. Lehman. Philadelphia: Muehlenberg Press and Fortress Press; St. Louis: Concordia, 1955-86.
LXX	Septuagint
MS(S)	manuscript(s)
NPNF[1]	*Nicene and Post-Nicene Fathers.* Series 1. Edited by Philip Schaff. 1886-90. 14 vols. Christian Classics Ethereal Library. http://www.ccel.org/fathers.html.

---

1. Abbreviations for ancient works primarily follow the conventions of *The SBL Handbook of Style* (Peabody, MA: Hendrickson, 1999), sec. 8.3, and occasionally W. H. Lampe, *A Patristic Greek Lexicon* (Oxford: Clarendon, 1961), xi-xlv.

NPNF²	*Nicene and Post-Nicene Fathers*. Series 2. Edited by Philip Schaff. 1890–1900. 14 vols. Christian Classics Ethereal Library. http://www.ccel.org/fathers.html.
NT	New Testament
OT	Old Testament
𝔓	symbol for papyrus manuscripts, always accompanied by a superscript number (e.g., 𝔓⁴⁶, the earliest extant collection of Paul's letters)
PG	Patrologia Graeca [=*Patrologiae Cursus Completus*: Series Graeca]. Edited by Jacques-Paul Migne, 162 vols. Paris, 1857-86.
PL	Patrologia Latina [=*Patrologiae Cursus Completus*: Series Latina]. Edited by Jacques-Paul Migne, 217 vols. Paris, 1844-46.
TLG	Thesaurus Linguae Graecae® Digital Library. Edited by Maria C. Pantelia. University of California, Irvine. http://www.tlg.uci.edu.

English Versions

CEB	Common English Bible
CSB	Christian Standard Bible
ESV	English Standard Version
GW	GOD'S WORD Translation
KJV	King James Version
LEB	Lexham English Bible
NABRE	New American Bible (Revised Edition)
NASB	New American Standard Bible (2020 update)
NASB1995	New American Standard Bible (1995 update)
NET	New English Translation
NIV	New International Version
NJB	New Jerusalem Bible
NKJV	New King James Version
NLT	New Living Translation
NRSVUE	New Revised Standard Version Updated Edition
REB	Revised English Bible
RSV	Revised Standard Version

Apocrypha

| 1 Macc. | 1 Maccabees |
| Sir. | Sirach/Ecclesiasticus |

Old Testament Pseudepigrapha

1 En.	*1 Enoch (Ethiopic Apocalypse)*
4 Ezra	*4 Ezra*
Jub.	*Jubilees*
T. Levi.	*Testament of Levi*

Jewish Writings

Dead Sea Scrolls

| 1QS IV | *Rule of the Community* (col. IV) |

Josephus

| *Ant.* | *Jewish Antiquities* |

Philo

| *Abr.* | *De Abrahamo* |

Rabbinic Works

'Abot	*'Abot*
'Abot R. Nat.	*'Abot de Rabbi Nathan*
Meg.	*Megillah*
Pirqe R. El	*Pirqe Rabbi Eliezer*
Ta'an.	*Ta'anit*
Tg. Ps.-J.	*Targum Pseudo-Jonathan*
Zebaḥ.	*Zebaḥim*

Apostolic Fathers

Barn.	*Barnabas.*
1 Clem.	*1 Clement*
Herm. Mand.	*Shepherd of Hermas, Mandate(s)*
Herm. Vis.	*Shepherd of Hermas, Vision(s)*
Ign. *Smyrn.*	Ignatius, *To the Smyrnaeans*
Ign. *Trall.*	Ignatius, *To the Trallians*
Mart. Pol.	*Martyrdom of Polycarp*
Pol. *Phil.*	Polycarp, *To the Philippians*

Other Church Fathers

Amphilochius of Iconium
　　Seleuc.　　　　　*Epistula Iambica ad Seleucum*
Augustine
　　Civ. Dei　　　　　*De civitate Dei*
　　Conf.　　　　　　*Confessionum libri XIII*
　　Doctr. chr.　　　　*De doctrina christiana*
　　Tract. ep. Jo.　　　*In epistulam Johannis ad Parthos tractatus*
Clement of Alexandria
　　Paed.　　　　　　*Paedagogus*
　　Strom.　　　　　*Stromata*
Cosmas Indicopleustes
　　Top.　　　　　　*Topographia christiana*
Cyprian
　　Ep.　　　　　　　*Epistulae*
　　Fort.　　　　　　*Ad Fortunatum*
　　Test.　　　　　　*Ad Quirinum*
Cyril of Jerusalem
　　Catech.　　　　　*Catechetical Lectures*
Epiphanius
　　Pan.　　　　　　*Panarion (Adversus haereses)*
Eusebius
　　Comm. Ps.　　　　*Commentarius in Psalmos*
　　Eccl. theol.　　　　*De ecclesiastica theologia*
　　Hist. eccl.　　　　*Historia ecclesiastica*
Gregory of Nyssa
　　Homilies　　　　　*Homilies on the Song of Songs*
Irenaeus
　　Haer.　　　　　　*Adversus haereses*
Jerome,
　　Epist.　　　　　　*Epistulae*
　　Helv.　　　　　　*Adversus Helvidium de Mariae virginitate perpetua*
　　Vir. ill.　　　　　*De viris illustribus*
John Chrysostom
　　Hom. Heb.　　　　*Homiliae in epistulam ad Hebraeos*
　　Hom. Rom.　　　　*Homiliae in epistulam ad Romanos*

Justin Martyr
    1 Apol.   *Apologia i*
Origen
    Cels.   *Contra Celsum*
    Comm. Jo.   *Commentarii in evangelium Joannis*
    Comm. Matt.   *Commentarium in evangelium Matthaei*
    Comm. Rom.   *Commentarii in Romanos*
    Fr. Jo.   *Fragmenta in evangelium Joannis*
    Hom. Exod.   *Homiliae in Exodum*
    Hom. Jer.   *Homiliae in Jeremiam*
    Or.   *De oration (Peri proseuchēs)*
    Sel. Deut.   *Selecta in Deuteronomium*
    Sel. Ps.   *Selecta in Psalmos*
Philaster
    Haer.   *Diversarum haereseon liber*
Rufinus
    Symb.   *Commentarius in symbolum apostolorum*
Tertullian
    Cult. fem.   *De cultu feminarum*
    Marc.   *Adversus Marcionem*
    Pud.   *De pudicitia*
Victorinus of Pettau
    Comm. Apoc.   *Commentarii in Apocalypsin*

Other Ancient Writers

Epictetus
    Diatr.   *Diatribai (Dissertationes)*
Quintilian
    Inst.   *Institutio oratoria*

PART I

Most Christians are familiar with the two major parts of the New Testament: the Gospels and the Epistles of Paul. The Acts of the Apostles, standing between these two collections, supplies a lively narrative of the apostolic witness in the earliest days of the church. Placed at the very end of the biblical canon, the book of Revelation has the dubious distinction of being the only document in the New Testament that Christians have obsessed over or, alternately, entirely ignored. Then there are the eight books that come between Paul's letters and the Revelation: Hebrews, James, 1–2 Peter, 1–3 John, and Jude. These forgotten books in the back of the Bible are reminiscent of the fabled "Island of Misfit Toys" in the television Christmas classic *Rudolf the Red-Nosed Reindeer* (1964). Nobody quite knows what to do with them. They are too often neglected and misunderstood. The reasons for this are complex and constitute what we might call the challenge of Hebrews and the Catholic Epistles.

1

The Challenge of Hebrews
and the Catholic Epistles

The ancient philosopher Antisthenes (ca. 446–ca. 366 BC) was once asked what learning is the most necessary. He replied, "The removal of what one needs to unlearn."[1] Since the rise of historical criticism over three hundred years ago, biblical scholars have learned interpretive habits that need to be unlearned. We will encounter some of them as we explore six challenges related to Hebrews and the Catholic Epistles (CE).

We begin with challenges related to Hebrews and the CE, not because we wish to find fault with them, but because we want to learn how to interpret them better. Before we can formulate an appropriate approach to reading and interpreting Hebrews and the CE, we must acknowledge the elephant in the room: these books have had a checkered history from ancient times until today. They have been susceptible to misunderstanding, neglect, and controversy. It is no wonder one scholar has called them "the ugly stepchildren" of the New Testament (NT).[2] Only once we have grasped their colorful and storied past can we begin to imagine anew how Hebrews and the CE may be appropriated as channels of divine grace and truth for the Christian church today.

The Challenge of Categorization

The formation of the NT canon involved assembling four major "collection units": (1) the Gospels, (2) the Acts of the Apostles and the Catholic Epistles (James, 1–2 Peter, 1–3 John, Jude), (3) Paul's letters (often fourteen

---

1. Diogenes Laertius, *Lives of Eminent Philosophers* 6.1.7, AT.
2. Blomberg 2016, 463.

in number, including Hebrews), and (4) the Revelation.[3] In chapter 3 we will contemplate the arrangement of Hebrews and the CE in our current Bibles and its significance for interpretation. Presently we will survey some of the ways modern scholarship organizes—or rather, reorganizes—the material in the NT.

Since the advent of historical criticism, scholarly approaches to the Bible have tended to disregard the canonical divisions of the NT. The fourfold Gospel canon (Matthew, Mark, Luke, and John) has given way to studying the Synoptic Gospels (Matthew, Mark, and Luke), on the one hand, and the Fourth Gospel (John), on the other. The Gospel of Luke and the Acts of the Apostles are often treated together as Luke's two-volume work (Luke–Acts). It is not uncommon to bring together the Gospel of John and the three Epistles of John (and sometimes Revelation) under a heading such as "Johannine Traditions."[4] The Epistles of Paul are something of an exception. Even a more critical approach that recognizes only seven authentic letters[5] would yet consider the six so-called deutero-Pauline letters[6] as part of the legacy of Paul's theological thinking. Hence, the Pauline corpus holds together, though in an attenuated fashion.[7]

Historical criticism also subjects Hebrews and the CE to its atomistic and disintegrative analysis. Hebrews has long been a castaway from the Pauline corpus. Scholars usually study it as a stand-alone document, having little in common with either the Pauline letters or the CE. Modern scholars virtually never acknowledge the CE as a coherent whole. Scholars generally study each letter in isolation from the others. Of course, the Johannine Epistles (1–3 John) are studied together due to their common stylistic and theological characteristics. Second Peter and Jude are regularly studied in tandem because of the apparent literary relationship between them. Even commentaries that cover 1 and 2 Peter in the same volume often do not treat them as belonging together.

---

3. Trobisch 2000, 26.

4. For example, Johnson 2010.

5. Romans, 1–2 Corinthians, Galatians, Philippians, 1 Thessalonians, Philemon.

6. Colossians, Ephesians, 2 Thessalonians, 1–2 Timothy, Titus.

7. So also Nienhuis and Wall 2013, 9-10n22.

Consequently, scholars usually regard Hebrews and the CE (often along with Revelation) as a mixed bag of documents thrown together at the end of the NT.[8] In introductions to the New Testament, after sections on the Gospels, Acts, and Paul's letters, it is common to find a section labeled "Other New Testament Writings," "Other Canonical Witnesses," "Letters by Other Church Leaders," or "Hebrews and the Catholic Epistles: Non-Pauline Christianity."[9] A recent collection of essays on Hebrews and the CE is appropriately titled *Muted Voices of the New Testament*.[10] David Nienhuis concludes, "Compared to the Gospel and Pauline collections, mainstream contemporary scholarship apparently finds it difficult to think of these seven letters [the CE] as much more than an amorphous grouping of 'other writings' with a limited sense of internal coherence."[11] Moreover, scholars primarily weigh the "otherness" of Hebrews and the CE over against the tacit superiority of the Pauline corpus.

Rarely will one find Hebrews *called* one of the Catholic or General Epistles.[12] Andrew Lincoln identifies Hebrews as "the first of what are frequently called the Catholic epistles," and he places it within the last of four NT divisions: "The Gospels, The Acts of the Apostles, The Letters of Paul, and The General Epistles and Revelation."[13] Such miscategorization creates an added layer of confusion and has no precedent in the ancient reception of the NT books. By the early fourth century, as we will see, Christians recognized *seven* letters in the canonical collection known as "the Catholic Epistles," but Hebrews was not among them.

Modern scholarship has often abandoned the ancient, canonical structure of the NT. Severing or reconfiguring relationships between NT books has surely contributed important insights, but it has also injected a measure of confusion. We propose that interpreters take a second look at Hebrews and the CE in their canonical context. We will pursue this line of inquiry in chapters 2 and 3.

---

8. Ibid., 5-8.
9. Respectively, Martin 1978; Johnson 2010; Marshall, Travis, and Paul 2016; Hagner 2012.
10. Hockey, Pierce, and Watson 2017.
11. Nienhuis 2017, 4.
12. McNeile 1953, 201; Varughese 2005, 298; Bateman 2013, 20.
13. Lincoln 2006, 1.

The Challenge of Authorship

Throughout the history of Christianity, people have questioned the authorship of every single one of our eight documents (Hebrews and the seven CE). The apostolic authorship of 1 Peter and 1 John was accepted as far back as our patristic sources take us (early second c.), but not as readily by many biblical scholars today. Even in ancient times the authorship of the remaining books was scrutinized. In one instance (2 Peter), there was widespread suspicion that the work was pseudonymous. In another (James), there was a claim by "some" that the letter was published by someone else in his name.[14] In other cases, questions focused on the precise identity of the named author.

With respect to the Epistles of James and Jude, the identity of their authors is often dependent on how one construes the makeup of the holy family. Eastern Christians, who believed that James and Jude were the stepbrothers of Jesus via Joseph's previous marriage, acknowledged that each letter was written by a "brother" of the Lord. Western Christians usually followed Jerome's view that these "brothers" of Jesus were really cousins, born of the Virgin's sister, another Mary. Both James and Jude were also numbered among the original twelve apostles: James son of Alphaeus and Thaddeus (Matt. 10:3; Mark 3:18; Thaddeus being equivalent to Judas son of James in Luke 6:16; Acts 1:13[15]). Most contemporary scholars identify the implied authors of James and Jude as two half brothers of Jesus among the four listed in Mark 6:3 (// Matt. 13:55), children born to Joseph and Mary after the birth of Jesus.

Both 2 and 3 John are addressed from a certain "elder." Christians have traditionally attributed the two letters—along with 1 John, the Fourth Gospel, and the Revelation—to the apostle John. Some attributed 2 and 3 John to another John in Ephesus known as John the Elder. Modern scholarship has dished up a smorgasbord of theories on the authorship of the Johannine writings that are too elaborate to survey here.[16]

---

14. Jerome, *Vir. ill.* 2 (*NPNF*[2] 3:361).

15. See also Jerome, *Helv.* 15 (*NPNF*[2] 6:340-41).

16. Especially, Brown 1979, 25-58; Brown 1982, 69-115; for summaries of compositional theories, see Culpepper 1998, 29-41; Burge 2013, 57-76.

The problem of authorship for the Epistle to the Hebrews is well known, as is Origen's oft-repeated pronouncement: "But who wrote the epistle, in truth, God knows."[17] The Eastern church strongly held to Pauline authorship from as early as the late second century, as evidenced by the inclusion of Hebrews in our earliest surviving collection of Paul's letters ($\mathfrak{P}^{46}$, ca. 200). The Western church equally strongly resisted Pauline authorship until around the turn of the fifth century. Tertullian (d. ca. 225) casually identified Barnabas as the author of Hebrews. Over the centuries many other possibilities proliferated. Among the ancients, common suggestions were Clement of Rome or Luke (as Paul's translator). Martin Luther (1483–1546) famously suggested Apollos. Adolf von Harnack (1851–1930) proposed Priscilla (assisted by Aquila), though few scholars have concurred.[18] Since Hebrews is formally anonymous, it is inappropriate to argue that it is a pseudo-Pauline writing, but even this has been proposed.[19]

James, 1–2 Peter, and Jude (whose salutations name an apostle or brother of Jesus as the author) are commonly considered pseudonymous by modern scholars. Issues of authorship are also essential to the upcoming section titled "The Challenge of Canonization" (p. 27).

The Challenge of Setting

Decades ago, William Lane published an article titled "Hebrews: A Sermon in Search of a Setting."[20] There, as well as in his popular[21] and full-length[22] commentaries, Lane proposed a reconstructed setting for Hebrews: it was written to beleaguered Christians in Rome sometime between the great fire of AD 64 and Nero's suicide in AD 68. As plausible as this theory is, there are not enough specific data in Hebrews to identify the time or geographical location of either the author or recipients with any certainty. The question of whether the letter was written before or after the destruction of Jerusalem's temple in AD 70 remains a point of contention. Internal evidence about

17. Eusebius, *Hist. eccl.* 6.25.14 (*NPNF*[2] 1:273).
18. Hoppin 2009.
19. Rothschild 2009.
20. Lane 1985b.
21. Lane 1985a, 21-25.
22. Lane 1991, lx-lxvi.

the letter's setting is frustratingly ambiguous. Take, for example, Hebrews 13:24*b*, "Those from Italy send you their greetings." Does it imply that the original readers were in Rome or that the author was writing from Rome?

John Chrysostom (ca. 347–407) held to the earliest known theory regarding the setting of Hebrews. The author (Paul) wrote from Rome to Jewish Christians in Jerusalem (and Palestine) who had long suffered at the hands of unbelieving Jews.[23] Since the 1700s, most scholars have argued for a Roman destination for Hebrews, but until more recently there were scholars who suggested Alexandria. As a further indication of the difficulty in nailing down the setting for Hebrews, there is even a debate about whether the recipients were Jewish, Gentile, or a mixed group of Christians. However, the consensus, going back to ancient commentators, is that they were Jewish Christians.

The challenge of determining setting extends to the CE. All but James and 1 Peter provide us with no information about the geographical location of the author or recipients. First John contains no opening address to identify either the author or intended readers. The only concrete reference to the situation addressed by the letter is the allusion to a schism that happened in the community (2:19). Second John is cryptically addressed "To the lady chosen by God and to her children" (v. 1), and 3 John to an otherwise unknown "Gaius" (v. 1). Only church tradition informs us that the author was in Ephesus and that his readers were in churches located somewhere in the Roman province of Asia.

Both 2 Peter and Jude have an address that identifies each letter's recipients in rather generic Christian terms (2 Pet. 1:1; Jude v. 1). In the case of Jude, the traditional view of authorship leads to the inference that the author was centered in Jerusalem and his readers somewhere in Judea, Galilee, and/or Syria. The author's use of Old Testament (OT) Pseudepigrapha (*1 Enoch* and the *Testament of Moses*) may also point to a first-century Judean setting. As for 2 Peter, acknowledging it as Peter's "second letter" (3:1) ties its intended audience to the same five geographical regions listed in 1 Peter 1:1.

James and 1 Peter are the most fully expressive concerning their addressees. Yet fundamental questions remain. James is addressed "To the twelve

---

23. John Chrysostom, *Hom. Heb.* "Argument and Summary of the Epistle" (*NPNF*[1] 14:363-65).

tribes in the dispersion [*en tē diaspora*]" (James 1:1, NRSVUE). But does this mean that James was writing to all Jews in the Diaspora? Or was he addressing himself only to Christian Jews? Or is the phrase "the twelve tribes in the dispersion" an appropriation of a stock Jewish identity marker to refer to all Christians, whether Jew or Gentile?

Likewise, Peter's address "To those who are elect exiles of the Dispersion [*diasporas*]" (1 Pet. 1:1, ESV) could relate to either Jewish or Gentile Christians. All three descriptors ("elect," "exiles," "Dispersion") belong to the heritage of Israel as depicted in the OT. The "Dispersion" has been subject to varying interpretations. Does it refer to Jewish Christians who live outside the promised land? Or is the author applying the "Dispersion"—historically related to the deportation of Judeans to Babylon (sixth c. BC)—to Gentile Christians who have experienced a kind of exile of their own? Many interpreters take the expression in a metaphorical sense to refer to the way believers live as exiles within wider Roman society. Others go even further to take it in the sense that believers are currently exiled from their true home in heaven.

We could write at length about the setting for each of our eight letters, but what we have presented here is enough to show that drawing up a complete picture of the occasion and setting for each letter is a considerable challenge.

The Challenge of Genre

Traditionally, all of Hebrews and the CE are called "letters" or "epistles." Understanding the epistolary genre of these NT documents is crucial to their interpretation.

Five of our biblical books are easily identifiable as ancient letters: 1–2 Peter, 2–3 John, and Jude. They have all three major components of an ancient letter: (1) letter opening with an address (sender to receiver) and greeting, (2) letter body, and (3) letter closing with concluding greetings or (in 2 Peter and Jude) a closing doxology. In its letter opening, 1 Peter also contains a thanksgiving or blessing (1:3-9), such as we find in Paul's letters.

The most neglected books of the NT are 2–3 John and Jude, in part due to their brevity (2 John: 245 words; 3 John: 219 words; Jude: 461 words).[24] Ironically, their small size is what makes them most like other ancient letters, which averaged about 87 words.[25] Even these letters exceed the average length; the rest of the NT letters far exceed it. The Letter to the Hebrews is the third largest letter in the NT (4,953 words) behind Romans (7,111 words) and 1 Corinthians (6,829 words).[26]

Hebrews and James present a kind of mirror image in epistolary form. Whereas James opens with a customary address and greeting, Hebrews does not. While James does not contain a standard letter closing, Hebrews contains the most extensive epistolary closing of any of our eight documents, complete with a benediction (13:20-21), final exhortation (v. 22), travelogue (v. 23), and closing greetings (vv. 24-25). Both Hebrews and James are similar in that their remaining bulk consists of exhortations (paraenesis) and teaching. Both are indebted to the patterns of logical argumentation from Greco-Roman rhetoric, though Hebrews does so with greater sophistication. James draws deeply from the Hebrew wisdom tradition. Scholars often identify each as either a homily or series of smaller homilies. The author of Hebrews identifies his own work as a "word of exhortation" (13:22), an expression used to label Paul's synagogue sermon in Acts 13:15.

First John poses the greatest challenge to determining its genre. It contains virtually no epistolary features whatsoever, apart from the author's frequent first-person references to writing (13x) and his affectionate address to his readers throughout ("Dear friends" [agapētoi], 6x). It has no standard letter opening (address and greeting) or closing (e.g., final greeting). Rather, it begins with a prologue (1:1-4)[27] and ends with a terse, final exhortation (5:21). Thus some scholars reach for the lowest common denominator by

---

24. See Just 2005.

25. Bateman 2013, 25.

26. Just 2005.

27. Among NT letters, only Hebrews and 1 John begin with a prologue, and both commence with a period—that is, a sentence composed of carefully balanced clauses (Heb. 1:1-4; 1 John 1:1-3a).

dubbing 1 John a "writing"[28] or "paper."[29] I. Howard Marshall concludes that it is a "written sermon or pastoral address."[30]

The Challenge of Theological Difficulties

Theological conundrums abound in the Bible. Often a given theological problem or puzzle exists more in the eye of the beholder or in the misunderstanding of the reader than in a fair-minded and informed interpretation of the text. Hebrews and the CE have their share of theological difficulties—some rankling readers since ancient times and others emerging solely among modern readers.

A primary theological difficulty in Hebrews is its strong impression on readers that they could lose their salvation. The letter contains five severe warnings against apostasy (2:1-4; 3:7–4:13; 5:11–6:12; 10:19-39; 12:14-29).[31] Since the Reformation, Protestants have wrangled over whether the warnings deal with a projected falling away from the faith that is serious and real (an Arminian or Wesleyan interpretation) or are merely rhetorical or hypothetical (a common Reformed or Calvinist interpretation).

What bothered ancient Christians, however, was the repeated claim of Hebrews that apostasy is irreversible, a second repentance impossible (6:4; 12:17). An early Christian writer, the Shepherd of Hermas (ca. 150), relaxed the rigorist position of Hebrews by allowing one postbaptismal opportunity for repentance from sin.[32] Tertullian railed against "that apocryphal 'Shepherd' of adulterers" and cited Hebrews 6:1, 4-6 in support of his position that there is no "second repentance" after baptism for serious sins such as fornication and adultery.[33] Montanists in the second century and Novatians in the third employed Hebrews to authorize their belief that Christians who had renounced their faith under persecution could not be restored to salvation or be readmitted into the church. So, in addition to doubts about the Pauline authorship of Hebrews, the writing's misappropriation by sectarians

---

28. Johnson 1993, 13.
29. Smalley 2015, xxxiii.
30. Marshall 1978, 14.
31. See Bateman 2007.
32. *Herm. Mand.* 4.3.1-7; see *Herm. Vis.* 2.2.4-5.
33. Tertullian, *Pud.* 20.

contributed to its rejection in the West.[34] In truth, Hebrews's concern about a point-of-no-return apostasy does not match the third-century controversies over the church's proper response to lapsed Christians who sought restoration.[35]

According to certain past interpreters, the Epistle of James presents theological difficulties of the highest order. There are two significant matters: a deficient Christology and an aberrant doctrine of salvation. The first, a deficient Christology, has mostly to do with what is *lacking* in James. The letter only mentions the "Lord Jesus Christ" twice (1:1; 2:1), and the other references to "the Lord" (*ho kyrios*) more likely concern God than Christ. Some scholars have proposed that James was originally a thoroughly Jewish work and that the references to the "Lord Jesus Christ" are later Christian interpolations. Virtually no one accepts this view today.[36] There is no textual evidence to support it. Yet it gives one pause to find, as Luther observed, that James "does not once mention the Passion, the Resurrection, or the Spirit of Christ."[37] The author is keen to provide his readers with wisdom teaching about righteous living, but he never holds up Jesus as the example. He points instead to OT figures such as Abraham (James 2:21, 23), Rahab (v. 25), Job (5:11), and Elijah (v. 17).

We can make two quick points in response to these difficulties. First, the two references to Jesus (1:1; 2:1) encapsulate a high Christology, since Jesus is designated as both "Lord" and "Christ." The expression "our glorious Lord Jesus Christ" may be rendered "our Lord Jesus Christ, the Lord of glory" (2:1, ESV; cf. KJV, RSV). Other translations such as "Jesus Christ, our glorified Lord" (NJB) and the paraphrastic "our Lord Jesus Christ, who has been resurrected in glory" (CEB) capture the sense that Jesus Christ is the incarnate, crucified, risen, and exalted Lord. Second, while James never invokes the life of Jesus as an ethical example, the letter's ethical instruction is saturated with Jesus's wisdom teaching, especially from the Sermon on the Mount.[38] The

---

34. Gamble 1985, 52; Koester 2001, 23. Gaius, a presbyter in Rome (early third c.), did not accept Hebrews in response to the Montanists' use of it (Photius, *Bibliotheca*, 48; see also Metzger 1987, 102). Philaster (d. ca. 397) reported that churches in the West did not read Hebrews because it lent itself to the Novatians' false view on repentance (*Haer.* 89).

35. See Anderson 2013, 190-91, 204-10.

36. See Davids 1982, 3, 5; Moo 2000, 12.

37. *LW* 35:395.

38. deSilva 2018, 725.

strong Jewish flavor of James speaks to its early Judean origins, while our two points about the identity and ethical teaching of Jesus favor its unambiguously *Christian* character.

The second theological difficulty in James has to do with the doctrine of salvation. We will have the opportunity to deal with this problem in chapter 6, so here we will focus on the problem itself without proposing any solution. James appears to contradict Paul's statements that salvation is by faith and *not* works (Rom. 3:27-28; 4:1-10; Gal. 2:16; 3:1-14; Eph. 2:8-9). James states that a faith that saves (2:14) is one that cooperates with and is perfected by works (v. 22). It is important to note that during the centuries of canon formation the church did not see Paul and James as contradictory but rather complementary on this point. Then, in the early sixteenth century, Martin Luther championed the doctrine of *sola fide* (faith alone)—an expression that does not occur in Paul (except in Luther's rendering of Rom. 3:28!); however, it does appear in James, but only to be negated: "You see that a person is considered righteous by what they do and *not* by faith alone" (James 2:24, italics added). Luther famously characterized James as "an epistle of straw" because "it has nothing of the nature of the gospel about it."[39] More specifically, Luther stated that James "is flatly against St. Paul and all the rest of Scripture in ascribing justification to works."[40] On another occasion, Luther lashed out at James because of its use by papists, writing, "I almost feel like throwing Jimmy into the stove."[41]

Perhaps the most curious theological difficulty is in 1 Peter. The author asserts that before Christ's heavenly exaltation (3:22), he "made proclamation to the imprisoned spirits" (v. 19). Three interpretations of this text have prevailed.[42] The first is the view that the preincarnate Christ preached through Noah to spirits who are now imprisoned in hell. A second view, reflected in the Apostles' Creed, is that Christ descended into hades to preach grace (and release) to imprisoned spirits who had disobeyed in the time of Noah. The third view is that Christ announced ultimate defeat to fallen angels who had

---

39. *LW* 35:362.
40. Ibid., 396-97.
41. *LW* 34:317; see Althaus 1966, 81.
42. Jobes 2011, 313.

been kept in chains in anticipation of being judged for leading Noah's generation into sin. This last view enjoys wide support among modern scholars because of its parallels to material in *1 Enoch*, also echoed in 2 Peter 2:4 and Jude v. 6.

We have already observed that 2 Peter had difficulty making it into the canon due to doubts about its authenticity (i.e., apostolic authorship). Though 2 Peter 1:4 expressly underwrites the Eastern church's doctrine of *theosis* and is "the high-water mark of the Christian revelation,"[43] a troubling theological problem presents itself in the third chapter of the letter. The sixth-century Nestorian monk, Cosmas Indicopleustes, wrote the eccentric work *Christian Topography* (ca. 547). In it he strenuously opposes a purported theological falsehood that could be derived from 2 Peter 3:7-13—that the present cosmos will be annihilated and replaced by new heavens and a new earth.[44] Following longstanding Eastern tradition, Cosmas interprets 2 Peter 3 to mean transformation and purification rather than dissolution. He uses 1 Corinthians 7:31 ("For the form [*to schēma*] of this world is passing away" [NASB1995]) as the skeleton key for unlocking such problem texts (including Ps. 102:26-28; Rev. 20:11; 21:1).[45] But for Cosmas, his ace in the hole against 2 Peter 3 is the letter's doubtful canonicity. Only the three greater CE (James, 1 Peter, and 1 John) were accepted by Syrian Christians.

Even the beloved letters of John—which tradition ascribes to the "Apostle of Love," John the son of Zebedee—contain some thorny issues. First John promotes a strong moralism that one could readily interpret as sinless perfection (2:1*a*; 3:6, 8, 9; 5:18; but see 1:8, 10; 5:16-17). The possibility of believers having "perfect love" (4:18; see 2:5; 4:12, 17) appealed to John Wesley (1703-91) and became one of the foundation stones for his doctrine of Christian perfection.[46] But interpreters of every stripe have struggled mightily to make sense of the Johannine teachings concerning the Christian's relationship to sin[47] (see ch. 7). What compounds the trouble for modern readers in

---

43. Bruce 1988, 251.
44. Cosmas Indicopleustes, *Top.* 10.
45. Irenaeus (*Haer.* 5.35.2; 5.36.1 [*ANF* 1:566]) was likely the first to marshal 1 Corinthians 7:31 as a key text in opposition to the Valentinian Gnostic doctrine of cosmic destruction.
46. Wesley 2015.
47. Brown 1982, 411-16; Kruse 2000, 126-32.

a pluralistic society is that such high morality and the accentuation of perfect love stand side by side with an inflexible theological exclusivism.[48] Worse yet, such exclusivity comes to expression in actual schism (2:19) and the elder's direct command to refuse hospitality to itinerant teachers who do not conform to orthodoxy (2 John v. 9)—a favor returned by his nemesis, Diotrephes (3 John vv. 9-10).

Jude is the only NT book that appeals to material from the so-called Pseudepigrapha. The Pseudepigrapha are works, often written under the pseudonyms of ancient Hebrew worthies, that expand the OT's historical, prophetic, apocalyptic, and wisdom literature. Written during the intertestamental period, none of these writings (with few exceptions) is considered part of canonical Scripture by any Jewish or Christian group.[49] Jude alludes to a story in *1 Enoch* 6–8 (Jude v. 6), another in the *Assumption of Moses* (Jude v. 9), and quotes *1 Enoch* 1.9 as a prophetic oracle (Jude vv. 14-15). This obviously raises the theological question about the boundaries of the biblical canon. According to Jerome, many rejected Jude because he quotes from the spurious book of *Enoch*.[50] Tertullian (d. ca. 225), however, held to *1 Enoch* as an authoritative prophecy. Thus the fact that Jude quotes *1 Enoch* presents decisive evidence for Jude's authenticity.[51] With this little conundrum about Jude and noncanonical *1 Enoch*, we appropriately turn to the final challenge concerning Hebrews and the CE: their canonization.

The Challenge of Canonization

The church's confession today concerning the twenty-seven books of the NT is unwavering and has been so for many centuries. It is quite a different matter when certain individuals or movements neglect certain biblical books and privilege others, thereby setting up a "canon within the canon." Examples of this impulse are Luther's demotion of Hebrews, James, Jude,

---

48. Culpepper 1998, 299-303.

49. For the OT Pseudepigrapha, see Charlesworth 1983-85; Bauckham, Davila, and Panayotov 2013. The Pseudepigrapha should not be confused with the Apocrypha. Also composed during the intertestamental period, the books (or parts of books) in the Apocrypha made their way into the Christian Bible via their inclusion in the Greek version of the OT, the Septuagint (LXX). Roman Catholics and Orthodox Christians accept the Apocrypha as part of the biblical canon (though of secondary authority, i.e., "deuterocanonical") while most Protestants reject them.

50. Jerome, *Vir. ill.* 4 (*NPNF*[2] 3:362).

51. Tertullian, *Cult. fem.* 1.3 (*ANF* 4:15-16).

and Revelation in the sixteenth century and, in the twentieth century, Ernst Käsemann's estimation of 2 Peter as "perhaps the most dubious writing in the canon."[52]

Isolated doubt about the relative value of a given NT book falls far short of an authoritative conciliar decision about the canon. Therefore, the *canonicity* of none of the twenty-seven books of the NT is currently in question. But the process of *canonization* during the first four or five Christian centuries was certainly untidy and for a time left the status of some books in jeopardy. The messiness of the process was in no small part related to the books we are presently studying.[53]

Hebrews

The canonicity of Hebrews may well have become a fait accompli sometime in the second century. At that time a Christian scribe in Egypt included Hebrews in an edition of Paul's letters. From around AD 200 onward, the place of Hebrews among Paul's Epistles—and therefore in the NT canon—was certain among Eastern Christians.

Our earliest evidence of the knowledge and usage of Hebrews comes from the West. The author of *1 Clement* (before 70 or ca. 96)[54] clearly incorporates material from Hebrews, though never explicitly identifies its author or acknowledges it as Scripture. *First Clement* 36:1-6 echoes Hebrews's majestic opening (esp. Heb. 1:3-4, 7, 13) and relies on "its distinctive presentation of Jesus as Son and high priest."[55] In the mid-second century, both the Shepherd of Hermas and Justin Martyr knew and used Hebrews. Justin calls Christ an "Apostle,"[56] such as only Hebrews does in the NT (Heb. 3:1).

---

52. Käsemann 1964, 169.

53. Our discussion of the reception of the books of Hebrews and the CE into the canon is necessarily brief. Readers may consult the major studies on the biblical canon for further information (Westcott 1896; Souter 1913; Lohse 1981; Bruce 1988; Metzger 1987; McDonald 2017, esp. 2:257-62 on Hebrews and the CE). Biblical commentaries will often include an introductory section about a book's canonization (e.g., for Hebrews: Lane 1991, cl-clv; Ellingworth 1993, 34-36; Koester 2001, 19-27). One may now also consult extensive treatments of the canonical history of the CE (Schlosser 2004; Nienhuis 2007, 29-97; Nienhuis and Wall 2013, 17-39, 77-79, 108-14, 171-74, 223-25; Lockett 2017, 59-90).

54. Thomas J. Herron (1989 and 2008) has made an argument for a pre-AD 70 date for *1 Clement*, considered persuasive by the notable expert on the Apostolic Fathers, Clayton Jefford (2006, 18-19). The consensus view is that *1 Clement* was written ca. AD 96 during the reign of Emperor Domitian.

55. Lane 1991, cli-clii.

56. Justin Martyr, *1 Apol.* 12, 63 (*ANF* 1:166, 184).

The earliest canonical list, the Muratorian Canon (ca. 175–ca. 200), lacks Hebrews. Around this same time, Irenaeus (ca. 135–ca. 202) comments on Hebrews in a nonextant work.[57] In Irenaeus's work *Against Heresies*, he refers to God's creation "by the word of his power," echoing Hebrews 1:3.[58] Hippolytus (ca. 176–ca. 236) seems to have known Hebrews, as well.[59] Photius (ca. 810–ca. 895) later reports that both Irenaeus and Hippolytus rejected the Pauline authorship of Hebrews,[60] an opinion shared by their contemporary, Gaius of Rome (ca. 200).[61] As for the early Latin theologians in Carthage, North Africa: Tertullian (d. ca. 225) idiosyncratically attributes Hebrews to Barnabas,[62] while Cyprian (d. 258) shows no familiarity with it whatsoever.

The earliest evidence of an Eastern tradition about the Pauline authorship of Hebrews springs from Alexandria in the early third century. The oldest extant codex containing Paul's letters, $\mathfrak{P}^{46}$ (ca. 200), includes Hebrews immediately after Romans. Clement of Alexandria (ca. 155-ca. 220), following his teacher Pantaenus (d. ca. 200), provides explanations for the presence of Hebrews among the Pauline letters, despite its formal, stylistic, and missional departures from the Apostle to the Gentiles. According to Clement, Paul omitted his usual prescript, "Paul the Apostle," so as neither to be off-putting to a suspicious Hebrew audience nor to trespass beyond the boundaries of his apostolic mission among the Gentiles (Gal. 2:7-9). Hebrews's deviation from Paul's writing style may be explained by the theory that Paul originally wrote in Hebrew, which Luke (or Clement of Rome) then translated into Greek.[63] For Origen (ca. 185–ca. 254), however, Hebrews's superior style makes Pauline authorship unlikely, though its contents belong to Paul's thought world. Ultimately, Origen happily counts Hebrews among Paul's writings while remaining agnostic about who wrote it.[64]

---

57. Eusebius, *Hist. eccl.* 5.26.3 (*NPNF²* 1:244-45).
58. Irenaeus, *Haer.* 2.30.9 (*ANF* 1:406).
59. Westcott 1896, 387.
60. Hippolytus, *Bibliotheca*, codices 121, 232.
61. Eusebius, *Hist. eccl.* 6.20.3 (*NPNF²* 1:268).
62. Tertullian, *Pud.* 20; de Boer 2014.
63. Eusebius, *Hist. eccl.* 6.14.2-4 (*NPNF²* 1:261); see 3.38.2-3; 6.25.14 (*NPNF²* 1:169, 273).
64. Ibid., 6.25.11-14 (*NPNF²* 1:273).

Eusebius (early fourth c.) regards Paul's fourteen Epistles—including Hebrews—as "obvious and plain."[65] Yet he is careful to acknowledge that the church of Rome rejected Hebrews as not being written by Paul.[66] Athanasius of Alexandria (ca. 296–373) is the first to list the twenty-seven books of our NT (no more, no less) in his *Thirty-Ninth Festal Letter* of AD 367, placing Hebrews among Paul's "fourteen Epistles." During his exile in Rome (early 340s), Athanasius may have influenced Roman acceptance of Hebrews as an authentic letter of Paul's.[67] Western theologians who spent considerable time in the East, such as Hilary of Poitiers (ca. 315–ca. 367), Rufinus (ca. 345–411), and Jerome (ca. 345–420), helped to push Western opinion about the canonicity of Hebrews to align with that of the East.

Even late in the fourth century, the Eastern churchman Amphilochius of Iconium (ca. 340–ca. 395) finds it necessary to bat away doubts about Hebrews as "spurious," insisting that "its grace is genuine."[68] Meanwhile, Jerome and Augustine (354–430) decisively steer the West toward acceptance of Hebrews into the canon, despite their doubts about its Pauline authorship. Accordingly, both list Hebrews at the end of the Pauline corpus, after Philemon.[69] Over his lifetime, Augustine became increasingly convinced that Hebrews is anonymous.[70] Jerome shared this decoupling of canonicity from authorship.[71] He noted its ancient acceptance in the East as Pauline, as well as alternative views of authorship (Clement or Barnabas), but then declared, "And it makes no difference whose it is, since it is from a churchman, and is celebrated in the daily readings of the Churches."[72]

The Western view of Hebrews at the end of the fourth century—that is, as canonical, even if not written by Paul—is reflected in the Third Council of Carthage (397; mirroring the Council of Hippo in 393). The canon list includes "the Epistles of Paul, thirteen; of the same to Hebrews, one Epistle."[73]

---

65. Ibid., 3.3.5 (LCL).
66. Ibid., 3.3.5; 6.20.3 (*NPNF²* 1:134, 268).
67. Bruce 1988, 221.
68. Amphilochius of Iconium, *Seleuc.* lines 308-9; Bruce 1988, 213.
69. Jerome, *Epist.* 53.9 (*NPNF²* 6:101); Augustine, *Doctr. chr.* 2.8.13 (*NPNF¹* 2:539).
70. Souter 1913, 191.
71. Bruce 1988, 227, 232.
72. Jerome, *Epist.* 129.3; Lincoln 2006, 4.
73. Metzger 1987, 315.

The Sixth Council of Carthage (419) erased the line of separation between Hebrews and the Pauline letters, listing "Fourteen Epistles of Paul."[74] However, it could not eradicate the persistent reservations about Pauline authorship in the West, which the likes of Erasmus, Luther, and Calvin would fan into flame in the sixteenth century.

The Catholic Epistles

When Eusebius completed his *Ecclesiastical History* (ca. 325), two facts about the NT canon had become certain since the time of Origen (d. 254). First, twenty-seven books could be enumerated among "the writings of the New Testament."[75] Second, in the interval between Origen and Eusebius, the seven letters—James, 1–2 Peter, 1–3 John, and Jude—were formed into a collection under the name "Catholic Epistles."[76] However, Eusebius's knowledge of historical sources and current church practice made it clear that the tally of NT books varied. Some churches and prominent church leaders regarded fewer than twenty-seven books to be authoritative. Others were using additional books besides them. A parade example is the great uncial manuscript from the fourth century, Codex Sinaiticus, which contains all twenty-seven NT books but appends the *Epistle of Barnabas* and a large portion of the *Shepherd of Hermas*.

Consequently, Eusebius was obliged to categorize books in such a way as to reflect the complexity of the situation.[77] His system of classification, a modification of Origen's,[78] differentiates several classes of books.[79]

The first category includes "accepted" or "recognized" books (homologoumena): the Gospels, Acts, Epistles of Paul (including Hebrews), 1 John, 1 Peter, and (tentatively) the Apocalypse of John. Thus the church widely acknowledged twenty-one or twenty-two books of the NT in the early fourth

---

74. Ibid., 238.

75. Eusebius, *Hist. eccl.*, 3.25.1-3 (*NPNF*[2] 1:155-56).

76. Ibid., 2.23.25 (*NPNF*[2] 1:128).

77. Ibid., 3.25.1-7 (*NPNF*[2] 1:155-57).

78. Lohse 1981, 23-24.

79. Eusebius's classification is not altogether clear. The following scholars have made a reasonably coherent construal of his categories: Lohse 1981, 23-24; Metzger 1987, 203-6; Bruce 1988, 198-200; Nienhuis 2007, 63-70; see also the dated but full discussion by Lawler and Oulton (Eusebius 1927-28, 2:100-104).

century. Elsewhere Eusebius refers to such books as "unquestionable" and "acknowledged by all."[80]

Eusebius's second category involves "disputed" books (antilegomena), but these books fall into two subcategories: (1) books that "nevertheless are recognized [gnōrimōn] by many"[81] and (2) books that are "rejected" (noutha).[82] Books both "disputed" yet "recognized by many" are James, Jude, 2 Peter, and 2–3 John. "Rejected" books are the *Acts of Paul, Shepherd of Hermas, Apocalypse of Peter, Epistle of Barnabas, Didache,* Apocalypse of John, and *Gospel of the Hebrews.*

Eusebius's third category includes apocryphal books that claim apostolic authorship or association.[83] Eusebius does not give a label to this category but comes close to it when he states that these books do not even rise to the level of the "rejected" books; they must rather be *paraitēteon*—that is, "cast aside."[84] These books do not have a literary style that is apostolic, nor do their contents align with orthodoxy. They are heretical fabrications.

Three points about Eusebius's classification of books are germane to our study. First, Hebrews is silently positioned among Paul's fourteen epistles in the category of universally "recognized" books (first category), even though Eusebius was well aware that it was contested, particularly in Rome. Second, two of the CE, 1 Peter and 1 John, are listed as universally "recognized" books (first category), while the remaining five CE (James, 2 Peter, 2–3 John, and Jude) constitute entirely the subclass of books that are "disputed" though "recognized by many" (second category, subcategory 1). Third, Eusebius places the Apocalypse of John in *both* the first category ("recognized") *and* subcategory 2 of the second category ("rejected")!

1 Peter and 1 John

It is not surprising that 1 Peter and 1 John are among the universally acknowledged books. They are attested in some of our earliest Christian

---

80. Eusebius, *Hist eccl.* 3.3.7 (Eusebius 1927-28, 1:66).
81. Ibid., 3.25.3.
82. Ibid., 3.25.4-5.
83. Ibid., 3.25.6-7.
84. Ibid., 3.25.7 (*NPNF*[1] 1:157).

sources, the Apostolic Fathers. We find echoes of both letters in the *Epistle of Barnabas*[85] and rather clear usage of them by Polycarp.[86] Eusebius confirms the knowledge of both letters in Asia Minor in the early second century, for he states that Papias (a contemporary of Polycarp) employed testimonies from 1 John and 1 Peter.[87] Late in the second century, Irenaeus is the first to cite both 1 Peter[88] and 1 John by name.[89] Interestingly, Irenaeus does not seem to distinguish between 1 and 2 John, leading scholars to believe that he viewed them as one book[90] or 2 John as a "covering letter" for 1 John.[91] Clement of Alexandria cites 1 John as "the larger Epistle," implying at least one other letter.[92] By the third century, 1 John makes its mark in the Latin West, while attestation for 1 Peter is scarce, as evidenced by its omission from the Muratorian Canon. Tertullian quotes 1 John forty or fifty times[93] but 1 Peter only twice.[94] Both 1 Peter and 1 John are acknowledged as undisputed writings by Origen in the early third century[95] and by Eusebius in the early fourth.[96]

James, 2 Peter, and 2–3 John

It is also not surprising that James, 2 Peter, 2–3 John, and Jude end up in Eusebius's "disputed" category. Undeniable testimony to the existence of James does not occur until Origen (d. 254).[97] Even late in the fourth century, Jerome reports that some believed it had been written by someone else in James's name.[98] Scholars disagree on whether there are any echoes of James in the earlier writings of *1 Clement* or the *Shepherd of Hermas* (among others). There is one possibly clear allusion to James 2:23 in Irenaeus,[99] and Clement

---

85. *Barn.* 5.6 (// 1 Pet. 1:2); 5.9-11 and 12:10 (// 1 John 4:2); 14.5 (// 1 John 3:4, 7, 8); see Brown 1982, 7.

86. Pol. *Phil.* 1.3 (// 1 Pet. 1:8, 12); 2.1 (// 1 Pet. 1:13, 21); 8.1-2 (// 1 Pet. 2:21, 22, 24; 4:16); 10.2 (// 1 Pet. 2:12); 7:1 (// 1 John 3:8; 4:2-3); 7:2 (// 1 John 2:7, 24; 3:11); see Michaels 1988, xxxii; Brown 1982, 9. Given the bulk of allusions, Metzger (1987, 62) states that Polycarp "must have known [1 Peter] practically by heart."

87. Eusebius, *Hist. eccl.* 3.39.17 (*NPNF*[2] 1:173).

88. Irenaeus, *Haer.* 4.9.2; 4.16.5; 5.7.2 (*ANF* 1:472, 482, 533).

89. Ibid., 1.16.3; 3.16.5, 8 (*ANF* 1:342, 442-43).

90. Brown 1982, 10.

91. Painter 2002, 42.

92. Clement of Alexandria, *Strom.* 2.15 (*ANF* 2:362).

93. Brown 1982, 10.

94. Westcott 1896, 269n2.

95. Eusebius, *Hist. eccl.* 6.25.5, 8, 10 (*NPNF*[2] 1:273).

96. Ibid., 3.3.1; 3.25.1-2 (*NPNF*[2] 1:133, 155-56).

97. Origen, *Comm. Jo.* 19.6; Origen, *Hom. Exod.* 15.25.

98. Jerome, *Vir. ill.* 2 (*NPNF*[2] 3:361).

99. Irenaeus, *Haer.* 4.16.2 (*ANF* 1:481).

of Alexandria may have written a commentary on all of the CE, including James;[100] but both claims are disputed.[101] The doubtful status of James in the East was already dissipating when Eusebius was writing his *Ecclesiastical History*, for elsewhere he cites it as an authoritative writing[102] or "Scripture" coming from "the holy Apostle."[103] From the time of Eusebius forward, "every major church father (Cyril, Athanasius, Epiphanius, Gregory [of Nyssa], and Amphilochius) and codex of the NT (Sinaiticus, Vaticanus, and Alexandrinus) place James as the lead letter in a collection of seven called 'catholic.'"[104]

Though for centuries James was scarcely used in the West and is missing from the Muratorian Canon (ca. 175–ca. 200), suddenly at the turn of the fifth century its canonical place became certain there too. During his exiles in Gaul (335/336) and Rome (337-46), Athanasius may have inclined the West toward acceptance of Hebrews and the five disputed CE.[105] It is even possible that Athanasius *introduced* James to the West.[106] Latin fathers such as Hilary of Poitiers (d. ca. 367), Ambrosiaster (late 4th c.), and Jerome and Augustine were pivotal in securing James's place within the canon.

Second Peter's canonical status was precarious all the way up to the time when Athanasius wrote his famous canon list in AD 367. The *Apocalypse of Peter* (ca. 110-ca. 140) may have used 2 Peter, and though there *might* be echoes of it in the Apostolic Fathers,[107] Origen is the first to express direct knowledge of it—though as a disputed letter.[108] The earliest manuscript to contain 2 Peter (as well as 1 Peter and Jude) is $\mathfrak{P}^{72}$, which may have been copied in Origen's lifetime.[109] It was once thought that Didymus the Blind (ca. 313-98), in a commentary on the CE dubiously attributed to him, marked 2 Peter as "counterfeit."[110] However, the discovery of attested commentaries by Didymus in 1941 at Toura, south of Cairo, reveals his use of 2 Peter as

---

100. Eusebius, *Hist. eccl.* 6.14.1 (*NPNF*² 1:261).

101. On Irenaeus, see Nienhuis 2007, 36; on Clement, see Nienhuis 2007, 48-50; Lockett 2017, 73-75.

102. Eusebius, *Eccl. theol.* 2.25.3; 3.2.12.

103. Eusebius, *Comm. Ps.*, PG 23:505.7-8; 23:1244.34; thus Westcott 1896, 432n2; Mayor 1910, lxvii.

104. Ninehuis and Wall 2013, 78.

105. Bruce 1988, 223.

106. Yates 2004.

107. Picirilli 1988. Regarding the *Apocalypse of Peter*, a recent study argues, rather, that 2 Peter made use of it (Grünstäudl 2013).

108. Eusebius, *Hist. eccl.* 6.25.8 (*NPNF*² 1:273).

109. Bruce 1988, 193; Lockett 2017, 81-82.

110. Bray 2000, 157-58.

"authentic and authoritative."[111] In the great fourth-century codices Sinaiti-cus and Vaticanus, it is ensconced among the twenty-seven NT books, and beyond the time of Athanasius's canonical list, any doubts expressed about it are isolated. Jerome is aware of skepticism concerning the Petrine authorship of 2 Peter due to its stylistic differences from 1 Peter[112] but offers the explana-tion that Peter used different amanuenses.[113]

The presence of 2 John was not strongly felt until the late second century, and that of 3 John was not felt at all until the early third century. Irenaeus is the first to quote 2 John as the work of "John, the disciple of the Lord"[114] but later quotes from both 1 and 2 John as from the selfsame letter.[115] The Muratorian Canon's reference in line 68 to "two of the above-mentioned (or, bearing the name of) John" is difficult to decipher. Most scholars believe that 1–2 John are intended by the wording,[116] but some read the evidence to mean that 2–3 John are being referenced in addition to the aforementioned 1 John quoted in lines 29-31.[117] In any case, Origen is the first to bear unambigu-ous witness to the grouping of all three Johannine Epistles, though reporting doubts about the authenticity of 2–3 John.[118] Origen's successor, Dionysius of Alexandria (d. ca. 264), distinguishes between "the Catholic Epistle" (i.e., 1 John) and "the reputed" 2–3 John.[119] Eusebius places 2–3 John among the "disputed" books due to the question of whether they were written by "the evangelist" or "another person of the same name."[120]

Among Latin theologians there are no definite references to 3 John until Jerome and Augustine. Even after all three epistles were included in the major canon lists in the late fourth and early fifth centuries, scholars could still regis-ter the persistent suggestion that 2–3 John were possibly authored by a certain John the Elder rather than the apostle John.[121]

---

111. Metzger 1987, 213; see Ehrman 1983.
112. Jerome, *Vir. ill.* 1 (*NPNF*² 3:361).
113. Jerome, *Epist.* 120.11.
114. Irenaeus, *Haer.* 1.16.3 (*ANF* 1:342).
115. Ibid., 3.16.5, 8 (*ANF* 1:442-43).
116. Manson 1947, 32-33; Bruce 1979, 18-19.
117. Lightfoot 1904, 99-10; Moffatt 1918, 478-79; supplementary note to Eusebius, *Eccl. hist.* 3.24.17 (*NPNF*² 1:388); Katz 1957.
118. Eusebius, *Hist. eccl.* 6.25.10 (*NPNF*² 1:273).
119. Ibid., 7.25.7, 10-11 (*NPNF*² 1:310).
120. Ibid., 6.25.3 (*NPNF*² 1:156); see 6:24.17 (*NPNF*² 1:154).
121. Jerome, *Vir. ill.* 9; Bede the Venerable 1985, 231.

Jude

Finally, we come to the canon history of the Epistle of Jude. There may be faint echoes of Jude in second-century Christian works,[122] but none distinct enough to indicate literary dependence.[123] If we assume the priority of Jude to 2 Peter, the earliest witness to Jude is 2 Peter (before AD 64 or, if pseudepigraphic, before AD 140).[124] Around the turn of the third century we find Jude in wide circulation: as far as Italy (Muratorian Canon) and Carthage (Tertullian) in the West, and Egypt in the East (Clement of Alexandria and Origen). Eusebius tells us that Clement of Alexandria in his (now lost) *Outlines* commented briefly on "all canonical Scripture, not omitting the disputed books," including "Jude and the other Catholic epistles."[125] Clement, as far as we know, is the first to quote from Jude by name.[126] Origen highly praises Jude as "a letter of a few lines . . . but filled with the healthful words of heavenly grace,"[127] and yet he also implies that it was not universally accepted.[128] Around AD 213 in Carthage, Tertullian quotes Jude as authoritative,[129] but later Cyprian (d. 258) does not make use of any of the five disputed CE.[130] In the early fourth century, Eusebius reports the scanty attestation to Jude's letter among the ancients.[131] This cause for hesitation is traded for other qualms even as the letter is achieving a place among the great codices and canon lists of the fourth and fifth centuries. As the division between canonical and noncanonical books becomes increasingly defined, Jude's own use of pseudepigraphal books becomes less tenable. It is incumbent upon a Greek commentator (previously mistaken for Didymus the Blind) to defend Jude's appropriation of the *Testament* (or *Assumption*) *of Moses*[132] and upon Jerome[133] and Augustine[134] to defend its appeal to *1 Enoch*. Charles Bigg wryly opines,

122. Guthrie 1990, 901, relying on Bigg 1901, 307-8.
123. Bauckham 1983, 16.
124. See Davids 2006, 130-31.
125. Eusebius, *Hist. eccl.* 6.14.1 (*NPNF²* 1:261); see also 6.13.6 (*NPNF²* 1:260).
126. Clement of Alexandria, *Paed.* 3.8.44-45; *Strom.* 3.2.11 (*ANF* 2:282, 383).
127. Origen, *Comm. Matt.* 10.17.40-43 (*ANF* 9:424).
128. Ibid., 17.30.82-83.
129. Tertullian, *Pud.* 20.
130. Metzger 1987, 161-62; Bruce 1988, 184-85.
131. Eusebius, *Hist. eccl.* 2.23.25.
132. PG 38:1811-18; see Mayor 1907, cxv; McDonald 2017, 262.
133. Jerome, *Vir. ill.* 4 (*NPNF²* 3:362).
134. Augustine, *Civ. Dei* 15.23 (*NPNF¹* 2:305).

"The offence of Jude was not so much that he made use of *Enoch*, as that he actually quoted the book by name."[135]

The Catholic Epistles in the Syrian Canon

Before concluding our brief canonical history of the CE, it is necessary to mention the status of these books in the ancient Syrian churches.[136] In the fifth century the Syriac Bible, the Peshitta, included the three greater CE (James, 1 Peter, 1 John). The four smaller CE (2 Peter, 2–3 John, Jude) and Revelation were excluded, leaving twenty-two books in the Syrian canon of the NT. The sixth-century Philoxenian version brought the Syriac NT into line with Greek manuscripts, thus adding in the smaller CE and Revelation.

Nevertheless, to this day the Church of the East (Nestorian) rejects the smaller CE. In the sixth century, the Nestorian theologian Paulus listed James along with the lesser CE and Revelation as books of inferior authority. Around AD 850, Isho'dad of Merv wrote a commentary on the twenty-two-book Syrian NT but rejected even the greater CE.[137] There were Greek-speaking Christians in the East who were influenced by the Syrian canon. John Chrysostom (ca. 347–407) appears to have held to the same NT canon as in the Peshitta, for among his eleven thousand quotations from the NT, there are none from 2 Peter, 2–3 John, Jude, or Revelation.[138] Note, too, Amphilochius's awareness that some receive seven CE and others only three.[139]

Hebrews, the Catholic Epistles, and Eusebius's Canonical Categories

We are now in a position to consider Eusebius's curious categorization of the NT books. Why does Hebrews rest securely among the universally acknowledged books, while the CE are divided between the acknowledged (1 Peter and 1 John) and the disputed (James, 2 Peter, 2–3 John, Jude) books? Why does Eusebius distinguish between two subcategories of disputed books

---

135. Bigg (1901, 310).
136. Metzger 1987, 218-23.
137. Bray 2000, xxi.
138. Metzger 1987, 214-15.
139. Amphilochius of Iconium, *Seleuc.* lines 310-14.

("recognized by many" vs. "rejected")? Why does he classify Revelation as both universally acknowledged *and* rejected?

Two factors are crucial to answering these questions. First, acting as an historian, Eusebius carefully sifts through opinions about the NT books going back to the earliest church fathers. Thus, for Revelation, he knows that at one time it was embraced enthusiastically but had become controversial in his own day. Second, Eusebius is acutely aware of the shape of the NT in the Greek manuscripts that were being used in the churches. For some time in the East, Hebrews was included in the Pauline corpus, so he has no problem listing it as a universally acknowledged book, despite pesky objections from Rome. He is aware of serious questions about the five disputed CE, but it would be inappropriate to classify them as "rejected," because he knows that they have been for some time circulating among a collection of "seven so-called catholic epistles."[140]

As an historian, it is incumbent upon Eusebius to record the stated reasons for excluding the disputed CE from the canon, but as a churchman, he is obliged to keep them in. In AD 330, Constantine commissioned Eusebius to produce fifty copies of the entire Bible in Greek. There is little doubt that these massive codices contained the same twenty-seven books found in the great fourth-century codices Sinaiticus and Vaticanus.[141]

Conclusion

This chapter has introduced many issues related to Hebrews and the CE by way of a series of challenges they present to us. There are three primary conclusions we can draw before looking more constructively at how to interpret these books.

First, the challenges we have surveyed provide the interpreter with a "situational awareness" about why these books have been subjected to neglect, misunderstanding, and controversy. An amorphous mass of problems can leave the interpreter with an attitude of cynicism or skepticism toward these books, but a deeper understanding of each interpretive challenge affords one the opportunity to deal with each issue patiently and intelligently.

---

140. Eusebius, *Hist. eccl.* 2.23.25 (*NPNF²* 1:128).
141. Bruce 1988, 204; Skeat 1999.

Second, the history of challenges concerning Hebrews and the CE reveals at many points the limitations of any historical investigation of these texts. For instance, interpreters must present modest conclusions concerning what we can know with certainty about such matters as the authorship and setting for most of these books.

Third, interpreters will do well to take a posture of faith in their attempts to negotiate the many challenges of interpreting Hebrews and the CE. Acknowledging them as part of the canon of Scripture is itself an act of faith. By God's providence, the church has seen fit to include even small and seemingly unimportant books in the canon (like 2–3 John and Jude). Jerome and Augustine's stance toward the authorship of Hebrews should serve as a pattern to emulate. While not discarding their critical judgment that Paul had not likely written the Epistle to the Hebrews, they embraced the writing nonetheless as part of the apostolic witness to the gospel, in part because of its Eastern inclusion among the Pauline corpus. After all, the goal of interpreting the Scriptures is not primarily to arrive at a set of objective facts about the production of each book (as important as this is) but to discover sacred truths that are means for people to know and love God. This will be important to keep in mind as we look further at how to read and interpret Hebrews and the CE.

2

The Identity and Significance
of Seven Catholic Epistles

In chapter 1 we laid out a veritable buffet of challenges associated with Hebrews and the Catholic Epistles. This opened our eyes to the complex history of their reception and interpretation. It also pointed to some of the roadblocks to interpreting these books from a purely modern, historical perspective. A more fruitful way of reading them is to understand how they fit into the Bible itself. Toward this end, the present chapter will address two fundamental questions concerning the CE. First, why are these letters given the title "Catholic Epistles"? Second, why is it significant that the church acknowledged a collection of *seven* such letters?

The Identity of the Catholic Epistles

Hebrews and the Catholic Epistles

The history of the NT canon shows us two things about the classification of Hebrews and the CE. First, Hebrews made its way into the canon by being included among the Pauline letters. Second, the CE collection took shape sometime in the third century between the time of Origen (ca. 200) and Eusebius (ca. 300). A distinction between Hebrews and the CE is immediately apparent in their titles. Hebrews, after the fashion of the titles in the earliest manuscripts of Paul's letters ("To the Romans," etc.), is named after its *recipients* ("To the Hebrews"). Titles of the CE have the names of their designated *authors* ("Epistle of James," etc.). As a canonical collection, the letters of Paul stand together as inspired Scripture under the banner of Paul's apostleship. The CE comprise another canonical collection of letters whose authority comes from their reputed authors, who were apostles in the earliest churches in Jerusalem and Judea—James, Peter, John, and Jude.

Use of the Term "Catholic"

The "Catholic Epistles" are also known in English as the "General Epistles." "Catholic" and "General" are English equivalents, respectively, of the original Greek term (*katholikos*) and its Latin translation (*generalis*). Curiously, the Latin Vulgate employs the title *Epistulae Catholicae*, not *Epistulae Generales*.[1]

We prefer to use the expression "Catholic Epistles" rather than "General Epistles." The word "general," while not an inaccurate rendering of *katholikos*, can strike English readers as rather vague. "General Epistles" is the title preferred by Protestants[2] and Eastern Orthodox[3] who wish to avoid any association with the Roman Catholic Church—even though the term "Catholic Epistles" does not owe its existence to the *Roman* Catholic Church per se. Since either expression requires clarification, on balance it is better to use the ancient title "Catholic Epistles."

How did these letters get the title "Catholic Epistles," and what does the title signify? The short answer is that we do not exactly know. The Greek word *katholikos* is derived from the expression *kath + holou* ("on the whole" or "in general"). Ancient Greek writers regularly used the word to mean "general" or "universal," often in tandem with what is "common" (*koinos*) or in contrast to what is "partial" (*merikos*) or "particular" (*idios*). The earliest Christian usage goes back to the Apostolic Fathers in the second century who refer to the "Catholic Church."[4] Individual churches in particular locations are contrasted with the "universal assembly" (*katholikē ekklēsia*) found "in every place"[5] or "throughout the world."[6]

"Catholic" as applied to letters occurs a number of times among the church fathers. The two earliest occurrences are crucially significant. First,

---

1. Plummer 1907, 1.
2. Crowe 2015, xvn1.
3. *The Orthodox Study Bible* 2008, xx.
4. Ign. *Smyrn.* 8.2; *Mart. Pol.* 1.1; 8.1; 16.2; 19.2.
5. *Mart. Pol.* 1.1.
6. Ibid., 8.1; 19.2.

Eusebius reports that Dionysius, bishop of Corinth (ca. AD 171),[7] wrote "catholic epistles . . . to the churches."[8] Dionysius wrote self-consciously with ecclesiastical authority, and his "inspired labors" were beneficial to other churches who solicited his spiritual counsel. The fact that he wrote *seven* catholic letters may be incidental.[9] We may infer from one passage that Dionysius had compiled his catholic letters into a collection for wide dissemination.[10] While not equating his writings with Holy Scripture, Dionysius pronounced a woe on "apostles of the devil" who had tampered with them.

Second, an oblique allusion to one of the CE may occur in the anti-Montanist screed by Apollonius of Ephesus (ca. 200), excerpted by Eusebius.[11] Apollonius blasts the Montanist leader Themiso (ca. 180)[12] for writing "a certain catholic epistle."[13] Many unanswered questions surround this long-lost letter. Was Themiso deliberately "aping the Apostle,"[14] hence purporting to write inspired Scripture? Did he himself style his letter as a "catholic epistle"?[15]

What apostle was Themiso (seen as) imitating? We will probably never know. Some scholars think he was impersonating the apostle Paul.[16] The unqualified moniker "the Apostle" often referred to Paul, but no letter of his is ever called "catholic." Since 1 Peter and 1 John are the earliest NT letters to have been called "catholic," Peter and John are more likely candidates. Thomas Barns made the outlandish proposal that Themiso was the pseudonymous author of both 1 and 2 Peter.[17] A far better case can be made for the apostle John as Themiso's exemplar.[18] After all, Dionysius of Alexandria

---

7. Salmon 1999.

8. Eusebius, *Hist. eccl.* 4.23.1 (*NPNF²* 1:200).

9. Eusebius does not call attention to the number of letters, and he notes that Dionysius wrote an additional letter to a prominent Christian lady, Chrysophora (*Hist. eccl.* 4.23.12 [*NPNF²* 1:202]).

10. Eusebius, *Hist. eccl.* 4.23.12 (*NPNF²* 1:201-2).

11. Ibid., 5.18 (*NPNF²* 1:235-37).

12. See Walls 1964, 438.

13. Eusebius, *Hist. eccl.* 5.18.5 (*NPNF²* 1:235).

14. Eusebius 1927-28, 1:163.

15. On whether the Montanists intended to write newly inspired Scriptures, see Walls 1964; Wright 1976, 19-20; Denzey 2001; Tabbernee 2007, 108-10.

16. Eusebius 1927-28, 2:177; Zahn 1888-89, 1:9-10; Harnack 1889, 28.

17. Barns 1903 and 1904.

18. Walls 1964, 440; Brown 1982, 3; Tabbernee 2007, 108.

acknowledged 1 John as "*the* Catholic Epistle."[19] For our purposes it will suffice to recognize that, whether or not Themiso arrogated himself to the level of one of the apostles, at the very least he sought to exercise the same degree of ecclesiastical authority that Dionysius of Corinth did in his "catholic letters."

There are a couple of other instances in which "catholic" is applied to writings other than the CE in the NT. Clement of Alexandria designates the letter issued from the apostolic council in Jerusalem (Acts 15:22-29) as "the Catholic epistle of all the apostles."[20] Origen identifies the *Epistle of Barnabas* as a catholic letter.[21] Origen is also the earliest unmistakable witness to 1 Peter[22] and especially 1 John[23] each as a "Catholic Epistle."[24] There is far less certainty about Jude's status as a catholic letter at the time of Origen or of his predecessor, Clement of Alexandria. The appellation could have been anachronistically applied to Jude by the translator of Origen's commentary on Romans, Rufinus,[25] or by Eusebius in his report concerning the contents of Clement's *Outlines*.[26] In any event, we have no solid record of the canonical collection of letters circulating under the name "Catholic Epistles" until the time of Eusebius in the early fourth century.

The Significance of the Title "Catholic Epistles"

Why exactly was the collection of the seven letters—James, 1–2 Peter, 1–3 John, and Jude—labeled "the *Catholic* Epistles"? This question generated far more discussion in the nineteenth and early twentieth centuries than it has subsequently.[27] There are four views.

First, the term "catholic" refers to this group of writings as "the common collection" (*katholikon syntagma*) of all the apostles (except Paul and his letter

---

19. Eusebius, *Hist. eccl.* 7.25.7, 10-11 (*NPNF*² 1:310), italics added; Brown 1982, 3n3; Katz 1957, 273.
20. Clement of Alexandria, *Strom.* 4.15 (*ANF* 2:427).
21. Origen, *Cels.* 1.63 (*ANF* 4:424).
22. Origen, *Sel. Ps.* 12.1128.56; Origen, *Comm. Jo.* 6.35.175; see Eusebius, *Hist. eccl.* 6.25.5 (*NPNF*² 1:273).
23. Origen, *Comm. Matt.* 17.19.60; Origen, *Comm. Jo.* 1.22.138; 2.23.149; 19.1.3; 20.13.99; Origen, *Fr. Jo.* 10.37; Origen, *Or.* 22.2.14; 22.4.12; Origen, *Hom. Jer.* 9.4.62; Origen, *Sel. Deut.* 12.817.14.
24. Nienhuis 2007, 53.
25. Origen, *Comm. Rom.* 5.1.29.
26. Eusebius, *Hist. eccl.* 6.14.1 (*NPNF*² 1:261).
27. For example, Ebrard 1860, 409-16; Hug 1836, 603-6; Reuss 1884, 306-7; Gloag 1887, 1-22; Salmond 1901; Plummer 1907, 1-10; but see now Webb 1992; Guthrie 2009.

collection). The focus is on their shared apostolic authorship. Hug[28] proposes this interpretation, leaning heavily on Clement of Alexandria's reference to the Jerusalem Council's "Catholic epistle of all the apostles."[29] Anticipating the objection that Origen also calls the *Epistle of Barnabas* "catholic," Hug notes the fluidity at that time regarding which epistles should belong to the common apostolic collection. This view, however, cannot account for the fact that "catholic" is also applied to manifestly *nonapostolic* letters such as those by Dionysius of Corinth or the heretic Themiso.

Second, the term refers to the ecclesiastical recognition of these letters as authoritative. In other words, "catholic" equates to "canonical." Michaelis proposes that the term "catholic" was affixed first to the two letters that were acknowledged early as authentic (1 Peter and 1 John) and then to the remaining five CE as doubts about them subsided.[30] A statement in Eusebius is sometimes cited to support this view. Eusebius rejects certain works falsely attributed to Peter, asserting that "we know [they] have not been universally accepted [*en katholikois*; or "among the catholic writings"]."[31] However, the expression *en katholikois* more likely means "among catholics" (AT) or "in Catholic tradition."[32]

This view falters on the fact that Eusebius can refer to "the [seven] so-called catholic epistles" while reporting that some of them are disputed.[33] It is impossible for the term "catholic," then, to denote what is "canonical." We find the term "catholic" also applied to works that never achieved canonicity (*Epistle of Barnabas*) or never could have (epistles of Dionysius of Corinth and Themiso).

It is true that in the Latin West the CE came to be known as the "Canonical Epistles." We find this title in Augustine (ca. 415), Pseudo-Jerome's Prologue to the "Canonical Epistles" in Codex Fuldensis (ca. 541-ca. 546), Junillus Africanus (fl. 541-49), Cassiodorus (485/490–ca. 580), as well as later authors.[34] We do not know the cause of this Western shift in terminology.

---

28. Hug 1836, 605-6.

29. Clement of Alexandria, *Strom.* 4.15 (*ANF* 2:427).

30. Michaelis 1802, 270.

31. Eusebius, *Hist. eccl.* 3.3.2. (*NPNF*[2] 1:134).

32. Eusebius 1926 and 1932, 1:193.

33. Eusebius, *Hist. Eccl.* 2.23.25 (*NPNF*[2] 1:128); cf. 3.25.1-3 (*NPNF*[2] 1:1155-56).

34. Salmond 1901, 360; Nienhuis 2007, 84.

Perhaps it was due to the connotation of ecclesiastical authority attached to the term "catholic" along with the impulse to shore up support for those letters in the CE collection, which in the West took a longer path toward canonicity.[35] Nevertheless, "Canonical Epistles" is unsuitable as a title for the CE in comparison to the collection of Paul's letters, since both are equally *canonical*. Salmond rightly concludes: "There is nothing in the facts to conflict with the idea that this ["catholic" = "canonical"] came in the course of time to be the sense. There is everything to rebut the assertion that it was the original and proper sense."[36]

Third, the term refers to the doctrinal purity contained in these letters. In other words, "catholic" implies their *orthodox* and *authoritative* character over against heretical writings. This view is a variation of the previous view, and it fails at the same points.

Fourth, the term "catholic" refers to the destination of the epistles, showing that they are designed for a broad or "general" audience. In contradistinction to Paul's letters, addressed to specific churches (in Rome, Corinth, Galatia, Ephesus, etc.) or individuals (Timothy, Titus, Philemon), the CE are intended for the church *catholic*. This meaning fits every application of the expression "catholic epistle(s)," whether to the Jerusalem Council's letter, the *Epistle of Barnabas*, 1 Peter, 1 John, the letters of Dionysius of Corinth, or even Themiso's heretical "catholic epistle."

This fourth view is expressly shared by ancient interpreters. Leontius of Byzantium (485–583) explains the title for the CE: "They were called 'Catholic' since they were not written to one nation, as were Paul's [letters], but generally to all."[37] Oecumenius (tenth c.) writes in his preface to James, "They are spoken of as 'Catholic' as if they are encyclicals. The company of the Lord's disciples address these epistles, not singling out one nation or city (as the divine Paul does, such as 'To the Romans' or 'To the Corinthians'), but generally to the faithful, whether to the Jews who are in the Diaspora, as also Peter does, or even to all who will ultimately be Christians under the

---

35. Guthrie 2009, 797.
36. Salmond 1901, 361.
37. Leontius of Byzantium, *De sectis*, 2.4, AT (PG 86:1204).

same faith."[38] An illuminating comment comes from a scholiast who, inferring from the different prescripts, states that James is at the head of the CE collection "because it is more catholic [katholikōtera] than Peter."[39] He seems to mean that, whereas 1 Peter's addressees are limited to five Roman provinces, James addresses himself to the Diaspora absolutely, without geographical limitations.

The exceptions to this fourth view occur among the CE themselves. The two smaller Johannine letters (2–3 John) are not addressed to a general audience, but to a specific church (or small network of churches; 2 John v. 1) and to an individual (3 John v. 1). How, then, may they fall under the banner of "Catholic Epistles"? In the case of 2 John, it is possible to *interpret* the letter as an encyclical. Clement of Alexandria asserts that 2 John is written "to virgins," in particular, "a certain Babylonian woman called Elekta, whose name stands for the election of the holy church."[40] What Clement takes as the name of the addressee (*Eklektē*, "chosen") is universalized to apply to the whole church. The "Gaius" of 3 John cannot be similarly generalized.[41]

In the Latin West there was a tradition that the destination of 1 John was "To the Parthians." Modern scholars have speculated whether this address was a garbling of Clement's reference to John's writing "to virgins" or vice versa (observe the similarity of "to virgins" [*pros parthenous*] and "to Parthians" [*pros Parthous*]).[42] There was no interpreter who held that all three Johannine letters were intended for the Parthians (only 1 John), nor was this ever a method of justifying 2–3 John as Catholic Epistles. What ultimately seems to have happened is that all three of the Johannine letters were included among the CE as letters written by the apostle John, even though generically 2–3 John do not count as encyclicals.

While the fourth view possesses the greatest explanatory scope and power, it requires some modification. There is a grain of truth in each of the other views, and they were doubtless formulated because the notion of the CE's

---

38. PG 106:453, AT.

39. Reuss 1884, 2:306.

40. Bray 2000, 231; from a fragment, in Latin translation, of Clement's otherwise lost *Outlines*.

41. For a recent example of apprehending both 1 and 2 John as encyclicals, but not 3 John, see Painter 2009, 249-51.

42. Brown 1982, 772-74.

identity as *simply* encyclicals is inadequate. Were it not for its prior inclusion among the Pauline corpus, Hebrews could have easily qualified as a "catholic" letter, given its lack of an epistolary prescript (like 1 John). The general address of the *Epistle of Barnabas* probably led Origen to describe it as a "catholic epistle." Yet it is doubtful that Origen would have so named it had he not believed that it was written by the very Barnabas who belonged to the apostolic age.

In the end, intrinsic to the Christian phenomena of "*catholic* epistles"—whether canonical or noncanonical, orthodox or heretical—was the conviction that only an author with sufficient spiritual authority (ecclesiastical or apostolic, as the case may be) was qualified to address the universal church. Not just any person at all (like the heretic Themiso in Apollonius's eyes) was *worthy* to pen such works (as Dionysius, the bishop of Corinth, was, and, even more significantly, the apostles). Such books not only reach a geographically broad range of Christian readers but also, in the case of the canonical collection of the CE, direct enduring inspiration and truth "even to all who will ultimately be Christians under the same faith" (Oecumenius).

The Significance of Seven Catholic Epistles

Christians in late antiquity were not altogether different from Christians today. They read the Bible with an eye toward applying Scripture to their own contexts. For this reason, Paul's letters presented a challenge. The apostle wrote to *particular* churches (and individuals) about *specific* problems within relatively unique sociohistorical circumstances.[43] The solution to the problem was to catholicize or universalize Paul. Dahl's study shows how this was done in two ways: number symbolism and textual adjustments. The first strategy (on which we will focus) was already applied to the plurality of the *four* Gospels to indicate their canonical unity as witnesses to the *one* gospel.[44] But what do we make of Paul's letter collection when (to borrow words from

---

43. Dahl 1962; Beker 1980, 23-36; Mitchell 2010.
44. For example, Irenaeus, *Haer.* 3.11.8 (*ANF* 1:429): four cherubim/living creatures; Cyprian, *Ep.* 72.10 (*ANF* 5:382): four rivers of Eden.

John Chrysostom) "we have only fourteen letters of his" and "carry them all around the world"?[45]

The Muratorian Canon illustrates how the ancient church dealt with the particularity of Paul's letters.[46] The compiler makes the "chronologically preposterous" claim[47] that Paul followed the lead of John the Revelator when he wrote "by name to only seven churches."[48] The numerical symbolism signifies that "there is one Church spread throughout the whole extent of the earth," for John, too, when writing to seven churches "nevertheless speaks to all."[49] Even Paul's letters to individuals are universally applicable, since "these are held sacred in the esteem of the Church catholic for the regulation of ecclesiastical discipline."[50] Other church fathers similarly correlate the symbolism of "seven" to the letters of Paul and the Apocalypse.[51] While not invoking number symbolism, Tertullian echoes the same thought concerning the titles to Paul's letters: "But of what consequence are the titles, since in writing to a certain church the apostle did in fact write to all?"[52]

By the time someone assembled the CE into a collection, there was already at hand a set of symbolic constructs for the existing canonical units (the Gospels and Paul's letters). From time immemorial in the ancient Near East and the Hellenistic world, the number seven was a symbol of perfection, fullness, or completeness.[53] The symbolic logic regarding the universality of Paul's letters to seven churches spills over into the reckoning of seven CE. Jerome states that "the apostle Paul writes to seven churches" *and* that "the apostles James, Peter, John, and Jude, have published seven epistles."[54]

Eastern fathers in the fourth century, beginning with Eusebius, all specifically note "seven" CE: Gregory of Nazianzus, Amphilochius, Cyril of Jerusalem, the Synod of Laodicea, and Athanasius.[55] The symmetry of sevenfold

---

45. John Chrysostom, *Hom. Rom.* 16:3 1.3 (PG 51:191); trans. Mitchell 2010, 130.
46. Stendahl 1962.
47. Bruce 1988, 164.
48. Muratorian Canon, lines 48-49; Metzger 1987, 305-7.
49. Muratorian Canon, lines 56-60.
50. Ibid., lines 60-63.
51. Victorinus of Pettau, *Comm. Apoc.* 1.16 (*ANF* 7:345); Cyprian, *Fort.* 11 (*ANF* 5:503); Cyprian, *Test.* 1.20 (*ANF* 5:513).
52. Tertullian, *Marc.* 5.17 (*ANF* 3:465).
53. Boring 2009.
54. Jerome, *Epist.* 53.9 (*NPNF²* 6:101-2).
55. Metzger 1987, 311-14.

scriptural units is made to work, even when the addition of Hebrews foils the seven-church wholeness of Paul's letters. The numerical symbolism is simply reconfigured, as in Amphilochius's description of the fourteen-letter Pauline corpus: "Twice seven epistles."[56] A much later author captures the symbolism as it applies to the CE. Commenting on the clause from the Nicene Creed, "one, holy, catholic, and apostolic church," George Sphrantzes (1401- ca. 1478) writes, "Even as there are seven Catholic Epistles written to all the faithful generally, so also it is written that there is a Catholic Church of all adherents of orthodox faith."[57]

Conclusion

While the number symbolism employed by ancient Christians may strike modern readers as forced and artificial, its significance is nonetheless important for interpretation. The NT canon has at its foundation the four Gospels, which narrate the inauguration of the new covenant in the incarnation, ministry, death, and resurrection of Jesus Christ. The Pauline Epistles (to seven churches or in fourteen [2 x 7] letters), the seven CE, and the Apocalypse (with its letters to seven churches) signify how the various apostolic witnesses unify to proclaim and appropriate the gospel of the kingdom for the whole church.[58] There are two main interpretive outcomes from our discussion of the sevenfold collection of the Catholic Epistles in this chapter.

First, the configuration of the NT books suggests that readers must carefully consider the relationships both within and between collections. For example, we should read James within the context of its other apostolic witnesses in the sevenfold CE collection and then also in conversation with the other NT collections. Premodern readers did this as a matter of course, since virtually no one owned a complete NT (let alone Bible) bound in one volume. Bulky, expensive codices containing the whole Bible were suitable for churches, not individuals. The latter acquired copies of canonical units, assembling them into a collection of collections that made up the entire

---

56. Amphilochius of Iconium, *Seleuc.* line 101.

57. George Sphrantzes, *Chronicon sive Maius*, p. 578, line 27 (Grecu, 1966 [TLG]), AT.

58. The Acts of the Apostles, being the odd one out for numerical symbolism, plays a pivotal role in welding together all the canonical units of the NT. We will discuss this in chapter 3.

"Divine Library."[59] Thus the ancients would naturally read the CE as one coherent collection of letters that interplayed with the other collections in the NT, and indeed, all of Scripture.

Second, the development of the NT collections, along with the accompanying number symbolism describing them, underscores the catholicity of the documents that make up the NT canon as well as their intended readership, the church. The seven Catholic Epistles correspond to the one, holy, catholic, apostolic church that reads them. When reading any of the letters of the NT, therefore, the church is not reading "someone else's mail."[60] We must approach these books (as well as the whole Bible) as God's Word and so as addressing not merely ancient persons and problems but all the faithful within their varied and complex situations.

This is easier said than done, and more could be said about how to negotiate the particularity and universality of NT letters. Suffice it to say that the *simultaneity* of Scripture—a hermeneutical term for the inspired capacity of Scripture to relate to the particularity of its ancient readers, as well as to adapt across times and cultures to all persons who belong to Christ's church—requires interpreters to attend to both the particularity and universality of texts. Focusing on one at the expense of the other is problematic. Sole attention to particularities yields a text that has no relevance for today but is only of antiquarian interest. Exclusive stress on universality dangerously sets the text adrift from its historical moorings and leads to flights of fancy in interpretation that have no resemblance to the Scripture as it stands written.

One way to interpret the Catholic Epistles (or any other collection of books in the Bible) is to note well the shape and sequence of each canonical collection, as well the relationships between canonical units. We will devote ourselves to this approach in the next chapter.

---

59. Jerome's term for the Bible (Westcott 1864, 5). Recall Augustine's famous "pick up and read" episode (*Conf.* 8.12.29), wherein he remembers an event involving a reading from "the Gospel" (= the fourfold Gospel canon) similar to his own reading in "the book of the Apostle" (a codex of Paul's Epistles).

60. Green 2007, 50-59; cf. Fee and Stuart 2014, 57-73.

3

Interpreting Hebrews and the Catholic Epistles in Canonical Context

We have already broached the matter of interpreting NT books in terms of the interrelationships within and between canonical collections. But are there strategies for how this may be done? A ready answer presents itself in the sequence of the NT books. If we appropriately conceive of the Scriptures as the "Divine Library," our navigation among the books of the Bible can be quite intuitive. From experience we have learned to expect that books in a given section of a library are related to one another more closely than they are to books in other sections. Books located on the same bookcase or bookshelf are yet more closely related to one another than they are to other books in the same section. Moreover, there will usually be a logical sequencing of materials (e.g., topically, chronologically, alphabetically, etc.) both between and within sections. One does not have to be a type A personality to recognize the organizational patterns at work.

In what follows we will explore two organizational features of the NT that bear upon the interpretation of Hebrews and the CE. We will work from the microlevel to the macrolevel. The first concerns the order of books within particular collections. The second regards the sequence of the book collections that make up the NT.

Hebrews and the Catholic Epistles in Canonical Sequence

Hebrews, the Catholic Epistles, and Order within Canonical Units

Before we explore the interpretive significance of the placement of individual books within their respective canonical collections, it is necessary to state two important caveats.

First, we must be on the alert for the rationale behind any sequencing of books. Sometimes the method of organization is functional, such as *stichometric* order—that is, when books are listed in descending order of length (as for the Pauline corpus). The interpretive or theological significance of such sequencing may be negligible—unless other organizational factors are also at work. This is all the more the case when the sequence is random. For example, the earliest witness to 1–2 Peter and Jude ($\mathfrak{P}^{72}$ [third or fourth c.])[1] includes them among a haphazard assortment of eight other (extrabiblical) pieces, with Jude in slot four and 1–2 Peter at the very end.[2] Most instances will not be like this outlier. Rarely is there no design to the arrangement. Rarer still are instances when a compiler, editor, or even ancient commentator *tells* or *explains* what the pattern is. At times, the rhyme or reason for a given sequence seems rather obvious; at other times, we must be cautious about speculating.

Second, we must keep in mind that the ordering of books into collections—complete with titles, prologues, book summaries, subscripts (end titles), colophons (end comments about the text's production or transmission), paragraph markers (e.g., *ekthesis*, the first line of each paragraph extending beyond the left margin), chapter divisions, *nomina sacra* (abbreviations of "sacred names"), and other reading aids—are additions to the original authors' writings. They are the result of editorial activity and are not part of the inspired biblical text. Admittedly, the NT texts do not come to us in any other way. All extant manuscripts are the result of editorial activity to

---

1. Though several verses from Jude are in $\mathfrak{P}^{78}$ (third c.).
2. Lockett 2017, 81-82.

one degree or another. There is disagreement about the extent to which such (paratextual) features, such as the arrangement of books, are determinative for interpretation.

Nienhuis and Wall understand "the *canonization* of biblical texts (and not their *composition*) as their 'point of origin' as the church's Scripture"[3] and hence lay great store by the final literary shape of the canon (untethered from considerations of authorial intent) that forms "*a textual analogue of the apostolic Rule of Faith.*"[4] Lockett views the editorial shaping by editors and compilers during the canonical process as the extension, amplification, and safeguarding of the authorial communicative intentions of the biblical writers.[5] "Canon consciousness" and "compilational consciousness" emerge from the texts themselves, and to varying degrees redactors and compilers were aware of the canonical process in which they were participating.[6] The content and shape of the individual texts (the products of the authors' communicative aims) contribute substantially to the ultimate shape of the collection to which they belong.

Goswell perceives the order of books as a phenomenon belonging to "an early stage in the reception history (*Rezeptionsgeschichte*) of Scripture."[7] This is especially so when one encounters divergent sequencing. "The existence of two different canonical orders warns the reader against prescribing one or another order as determinative for interpretation. To give exclusive rights to any one order of books would be to fail to see the character of paratext as (uninspired) commentary on the text."[8] Competing arrangements present to readers "exegetical alternatives" that enrich our interpretation of Scripture rather than foreclose all but one reading of the biblical material.

Our own view is closer to Lockett's, tempered by the cautious approach of Goswell.[9] We are convinced that the final form of the canon has been providentially configured to facilitate faithful interpretation of the Scriptures.

---

3. Nienhuis and Wall 2013, 11.
4. Ibid., 13; italics are original.
5. Lockett 2017, 42-58 and passim.
6. Ibid.
7. Goswell 2013, 460.
8. Goswell 2010, 235.
9. Goswell (2016a, 748) moves nearer to Lockett's view in writing that the ordering of biblical books by ancient readers was a "process of *recognizing* meaning . . . rather than *giving* meaning."

Those who desire to read and interpret the Scriptures faithfully can rely on the canonical order of the NT found in virtually any modern English version of the Bible (whether published under the auspices of Catholic, Eastern Orthodox, or Protestant translators or editors). The traditional order of the NT books is the same in all of them. Besides, most readers will want to arrive at interpretive closure on their own and may not have the inclination (or perhaps the tools) to research the history of the NT canon for additional interpretive options. So, while not shying away from exploring alternative canonical sequences, we will ultimately defer to the weight of the traditional order of books. As a matter of pastoral counsel, readers may be assured that they will not go wrong with sticking to this order as they seek to understand God's Word and pursue the way of Christian discipleship.

The Order of Hebrews in the Pauline Corpus

As we have seen, Hebrews did not enjoy wide acceptance in the West until the fifth century, precisely because it was not admitted among Paul's letters. By AD 200 it was firmly established within the Pauline corpus in Egypt. In the NT manuscripts that have come down to us, Hebrews is without exception found traveling along with(in) the Pauline corpus. However, one does not always find it in the same *place* among Paul's letters.

We find the Epistle to the Hebrews in nine different locations throughout copies of the Pauline corpus. In his seminal study, Hatch organizes the variety of placements into three categories.[10]

The first category involves variations in which Hebrews is included among Paul's ecclesiastical letters (Romans–2 Thessalonians). The most consequential is Hebrews's placement immediately after Romans in $\mathfrak{P}^{46}$ (ca. 200), as well as in nine minuscule MSS and a Syrian canon from ca. 400. An Alexandrian scribe probably positioned Hebrews between Romans and 1 Corinthians in $\mathfrak{P}^{46}$ for a theological reason, since a purely stichometric ordering (i.e., in length, from larger to smaller) would preclude Hebrews from such pride of place.[11] Perhaps the compiler wished to privilege Romans and

---

10. Hatch 1936. While largely following Hatch's synthesis of the evidence, we have also consulted Metzger's updated and enlarged text-critical inventory (1994, 591-92).

11. But see Trobisch 1994, 17.

Hebrews as Paul's two greatest theological expositions.[12] It is possible that the Alexandrian editor was blatantly supporting Paul's authorship of Hebrews, in direct opposition to the rejection of the same at Rome.[13] This order did not become widespread. The evidence suggests at a minimum that Hebrews was sometimes placed second among Paul's letters in Egypt (third c.) as well as in Syria (fourth c.).

Hebrews is also found after 2 Corinthians (i.e., in stichometric order), after Galatians,[14] after Ephesians or Colossians (perhaps due to different stichometric calculations[15]), and less often after Titus.

All but the last of the above variations in sequence (i.e., after Titus) position Hebrews among Paul's letters to churches. The manuscripts in this category bear witness to the Eastern acceptance of Hebrews among Paul's ecclesiastical letters since around the turn of the third century.

Second, we find Hebrews at the close of Paul's letters to churches (after 2 Thessalonians) in ten uncial MSS (including Codex Sinaiticus and Codex Vaticanus), in more than eighty minuscule MSS, and in four different ancient versions (but not in Latin or Syriac). Thus, whereas in third-century Egypt one would have more likely found MSS in which Hebrews followed either Romans or 2 Corinthians, by the fourth century the position of Hebrews slipped to the end of Paul's ecclesiastical letters. The prevalence of this sequencing may have originated with an Alexandrian edition of the NT produced by Hesychius (fl. ca. 300).[16] The canon list of Athanasius (AD 367) and the Euthalian prologue to the Pauline Epistles both attest to the placement of Hebrews after 2 Thessalonians, as do many other witnesses.[17]

The change in Hebrews's position was arguably a concession to Western resistance to its admission into the canon as one of Paul's letters. As we have seen, doubts about Hebrews's authorship were noted even by *Eastern* figures

---

12. Hatch 1936, 134. Thoroughly modern is the idea that Hebrews would fit alongside Romans because it was addressed to Jewish-Christian house churches at Rome (note also the "from Italy" language in Rom. 18:2 and Heb. 13:24) or that both epistles approach their arguments within the context of Second Temple Judaism (see Goswell 2016b, 749).

13. Mason 1968.

14. Metzger 1994, 591n2.

15. See Metzger 1987, 298.

16. Hatch 1936, 140; Mason 1968, 131.

17. Hatch 1936, 138-43.

(Origen, Eusebius, and Amphilochius). There is also the matter (already pondered by Pantaenus and Clement of Alexandria) that the epistle was thought to be addressed to Jewish Christians in the Holy Land. This made Hebrews ill-suited as a letter to one of Paul's churches from his mission to Greco-Roman cities. Its title "To the Hebrews" denotes a people or ethnic group, not a city or region such as we find in the titles to Paul's ecclesiastical letters.[18]

Placing Hebrews after 2 Thessalonians catered to the majority of Eastern Christians who believed Hebrews belonged among Paul's ecclesiastical letters, as well as to Western Christians who did not so believe. The early and wide support for this placement is followed by over a half dozen modern critical editions of the Greek New Testament, including Westcott and Hort's text.[19] It was contemplated but ultimately declined as the published order in the recent Tyndale House *Greek New Testament*.[20]

Third, we find Hebrews at the close of the entire Pauline corpus (after Philemon) in seven uncial MSS, the vast majority of minuscule MSS, and in a number of ancient versions, not least the Latin Vulgate. The Greek textual tradition for this sequence (the so-called Byzantine text type) traces back to the recension of the NT text attributed to Lucian of Antioch (d. 312).[21] The placement of Hebrews after Philemon constituted a compromise between Eastern and Western estimations of the epistle and thereby paved the way for its universal acceptance in the canon. A terminal position in the Pauline corpus deferred both to Greeks who wished to own Hebrews as Paul's (or reserve their judgment, as Origen did) and to Latins who persisted in casting doubt on its Pauline origins.

Western resistance to Hebrews had already prompted third-century Egyptian Christians to place the epistle at the close of Paul's letters to churches. Western pressure must have been keenly felt in the early fourth century for the editors in Antioch to take the bold (conciliatory?) action of placing Hebrews dead last in the Pauline collection. In nearby Asia Minor, Amphilochius of Iconium (ca. 340-ca. 395) shows evidence of the East-West tug-of-war that

---

18. Goswell 2016b, 752-53.
19. Metzger 1994, 592.
20. Jongkind and Williams 2017, 512.
21. Hatch 1936, 143.

was still going on in his day. He places Hebrews after Philemon (doubtless following the Byzantine textual tradition) but defends Hebrews against the claim that it is "spurious."[22] What is more, he seems behooved to replace the seven-church symbolism introduced by the Muratorian Canon (which Mason argues was designed to preclude Hebrews from Paul's letters[23]) with a "twice seven Epistles" rubric that authorizes a fourteen-letter Pauline corpus.[24] His contemporary, Epiphanius of Salamis (315–403), was acquainted with some MSS that place Hebrews after 2 Thessalonians, as well as others that place Hebrews after Philemon.[25] Jerome, too, was aware of both placements but selected the terminal placement of Hebrews for the Latin Vulgate.

The positioning of Hebrews at the end of the Pauline corpus providentially granted it a far greater function than if it had remained embedded elsewhere among Paul's letters. Hebrews would eventually come into its own as a distinctive voice within the NT canon. This may not have happened if Hebrews had not ultimately landed in its current position at the outer edge of Paul's letters. We will have more to say about the role of Hebrews once we have completed our examination of the canonical sequence of the Catholic Epistles.

The Order of the Catholic Epistles

On the surface, the varying arrangements of the CE appear as a welter of possibilities (see table 3.1). However, two basic patterns emerge. First, we have the common Eastern (and eventually universal) order found in our Bibles today (sequence *a*). Here the Epistle of James occupies first place. Sequence *g* is like it in keeping the priority of James, except that it brings Jude into proximity with it. Second, over half of the sequences give Peter priority. This order reflects a Western origin. Readers may discern additional factors that may contribute to the various sequences of the CE: descending order of length (*b* and *f*, as well as the order of the Petrine and Johannine letters in every sequence); keeping the apostles Peter and John together (*a*, *b*, *d*, *f*, *g*); and keeping the brothers of the Lord, James and Jude, together (*b*, *d*, *e*, *f*, *g*). Among the attested sequences we never find Jude in first place or 1–2 Peter last.

---

22. Amphilochius of Iconium, *Seleuc.* lines 308-9.
23. Mason 1968, 83-119.
24. Amphilochius of Iconium, *Seleuc.* line 301.
25. Epiphanius, *Pan.* 3.42 (Epiphanius 2009, 360).

Theoretically, the seven CE could be ordered in 5,040 possible permutations. Realistically, 1–2 Peter and 1–3 John always count as single units, so that James, Peter, John, and Jude could be listed in twenty-four different possible ways.[26] Statistically, then, the seven attested sequences (*a* through *g*) account for less than 30 percent of the possibilities. If we bracket out *g* (because it is attested in only one late MS) and *e* (whose only witness, Rufinus, varies from *c* by transposing 1–3 John and Jude to produce the extraordinarily rare instance of 1–3 John standing next to Revelation), the five remaining permutations constitute only a little over one-fifth of the twenty-four possibilities.

TABLE 3.1. DIFFERENT ARRANGEMENTS OF THE CATHOLIC EPISTLES

The following table displays the seven different arrangements of the CE known to us from MSS of the NT and from patristic sources. This table relies on data from Metzger (1987, 299-300), Nienhuis (2007, 91-95), and additional research and observations.

	Order	Witnesses	Organizing Factors
a.	James 1–2 Peter 1–3 John Jude	Codex Sinaiticus (fourth c.), Codex Vaticanus (fourth c.), Codex Alexandrinus (fifth c.); Codex Fuldensis (ca. 546); Cyril of Jerusalem (ca. 350); Synod of Laodicea (ca. 363); Athanasius (367); Epiphanius (*Pan.* 3.369.23 [AD 374-77; Epiphanius 2013, 536]); Gregory of Nazianzus (d. 389); Amphilochius of Iconium (d. ca. 395); Jerome (d. 420); Bede the Venerable (d. 735); Nicephorus (d. 828)	The order of the "Pillars" (Gal. 2:9): James, Cephas (= Peter), and John; brothers of the Lord (James and Jude) enclose the CE; apostles Peter and John together (as per Acts 3:1, 3, 11; 4:13, 19; 8:14).
b.	1–2 Peter 1–3 John James Jude	Council of Carthage (397); Apostolic Canon no. 85 (ca. 350-ca. 380); a Latin canon of the sixth or seventh c.	Primacy of Peter; apostles Peter and John together; brothers of the Lord (James and Jude) together. Length might determine this order: 1–2 Peter (403 stichoi); 1–3 John (332); James (247); Jude (71).

---

26. Lockett 2017, 101.

c.	1–2 Peter James 1–3 John Jude	Codex Y (ninth or tenth c.); Catalogue Claromontanus (sixth c.); Decretum Gelasianum (sixth c.)	Transposition of James and 1–2 Peter to denote Peter's primacy.
d.	1–2 Peter 1–3 John Jude James	Philaster (ca. 397); Augustine (*Doctr. chr.* 2.13 [ca. 397; *NPNF*[1] 2:539]); Cassiodorus (d. ca. 580)	Primacy of Peter; apostles Peter and John together; Jude and James together.
e.	1–2 Peter James Jude 1–3 John	Rufinus (*Symb.* 37 [ca. 404; *NPNF*[2] 3:558])	Primacy of Peter; brothers of the Lord in the middle; Epistles of John placed next to the "Revelation of John."
f.	1–3 John 1–2 Peter Jude James	Innocent I (405); Isidore of Seville (d. 636)	The number of epistles from each author in descending order: Three from John, two from Peter, and one each from Jude and James.
g.	James Jude 1–2 Peter 1–3 John	MS 326 (12th c.)	Primacy of James; brothers of the Lord together; apostles Peter and John together.

The order of the CE under this analysis is relatively stable. The common Eastern order (*a*) is the earliest, and it would become the most widespread through the influence of the Byzantine textual tradition and the Latin Vulgate. Western departures from the Eastern order were driven primarily by concerns for the primacy of Peter (*b, c, d, e*) or by the placement of writings by apostles prior to those by nonapostles (*b, d, f*) such as we find in the Western order of the Gospels.[27] Our earliest witness to the Latin Vulgate, Codex Fuldensis (AD 546), contains a "Prologue to the Canonical Epistles" purportedly composed by Jerome (though it was not[28]). Its opening lines supply a sixth-century testimony to the rationale for the Latin order of the CE (the primacy of Peter) *and* its realignment with the Eastern order (as was also done with the Gospels):

> The seven Canonical Epistles among the Greeks (who in wisdom follow the orthodox faith) do not have the same order as is found in the Latin

---

27. Goswell 2017, 144.
28. Chapman 1908, 262-67.

codices, where Peter, being preeminent among the apostles, has his two epistles first. However, even as we have corrected the Gospels into their proper order, with God's help we have done the same with these. First there is one of James, then two of Peter, three of John, and one of Jude.[29] Therefore, the Eastern order has priority. The other sequences are deviations from it that reflect the concerns of Latin Christians.

Neither stichometric order nor the priority of Peter (or apostles from among the Twelve) is determinative for the earliest sequence of the CE (*a*). One could trace a chronological sequence, as Bede the Venerable does,[30] based upon traditions concerning the times of death for James (in the thirtieth year after the Lord's passion), Peter (in the thirty-eighth), and John (during Domitian's reign), but this rationale is not immediately apparent or widespread.

In the preface to his commentary on the CE, Bede's first pair of explanations for their order is in touch with more ancient traditions.[31] First, he states, "James is placed first among these for the reason that he received the government of the church of Jerusalem, from where the source and beginning of the preaching of the Gospel took place and spread throughout the entire world." Second, "The apostle Paul also shows respect for this see [the seat of a bishop's office] when in naming him he says, *James, Cephas, and John, who appeared to be pillars* [Gal. 2:9]."[32]

The diglot Greek-Latin MS, Codex Claromontanus (sixth c.), provides confirmation for this explanation. It preserves a table of contents (whose ancestor could have originated in Alexandria [ca. 300]) that follows sequence *c* in table 3.1. What is instructive is that the same MS has a variant reading of the list of "the pillars" (Gal. 2:9) in an order that *matches* the sequence of the first three CE authors in the table of contents: Peter (instead of Cephas), James, and John. Together, Bede and Codex Claromontanus demonstrate a linkage between the order of the "pillars" in Galatians 2:9 and the order of the CE.

The sequence of the pillar apostles in Galatians 2:9, then, acts as the primary principle of organization for the order of the CE. The order is buttressed by the preeminence of James in the governance of the early church,

29. PL 29:821-25, AT.
30. Bede the Venerable 1985, 4.
31. For example, Jerome, *Vir. ill.* 2; see Bede the Venerable 1985, 5n1.
32. Bede the Venerable 1985, 3.

which is in evidence in the Acts of the Apostles. In Luke's narrative, Peter implicitly acknowledges James's ecclesiastical authority in Acts 12:17. James presides over the Jerusalem Council in Acts 15, which concerned the extent of Gentile believers' adherence to the Mosaic law. He declares the final word on the controversy and commissions an encyclical letter to announce the resolutions of the council. Finally, James is chief among the church elders who attempt to defuse a potentially explosive clash between Paul and those who accused the minister to the Gentiles of preaching that Jewish as well as Gentile believers in Jesus ought to abandon Torah observance (21:17-26).

If James acted as the administrative head of the church, Peter was the most important apostolic witness to "the truth of the gospel" (Gal. 2:14; see also 1:18-19) and the lead apostle from among the Twelve who were with Jesus throughout his ministry (Matt. 10:1-4 // Mark 3:13-19 // Luke 6:12-16 // Acts 1:13; see vv. 20-22). There is no need for us to rehearse all the particulars of Peter's prominence in roughly the first half of Acts as the chief representative of the apostolic witnesses to Jesus's resurrection.

John's place after Peter in both Galatians 2:9 and in the order of the CE coheres with their friendly rivalry implied in the Fourth Gospel[33] and their frequent pairing in Luke and Acts.[34] Peter and John were in the innermost circle of Jesus's disciples who were given an exclusive preview of the Lord's glorification at the transfiguration (Matt. 17:1-8 // Mark 9:2-10 // Luke 9:28-36)—an event whose eye-and-ear-witness character is highlighted in 2 Peter 1:16-18. Is it mere coincidence that the prologue of 1 John (1:1-4)—"That which was from the beginning, which we have heard, which we have seen with our eyes . . ."—echoes the *only* speech in Acts (4:19-20) attributed to Peter *and* John jointly: "We cannot keep from speaking about what we have seen and heard"? The theme of eyewitness testimony joins together 2 Peter and 1 John within the CE.

The precedence of "the pillars," with James's ascendancy as the ecclesiastical leader, accounts for the placement of James as "the first of the so-called catholic epistles"[35] and Jude as the "seventh" (Gregory of Nazianzus;

---

33. John 13:21-30; 18:15-18; 20:1-10; 21:15-24; thus, Goswell 2010, 239.
34. Luke 8:51; 9:28; 22:8; Acts 1:13; 3:1, 3-4, 11; 4:1, 3, 7, 13, 19, 23; 8:14, 17, 25.
35. Eusebius, *Hist. eccl.* 2.23.25 (*NPNF²* 1:128).

Amphilochius of Iconium). By any account, Jude was an important figure in the early Jesus movement (being a brother of the Lord mentioned by name in Matt. 13:55 // Mark 6:3), but he operated in the shadow of the apostles. He was present with his brothers, as was Mary the mother of Jesus (Acts 1:14), alongside the Eleven (soon to be twelve again; vv. 12-26) in the nucleus of the nascent church. Almost certainly he was one of "the Lord's brothers" whom Paul mentions as itinerant missionaries (1 Cor. 9:5).

Elements of Jude's letter show how it fits in the seventh position among the CE. Though maximally separated spatially from James in the collection, Jude's self-identification as "a brother of James" (Jude v. 1) draws it into intimate relationship with James (who shares with Jude the identity as a "servant" of Jesus Christ [James 1:1; Jude v. 1]). Therefore, the epistles from James and Jude, the brothers of the Lord, enclose the corpus of the CE and bring into view the provenance of all the authors of the CE in connection with the primitive Jewish church at Jerusalem. Both James and Jude close with exhortations about preventing believers from falling away from the faith (James 5:19-20; Jude vv. 20-25). Jude's concern for staying true to the faith builds strong ties with 2 Peter and the Johannine Epistles. The well-known literary relationship between 2 Peter and Jude (regardless of the direction of literary dependence) creates further cohesion in the corpus of the CE. Jude's appropriation of apocalyptic sources (vv. 9, 14) and its eschatological orientation (e.g., eternal destiny, vv. 7, 13, 21; "in the last times," v. 18) make it most suited in the position immediately before the Apocalypse, rather than in a position that would interfere with the James-Peter-John sequence of Galatians 2:9.[36]

Our principal observations about the relationships between the stated authors of the CE are depicted in figure 3.1. The corpus of the CE stands as a collective witness to the way believers in the Lord Jesus Christ ought to live their lives in accordance with the gospel of the kingdom. The testimony in these seven letters originates from the most authoritative figures of the primitive Jerusalem church—who were eyewitnesses of Jesus's life and ministry.[37] Implicitly,

---

36. Goswell 2010, 240.

37. There is reason to believe that the CE were first brought together as a canonical collection in Jerusalem (Chase 1902, 136-37). Cyril of Jerusalem provides the earliest full-throated recognition of "the seven Catholic Epistles" (*Catech.* 4.33-37 [*NPNF²* 7:26-28]), and using a process of elimination, it is unlikely that the collection would have originated in Alexandria, Caesarea, Antioch, or anywhere further West.

then, their epistolary witness is intended to complement the epistolary contributions of Paul. We will have more to say about the interrelationships between the books of the NT once we have explored the canonical sequences of the epistolary collections, to which we will turn in the next section.

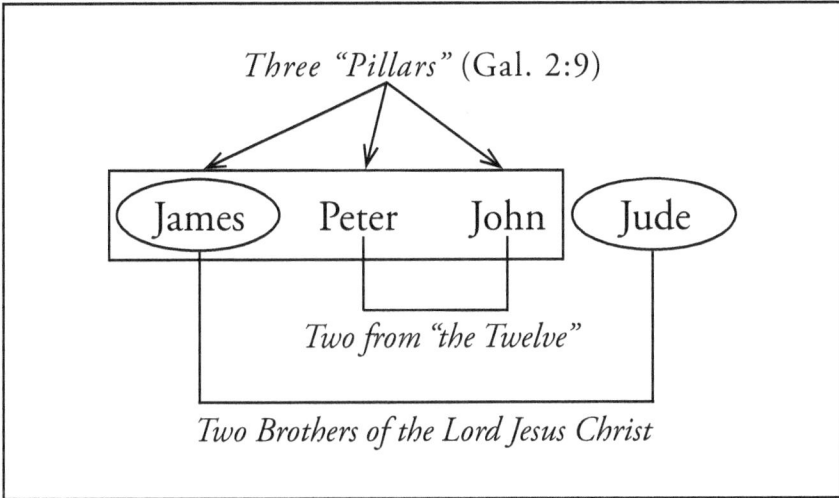

Three "Pillars" (Gal. 2:9)

James Peter John Jude

Two from "the Twelve"

Two Brothers of the Lord Jesus Christ

Fig. 3.1. Four early church figures and the order of the Catholic Epistles

The New Testament Letter Collections in Canonical Sequence

Only 59 Greek manuscripts contain the entire NT, and another 150 contain the entire NT minus Revelation. Most of the 5,800-plus total manuscripts contain sections or canonical units of the NT.[38] Thus less than 4 percent of the NT witnesses (209 MSS) contain roughly the whole NT in one volume (often without Revelation). Prior to the invention of the printing press, few Christians in the history of the church ever held in their hands a complete NT (or Bible!). As we have seen, the NT is a collection of collections, and understanding the arrangement of these collections helps us to better navigate the "Divine Library" of the Holy Scriptures.

One feature of the development of the NT canon is the regular appearance of the Acts of the Apostles and the CE bound together in one codex

---

38. About 2,150 MSS and fragments contain the four Gospels, 580-plus contain Paul's letters, 450-plus contain the Acts and the CE together, and not quite 230 have only Revelation (Aland and Aland 1989, 83).

(usually in that order, though sometimes Acts follows the CE; and there are instances of Acts affixed to the four Gospels). The pairing of Acts and the CE is so frequent that in critical editions of the NT (such as Nestle-Aland's *Novum Testamentum Graece*) the letter *a* (= *apostolos*) indicates MSS containing Acts plus the CE. It was also customary among Byzantine Christians to bundle together Acts plus the CE plus the Pauline letters into one MS, which they called a *praxapostolos*.[39]

For a long time the "Eastern order" of the NT books was as follows: Gospels, Acts, CE, Paul's letters, and (when present) Revelation. This is the order we find in Codex Vaticanus (fourth c.), Codex Alexandrinus (fifth c.), in a multitude of Greek MSS, as well as in the canon lists of Cyril of Jerusalem, Athanasius, and the Council of Laodicea. The support for this order, in which Acts and the CE *precede* Paul's letters, is strong enough to be adopted in the recent Tyndale House *Greek New Testament*.[40] However, there was also a strong tradition in Anatolia,[41] which held to the "received" sequence, as evidenced by the canon lists of Amphilochius of Iconium and Gregory of Nazianzus, but also by Jerome in Bethlehem. Jerome's Latin Vulgate strongly influenced the order of the biblical books as we find them today.

The Eastern order demonstrates the gravitational force of the Acts of the Apostles on the NT letter collections. The narrative flow of the Acts of the Apostles commends the placing of the CE collection first, followed by the Pauline corpus. Roughly, the first half of Acts (chs. 1–12) is devoted to the ministry of "the apostles" in Jerusalem, Judea, and Samaria, focusing especially on their chief spokesman, Peter (and to a lesser degree John). The word "apostles" occurs fifty-seven times in Acts (chs. 1–2, 4–6, 8–9, and 15) in connection with the Jerusalem apostles and only twice in reference to Paul and Barnabas (14:4, 14). We have already noted the prominence of James as an ecclesiastical authority in Jerusalem and the implicit presence of Jude among the other brothers of Jesus in Acts 1:14. The early history in Acts naturally corresponds to the epistolary deposit of the major figures

---

39. Parker 2008, 283.

40. Jongkind and Williams 2017, iv and 512; also in seven previous critical editions of the Greek NT (Metzger 1987, 296n2). Codex Sinaiticus (fourth c.) is closer to today's "received" order but still shows the tendency for Acts and the CE to travel together: Gospels, Paul's letters, Acts, CE, Revelation.

41. Influenced by the Lucianic text of the NT and/or the Syrian canon.

from among the Jerusalem church leaders and apostles: the CE. Roughly, the second half of Acts (13–28) is devoted to the mission of Paul the apostle. Paul's letter collection obviously correlates with this part of Luke's historical account. Cyril of Jerusalem understood the relationship of the NT letters in this very chronological relationship in line with the narrative of Acts. He lists the NT in the Eastern order (minus Revelation), marking Paul's letters as "a seal upon them all, and the last work of the disciples."[42]

However, there is an alternative logic for ordering the NT books in the "received" sequence. The Acts of the Apostles leaves off abruptly with Paul detained at Rome (28:16-31). The Pauline corpus begins with Paul writing to churches at Rome (Rom. 1:7). The Epistle to the Romans, furthermore, provides Paul's exposition of the gospel in full, including the justification for his mission practice—described repeatedly in Acts—of bringing the gospel "first to the Jew, then to the Gentile" (Rom. 1:16; 2:9, 10), namely, that righteousness comes through faith rather than ethnic identity (1:16-17). In Acts 28, after appealing to Jews at Rome with the kingdom message about Jesus, Paul interprets the rejection of the gospel by some of them as an opportunity for the success of the mission to the Gentiles (vv. 23-28). This in a nutshell is the message of the central section of Romans (chs. 9–11), in which Paul wrestles with the problem of the hardening of his own Jewish people in contrast to the reception of the gospel among many Gentiles.[43]

The "received" canonical order, therefore, guides the reader from the missionary career of Paul in the latter half of Acts into the epistolary witness of Paul in his letter collection. Then, upon reaching the CE, the reader doubles back to the earliest witnesses to the Lord Jesus whose activities are recounted in the first half of Acts. Epiphanius echoes a similar chronological relationship between Acts and the two NT letter collections. He writes about looking in "the four holy Gospels, the fourteen letters of the holy apostle Paul, and in the Catholic Epistles of James and Peter and John and Jude before these [*pro toutōn*, i.e., before Paul's letters], together with the Acts of the Apostles in their times."[44] It is unclear whether Epiphanius intends to list the CE and

42. Cyril of Jerusalem, *Catech.* 4.36 (*NPNF*[2] 7:28).
43. For further links between Acts and Romans, see Emerson 2013, 68-74; Wall and Lemcio 1992, 152.
44. Epiphanius, *Pan.* 3.369.21-23 (TLG 2021:002:2286467), AT.

Acts before Paul's letters.[45] He seems to have it both ways by *listing* Paul's letters before the CE and Acts but then *saying* that the latter belongs before the former! His statement about the Acts of the Apostles "in their times" is equally ambiguous, since it could refer to the times of the authors of the CE or to the *respective* times of both the authors of the CE and Paul. Either way, he is connecting the chronology of Acts with the CE (or with both the CE and the Pauline corpus).

There are two additional factors that contribute to the logic of the "received" canonical order. One involves internal evidence from the CE collection itself; the other, a theological link between Hebrews and Acts. We propose that the canonical order—the Pauline corpus (closed out by Hebrews) followed by the CE—creates a chiastic symmetry with the narrative sequence of Acts (fig. 3.2). Let us begin by considering the first set of evidence from within the CE collection.

Coherence of the Canonical Order: Internal Evidence in the Catholic Epistles

There are two specific instances when the CE *presuppose* knowledge of the Pauline letters.

The first is James's discussion of faith and works (2:14-26). There is hardly any doubt that James is reacting to a teaching that resembles or misconstrues Paul's teaching in Romans and Galatians. At least on a textual level, James 2:21, 24 share a cluster of key terms with Pauline texts such as Romans 4:2 and Galatians 2:16 ("Abraham," "justified," "faith," "works" [NASB]), and both James and Paul appeal to the same text from Genesis 15:6. It strains credulity to believe that the multiple points of contact between James and Paul are sheer coincidences.[46] We do not need to resolve the historical (and hermeneutical) question of whether James was engaging in direct anti-Pauline polemic or in the correction of a false interpretation of Paul's doctrine (we think the latter). What is important to know is that as canonical readers we have no access either to Paul's teaching or our inferences concerning a

---

45. Bruce suggests this possibility (1988, 213).
46. Hagner 2012, 680.

distorted version of Paul's teaching in isolation from the collection of Paul's letters. The fact that readers can even discern the need to negotiate between the Pauline and Jacobean discussions of faith and works is necessitated by the existence of both sets of texts. Given the identical terminology and shared proof text from Genesis 15:6, one is hard pressed to tell what *other* teaching James could be criticizing except some version of Paul's. On the canonical level, then, James's discussion of faith and works presupposes the teaching in Paul's letters; and the canonical order (Paul's letters, then the CE) facilitates readers' apprehension of James's teaching by exposing them in advance to Paul's teaching in his letters.

The second piece of evidence is more straightforward. The author of 2 Peter explicitly refers to Paul writing "in all his letters" (3:15-16)—"all" implying that there is a whole collection of them. There is no need to answer the historical questions this raises concerning the authorship of 2 Peter. The original readers must have had a prior knowledge of the Pauline letters for this reference to make sense. More to the point, readers of the Pauline corpus and the CE in their canonical order cannot help but read 2 Peter 3:15-16 as a reference to the Pauline letter collection that *precedes* the CE.

We could discuss additional data pointing to the CE as a canonical collection that presumes a Pauline corpus in connection with its own reception and interpretation, such as the way 1 Peter seems to appropriate Pauline epistolary and theological elements that would have been familiar to readers.[47] However, our examples above sufficiently show that the CE fit nicely within the canonical order: Acts—Paul—CE.

Coherence of the Canonical Order: Hebrews at the End of the Pauline Corpus

Another line of evidence indicates the appropriateness of Hebrews at the end of Paul's letters, thus forming a transition between the Pauline corpus and the CE. If indeed the narrative flow of the Acts of the Apostles has any coherent linkage with the placement of the NT letter collections—with the Pauline and CE collections corresponding in inverse order to the narrative

---

47. See Michaels 1988, xliii-xliv.

progression of early church history—then might Hebrews find its place in correlation to a central turning point of the story?

William Manson develops previous observations about the resemblance of the theology of Hebrews with that of Stephen in Acts 6–7. He finds no fewer than eight[48] correlations between Hebrews and Stephen's theological emphases:

> *a.* the attitude of Stephen to the Cultus and Law of Judaism;
>
> *b.* his declaration that Jesus means to change and supersede these things;
>
> *c.* his sense of divine call to the people of God being a call to "Go out";
>
> *d.* his stress on the ever-shifting scene in Israel's life, and on the ever-renewed homelessness of the faithful;
>
> *e.* his thought of God's Word as "living";
>
> *f.* his incidental allusion to Joshua in connection with the promise of God's "Rest";
>
> *g.* his idea of the "angels" being the ordainers of God's Law;
>
> *h.* his directing of his eyes to Heaven and to Jesus.[49]

Our task is not to authenticate a historical reconstruction showing the trajectory between Hebrews and the Hellenistic-Jewish Christians in Jerusalem (the "seven" of Acts 6:5), with Stephen being the chief exponent of the theological principles that would drive the Christian world mission beyond the narrow confines of Jerusalem and Judea.[50]

The *theological* nexus between Stephen and Hebrews, however, is unmistakable. Hebrews formulates Stephen's first principles in exegetical thickness and theological richness: the eschatological dawn of the Messiah and the blessings of the new covenant fulfill and supersede the Mosaic legislation and cultus. Hellenistic-Jewish Christians radiating from the "seven" in Jerusalem implemented the implications of these truths for Christian mission (Acts 8:1, 4; 11:19-20). The author of Hebrews realized how the realities of Christ's

---

48. A ninth correlation, though not exclusive to Stephen (see Acts 2:22, 43; 4:30; 5:12; 14:3; 15:12), involves the "wonders and signs" he performed (6:8); compare Hebrews's reference to such miraculous acts as divine testimony (2:4) and "powers of the coming age" (6:5). Lincoln Hurst (1990, 94) adds another: the citation of Exodus 25:40 in both Acts 7:44 and Hebrews 8:5.

49. Manson 1951, 36.

50. For a critique of Manson's historical reconstruction, see Childs 1994, 412, and more fully Hurst 1990, 89-106.

eternal priesthood and heavenly sanctuary were indispensable to Christian identity and discipleship.[51]

A canonical angle of vision understands Hebrews as belonging not merely to the outer edges of the Pauline ambit but at the theological nerve center of early Christian faith. The intertextual and theological links between Acts 6–7 and Hebrews situate Hebrews within the matrix of Hellenistic-Jewish Christianity that originally formed a "cultural bridge between the Aramaic-speaking ministry of Jesus and the early Jerusalem Church and Paul's urban ministry to Greek-speaking Gentile centers."[52] Analogously, the Epistle to the Hebrews serves as a middle point between the Pauline corpus and the CE in a mirror image of the narrative of Acts (see fig. 3.2).

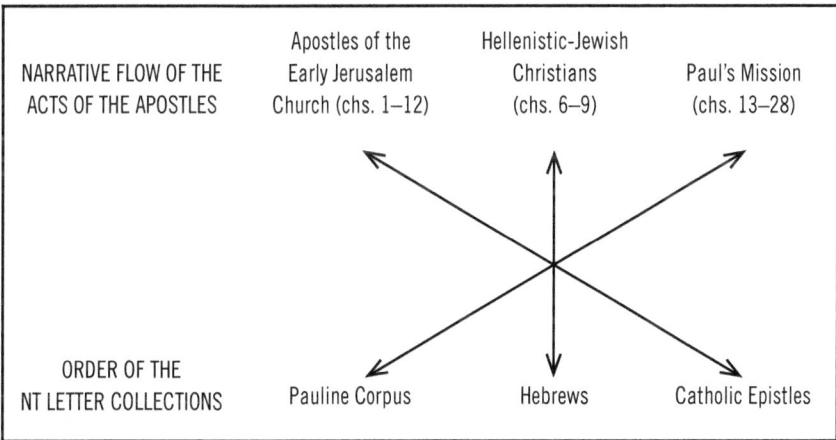

	Apostles of the	Hellenistic-Jewish	
NARRATIVE FLOW OF THE	Early Jerusalem	Christians	Paul's Mission
ACTS OF THE APOSTLES	Church (chs. 1–12)	(chs. 6–9)	(chs. 13–28)
ORDER OF THE			
NT LETTER COLLECTIONS	Pauline Corpus	Hebrews	Catholic Epistles

Fig. 3.2. Chiastic arrangement of the story in Acts and the NT letter collections

This illustrates the appropriateness of the canonical ordering of the NT letter collections in conjunction with the narrative logic of the Acts of the Apostles. We are now in a position to look at how to interpret Hebrews and the CE in light of the relationships we have traced between the NT letter collections.

---

51. For further explication of Hebrews's place within the Hellenistic-Jewish Christian tradition of Stephen, see Lane 1991, cxlvii-cl.

52. Lane 1991, cxlvi.

Interpreting the Catholic Epistles Canonically: Hebrews as a Segue

We will now pursue two goals, based upon what we know concerning the arrangement of the NT letter collections in relation to the narrative flow of Acts. We will explore the ways Hebrews functions as a segue from Paul's letters to the CE and then also describe the animating themes that hold together the seven CE as a collection.

Hebrews in Relation to the Pauline Letters

Modern scholarship accentuates the distinctive features of Hebrews to such a degree that the numerous commonalities between Paul and Hebrews are too often forgotten. Hurst lists over two dozen points of contact between them (see table 3.2 below).[53] The common ground between Paul and Hebrews spans their theological beliefs (especially Christology), conceptions of the Christian life, future hope, and some epistolary conventions. We can also see similarities in how Paul and Hebrews utilize the same OT texts, such as Psalm 8,[54] Deuteronomy 32:35,[55] and Habakkuk 2:4.[56]

TABLE 3.2. COMMON GROUND BETWEEN PAUL AND HEBREWS

The data in the following table has been adapted and expanded from Hurst 1990, 108.

Common Elements	Hebrews	Paul
Christ's incarnation, including his prior glory and role in creating and sustaining the cosmos	1:2, 3, 6	1 Cor. 8:6; 2 Cor. 4:4; Col. 1:15-17
Christ as "the firstborn" / believers as siblings of "the firstborn"	1:6 / 2:11-12; 12:23	Col. 1:15, 18 / Rom. 8:29

---

53. Hurst 1990, 108.

54. Hebrews 2:6-10; 1 Corinthians 15:22-28; see Philippians 3:21—in conjunction with Psalm 110:1 (Heb. 1:13; 1 Cor. 15:25, 27).

55. Hebrews 10:30; Romans 12:19.

56. Hebrews 10:38; Romans 1:17; Galatians 3:11.

Christ's humiliation	2:14-17	Rom. 8:3; Gal. 4:4; Phil. 2:7
Christ's obedience	5:8	Rom. 5:19; Phil. 2:8
Christ's sacrificial offering of himself for us	9:14, 26-28; 10:12	1 Cor. 5:7; Gal. 2:20; Eph. 5:2
Christ's death as a "sacrifice of atonement" (*hilastērion*; *hilaskesthai*)	2:17; 9:5	Rom. 3:25
Christ's death as "redemption" for sin	9:15	Rom. 3:24; 1 Cor. 1:30; Eph. 1:7; Col. 1:14
Christ's death and exaltation as the conquest over the devil and the power of death	2:14	Rom. 5:17, 21; 6:9; 1 Cor. 15:26; Col. 2:15; 2 Tim. 1:10
Christ's inheritance of a superior name	1:14	Phil. 2:9-11
Christ's intercession for us	7:25	Rom. 8:34
Christ as our brother / Christ and believers as (co-)heirs	2:11 / 1:4, 14; 9:15	Rom. 8:29 / Rom. 8:17
Superiority of the new covenant	8:6, 13; see 7:22	2 Cor. 3:9-18
The "foundation" of Christian teaching	6:1	1 Cor. 3:10-12
"Signs and wonders" and the distribution of the gifts of the Spirit	2:4	1 Cor. 12:11; 2 Cor. 12:12
Abraham's welcoming the promise "from a distance" or his being "pre-evangelized"	11:13	Gal. 3:8
Abraham's faith as an example	6:12-15; 11:11, 17-19	Rom. 4:17-20; Gal. 3:6-9
Believers as "Abraham's descendants"	2:16	Rom. 9:7-8; Gal. 3:7, 29
Deterrent example of Israel's faithless wilderness generation	3:7–4:11	1 Cor. 10:1-11
"Milk" associated with immaturity; "meat," with being "mature" (*teleioi*)	5:12-14	1 Cor. 3:2; 14:20
Conversion as enlightenment	6:4; 10:32	2 Cor. 4:4
"Righteousness that is in keeping with faith"	11:7	Rom. 4:13; 9:30; Phil. 3:9
Christian life as a race	12:1	1 Cor. 9:24-26
Christians living in expectation (*apekdechesthai*) of Christ's second coming or future hope	9:28	Rom. 8:19, 23, 25; 1 Cor. 1:7; Gal.5:5; Phil. 3:20

Similar closing epistolary features and distinctive "Pauline" expressions	"God of peace" (13:20)	Rom. 15:33; 16:20
	"Lord Jesus" (v. 20)	14:14; 16:20
	"equip you with everything good for doing his will" (v. 21)	12:2
	"through Jesus Christ" (v. 21)	1:8; 2:16; 5:21; 7:25
	ascribing glory to God (v. 21)	11:36; 16:27; Gal. 1:5; Eph. 1:5-6; Phil. 1:11; 4:20
	reference to Timothy (v. 23)	Rom. 16:21; 1 Cor. 16:10, etc.
	closing "grace" greeting (v. 25)	1 Cor. 16:24; 2 Cor. 13:13; Gal. 6:18; Eph. 6:24, etc.

It is no wonder Origen's impression was that Hebrews expresses the thoughts of Paul the apostle but in the literary style of an unknown author.

Yet Hebrews differs from Paul's letters in many ways, both in style and content. Not only is the author's command of Greek style and rhetoric superior (as Origen well recognized), but also his method of argumentation and overall theological approach are quite different from Paul's. We may mention Hebrews's effective interchange of exposition and exhortation throughout, varying from Paul's custom of reserving paraenesis for the latter portion of letters (e.g., Rom. 12–15; Eph. 4–6). Hebrews's quotations of longer passages (e.g., Ps. 95:7-11 in Heb. 3:7-11; Jer. 31:31-34 in Heb. 8:8-12) to serve as launching pads for careful exegesis and application, as well as his extensive recital of OT history (Heb. 11:1-40), bear little resemblance to Pauline interpretive practice.

Hebrews carries out a sustained comparison and contrast between "the first covenant" (8:7; 9:15, 18; see 8:9) and "the new covenant" (8:6, 8, 13; 9:15; 12:24), but he does so in a way that finely balances elements of continuity and discontinuity. Paul is inclined to stress the radical discontinuity between the two covenants: law versus grace, works of the law versus faith, flesh versus Spirit, slavery versus freedom, death versus life, and so on. It is more often the case that Hebrews expresses discontinuity in terms of the new-covenant benefits being "better" (1:4; 6:9; 7:7, 19, 22; 8:6; 9:23; 10:34; 11:16, 35, 40; 12:24). Both Paul and Hebrews understand the transition from old to new as coming in God's eschatological revelation through the Son. But the discontinuities in Hebrews could never be twisted by the likes of Marcion, who exploited Paul's teachings to argue for a complete rupture between the old and new.[57] This is true for several reasons.[58]

First, Hebrews has a vested interest in not being perceived as "trashing" the old covenant, because he addressed an audience comprised of *Jewish* Christians. In contrast, Paul's intended readers were Gentile Christians. Paul also has in mind the distressing reality of Jewish "hardening" or resistance to the gospel.[59]

Second, the author of Hebrews, with his keen exegetical eye, detects the explicit and implicit ways in which *God* reveals in the Hebrew Scriptures how obsolescence was built into the old covenant. The very fact that the Lord announces his intentions in Jeremiah 31:31-34 to establish a "new covenant" indicates the defectiveness and eventual expiration of the first covenant (Heb. 8:7, 13).

Third, Hebrews's unique contribution to NT Christology—Jesus as high priest—entails continuity as well as discontinuity. Priesthood exists through divine initiative (5:1-6), and a change in the priesthood necessitates an alteration of the law too (7:12). At the same time, in the theology of Hebrews the covenantal framework of priesthood, sanctuary, and bloody sacrifice is preserved, not eradicated. From Hebrews's perspective, all the trappings of the first covenant are transitory and ineffective shadows of the true, perfect, and eternal realities of the new covenant (8:5; 9:11; 10:1).[60]

All of this supports Hebrews's transitional status at the edge of the Pauline corpus. Much of what we find in Hebrews is compatible with the

---

57. For Marcion, the second-century Christian heretic, the break between old and new was fundamentally theological (a different "god" for each covenant) and required the wholesale rejection of the old exclusively in favor of the new. Paul would have been appalled at the perversion of his teaching in the service of an utter demolition of God's covenants and promises to ancestral Israel (see Rom. 9:2-5).

58. For an accessible treatment of the continuities and discontinuities found in all of the NT authors, see Hagner 2018.

59. This is a major component in Paul's only extended discussion of "the new covenant" in 2 Corinthians 3:1-18; for his most strident castigation of Jewish unbelievers, see 1 Thessalonians 2:14-16.

60. See Lehne 1990, 97-104.

teachings of the apostle Paul, while being a tour de force of theological exposition and pastoral encouragement that extends beyond the bounds of Paul's known work.

Hebrews as a Segue to the Catholic Epistles

In its canonical placement, Hebrews functions as a transition from Paul's letters to the CE collection. It does so in a number of ways.

First, and perhaps most obviously, it does not share the fullness of the epistolary genre that Paul masterfully executes in his letters. Hebrews as a "word of exhortation" stands closer to the sermonic form we find in James and 1 John (see "The Challenge of Genre" in ch. 1, p. 21).

Second, Hebrews's posture toward the original followers of Jesus takes on fresh meaning when viewed through a canonical lens. Paul surely gives "those who were apostles before I was" their due (Gal. 1:17) and acknowledges himself as the last apostolic witness to Jesus's resurrection and "the least of the apostles" because of his former persecution of the church (1 Cor. 15:8; see vv. 1-11). His relationship to the Jerusalem "pillars" was not adversarial (Gal. 2:1-10), but neither was it without conflict (vv. 11-21). Paul was insistent that his apostleship and preaching of the gospel were not derived from the Jerusalem apostles but independently established through a revelation of Christ (1:1, 11-12; 1 Cor. 9:1-2). Consequently, Hebrews 2:3 has struck interpreters as being uncharacteristic of Paul: "This salvation, which was first announced by the Lord, was confirmed to us by those who heard him." Paul would have never included himself ("to us") among those who needed confirmation of the truth of the gospel (Gal. 2:6). But when we read this statement about the authoritative pedigree of the first gospel witnesses in light of Hebrews's placement within the canon, it orients readers toward the validating testimony of the firsthand hearers of Jesus and, by extension, the authors of the CE.

Third, Hebrews supplies a systematic presentation of the "new covenant" faith within the wide sweep of salvation history, from "long ago" up until "these last days" (Heb. 1:1-2*a*, NASB).[61] Hebrews brings to fuller expression several major themes (along with some minor notes) that are in the CE. Even if individual letters of the CE develop certain themes distinctively (or not as comprehensively or not at all), Hebrews provides a framework for configuring and pondering many aspects of theology and practice in the CE. There are also instances when the CE fill out or adapt truths within new horizons. This is as one would expect, because all NT letters involve authors and hearers who are in varying historical, social, and ecclesial contexts.

The themes that draw Hebrews and the CE together are not merely tangential matters but vital concerns at the heart of their respective messages. The themes relate to Christology, eschatology, ecclesiology, and the normative Christian life as one of perfection, holiness, or godliness centered around faith(fulness).

Christology. Hebrews has one of the most fulsome portraits of Jesus Christ among the NT letters. The author gives us a clear vision of Jesus Christ as fully divine and fully human. I have written elsewhere,

> Hebrews relates a complete picture of Christ's life: preexistence (1:2; 10:5), incarnation (2:14-18; 5:5-7), suffering and death (2:9-10, 18; 5:8; 9:15, 26; 12:2; 13:12), resurrection (13:20), exaltation (1:3, 13; 4:14; 7:26; 8:1; 9:24; 10:12; 12:2), heavenly intercession (7:25; see 2:18; 4:15-16; 8:1-2; 12:24), and second coming to bring salvation and judgment (9:27-28; 10:25, 37-39).[62]

By showing forth Jesus as both Son and high priest—in his preexistent divine glory and in his perfection as a flesh-and-blood human being through suffering and obedience to God—Hebrews reveals Christ as the one who is at once the definitive sacrifice for sins *and* the supreme example of devotion to God. He is "the pioneer and perfecter of faith" (12:2).

The canonical proximity of Hebrews to the CE allows Hebrews to serve as a more complete representation of the common store of christological understanding, much of which is assumed in the CE. Thus when we encounter

---

61. It is worth noting that the Pauline corpus begins and ends with the two most comprehensive expositions of the gospel (Romans and Hebrews), in touch with questions about Christ's work in relationship to God's purposes for humanity, the fulfillment of God's dealings with the people of Israel, and the destiny of the whole created order.

62. Anderson 2013, 50.

James's reference to "the Lord Jesus Christ" (1:1) and "our glorious Lord Jesus Christ" (2:1), we will not go wrong in taking these phrases as shorthand for Hebrews's depiction of Jesus's being crowned with glory and honor after his suffering of death (2:5-9, citing Ps. 8:5-7). Hebrews's "main point" is Jesus's exaltation as high priest, "who sat down at the right hand of the throne of the Majesty in heaven" (8:1, citing Ps. 110:1).

First Peter shares with Hebrews the twofold scheme of the Messiah's "sufferings" and "the glories that would follow" (1 Pet. 1:11; see Luke 24:26), as well as a cultic understanding of Christ's atoning death (e.g., "sprinkled . . . blood" [1 Pet 1:2; see Heb. 12:24]; "with the precious blood of Christ, a lamb without blemish or defect" [1 Pet. 1:19; see Heb. 7:26; 9:14]). The author of 2 Peter trains his focus on his eyewitness experience of the transfiguration, a proleptic vision of Christ's suffering and consequent glory (1:16-18). The eschatological fulfillment in Christ's atoning death ("before the creation [lit. "foundation"] of the world, . . . revealed in these last times" [1 Pet. 1:20; see Heb. 9:26]) is also present in 1 John. Jesus "was revealed to take away sins" (1 John 3:5, NRSVUE). "The reason the Son of God appeared was to destroy the devil's work" (3:8; see Heb. 2:14-18; 9:26, 28). Jesus's death is an "atoning sacrifice" for sins (1 John 2:2; 4:10; see Heb. 2:17). The Johannine Epistles also share with Hebrews the emphasis upon the humanity of Jesus. If our "confession" in Hebrews concerns the divine-human apostle and high priest (3:1; see 2:14-18), in 1–2 John it is an acknowledgment that "Jesus Christ has come in the flesh" (1 John 4:2; 2 John v. 7).

Even in Jude we see pointers to the sort of high Christology we find in Hebrews. Jesus Christ is "our only Sovereign and Lord" (v. 4). "Jesus" is the preexistent one who saved a people out of Egypt (v. 5; see Heb. 11:26).[63] "Jesus Christ our Lord" is named in connection with the glory, majesty, power, and authority of God (Jude v. 25) not dissimilar to how Hebrews speaks of the Son as seated "at the right hand of the Majesty in heaven" (Heb. 1:3; 8:1). Incidentally, only Hebrews (1:3; 8:1) and Jude (v. 25) refer to the divine "Majesty" using the same rare term (*megalōsynē*).

---

63. "Jesus" is the reading in the latest edition (28th) of the Nestle-Aland Greek text.

A rather significant christological tie that binds together Hebrews and the CE is the emphasis on Christ as our supreme moral example. This truth is not absent from Paul's teaching (1 Cor. 11:1; Eph. 4:32–5:2; 1 Thess. 1:6), and it is implicit in the biographical portraits of Jesus in the Gospels. In Hebrews, Jesus's entire life of reverent submission to God (5:7-10), culminating in his obedience to God's will in offering himself as a sacrifice (10:1-10), perfects him as "the pioneer and perfecter of faith" (12:2). This theme is not explicit in James (not even in the mention of the murder of "the righteous one" in James 5:6, NRSVUE). However, James is thoroughly indebted to Jesus's wisdom *teaching*. He exclusively appeals to OT figures, not Jesus, as examples (2:21, 23; 2:25; 5:11, 17). But canonical readers will readily apprehend these exemplars as members of the "cloud of witnesses" from the OT whose faithfulness comes to its fullest expression in Jesus (Heb. 11:1–12:2).

First Peter is replete with the theme of Jesus as the exemplary righteous sufferer (1:10-12; 2:21-25; 3:15-18; 4:1, 13; 5:1). The image of Isaiah's suffering servant of the Lord stands behind 1 Peter's portrayal of Jesus. First Peter and Hebrews share the designation of Jesus as the shepherd who guides the sheep (Heb. 13:20; 1 Pet. 2:25; 5:4; see John 10:11, 14; Rev. 7:17).

First John could not be clearer in presenting Jesus as the pattern for Christian discipleship: "Whoever claims to live in him must live as Jesus did" (2:6); being born of God involves a family likeness with God's Son in performing righteousness rather than sin (2:28–3:10); because Jesus "laid down his life for us," we ought "to lay down our lives" for one another (3:16); and the perfection of God's love among believers constitutes their Christlikeness: "as he is, so are we in this world" (4:17, NRSVUE). Those who do not properly confess Christ in their doctrine and lifestyle are "antichrists" (2:18, 22; 4:3; 2 John v. 7).

Second Peter and Jude focus attention on the future coming of Jesus, rather than on the example of his earthly life, as an incentive for holy living. Yet Christ's example for the conduct of disciples is implicit when these authors denounce false teachers who deny the Lord precisely through their licentious behavior (2 Pet. 2:1; Jude v. 4).

Eschatology. Hebrews is at one with the rest of the NT in understanding the Christ event and the resultant Christian community as located near to the end of all things. This is encapsulated in Hebrews 9:26, 28: Christ appeared "at the culmination of the ages" to atone for sin, and we eagerly await his second coming to bring final salvation and judgment. The CE concur with the view that Christ's first coming is an eschatological fulfillment (of OT prophecy: 1 Pet. 1:10-12, 20; 3:20-22; 2 Pet. 1:19-21) and that Christians should live godly lives in anticipation of the judgment and salvation at Christ's second coming (James 5:7-9; 1 Pet. 1:3-5, 13-17; 4:5-7, 13; 5:1, 4, 10; 2 Pet. 2:9; 3:1-16; 1 John 2:28; 3:2-3; Jude vv. 1, 6, 14-15, 21, 24-25).

An eschatological theme central to Hebrews and illuminating for the CE is that of the "new covenant." No other NT writer develops this idea like Hebrews (but cf. 2 Cor. 3:9-18). For Hebrews the new covenant is the overarching achievement of Christ's saving work through his high priestly ministry in the heavenly sanctuary. The prophecy concerning the new covenant in Jeremiah 31:31-34 enfolds the central arguments of Hebrews. The passage is quoted at length in Hebrews 8:8-12. It is then revisited via "pull quotes" in 10:16-17 to highlight key points—namely, that the new-covenant ministry of Christ, our high priest, brings inward conformity to God's revealed will and the decisive removal of sins.

Again, Hebrews's teaching informs the understanding of canonical readers as they turn to the CE. Douglas Moo detects in the mention of "the implanted word" in James 1:21 (NRSVUE) an echo of Jeremiah's new-covenant promise of the law written on believers' hearts.[64] Likewise, "the perfect law that gives freedom" (James 1:25) or "the royal law" of loving one's neighbor (2:8; see v. 12) expresses the kingdom ethic under the new covenant.[65]

First Peter 1:2 obliquely refers to the new covenant when speaking of being "sprinkled" with Jesus's blood, since this is a covenant-inaugurating action reminiscent of Moses's inauguration of the first covenant (Exod. 24:8, a passage quoted by Hebrews [9:20]; note also Jesus's words about "the new covenant in my blood" [Luke 22:20; 1 Cor. 11:25]). The covenantal ideas of God's electing grace (1 Pet. 1:1-2) and the sanctifying work of the Spirit (Ezek. 36:25-27) confirm this identification.

---

64. Moo 2000, 87.
65. Ibid., 117; Jobes 2011, 203-6.

The Johannine Epistles breathe the air of the new covenant in their emphasis upon believers' intimate knowledge of God (1 John 2:3-4, 13-14, 20-21; 3:19; 4:6-8, 16; 5:20; 2 John v. 1; see Jer. 31:34), possession of the anointing/Spirit (1 John 2:20, 27; 3:24; 4:13; 5:6, 8; see Ezek. 36:25-27), and corresponding performance of the commandment that is old and new (1 John 2:4, 7-8; 3:22-24; 5:2; 2 John vv. 4-6; see Jer. 31:33).[66]

Second Peter and Jude, too, while not directly invoking the new-covenant promises (though possibly in 2 Pet. 1:4),[67] assure their readers that believers may avail themselves of the keeping love and stabilizing power of God that are the exclusive province of the new covenant (2 Pet. 3:17; Jude vv. 1, 21, 24).

A significant eschatological theme concerns what systematic theologians call "the eternal state." This theme is abundant in Hebrews but not evenly represented in the CE. To be fair, it is not evenly represented throughout the NT. Hebrews describes the final hope for believers under such images as divine rest (3:11, 18; 4:1, 3, 5-6, 8, 10, 11), the inner sanctuary where Christ our forerunner has already entered (6:19-20), the heavenly homeland (11:16), and especially the New Jerusalem (12:22): "the city with foundations, whose architect and builder is God" (11:10; see v. 16); "the city of the living God" (12:22); "the city that is to come," a lasting city (13:14).

Such specificity concerning the *place* of our future hope is largely absent from the CE—except in 2 Peter. The promise for believers is usually more general, like a "crown of life" (James 1:12) or "eternal life" (1 John 2:25; Jude v. 21), to which one may compare 2 Peter's reference to participating in the divine nature (i.e., sharing in immortality, in contrast to the world's corruption [2 Pet. 1:4; see 2:20]). Obversely, the fate of fallen angels is surprisingly detailed in 2 Peter (2:4) and Jude (v. 6): they are fastened with gloomy chains in the deepest part of the underworld awaiting the final judgment. "Blackest darkness" (2 Pet. 2:17; Jude v. 13) or the "eternal fire" of God's judgment is reserved for false teachers or apostates (Jude v. 7; see v. 23; Heb. 10:27; 12:29). As for believers, both James and 1 Peter share with Hebrews

---

66. Brown 1982, 279-80, 284, 286, 349, 370, 375, etc.
67. See Osborne 2011, 289.

the covenantal idea of salvation as an inheritance.[68] Similarly, 2 Peter relates the promise of entrance into "the eternal kingdom" (1:11).

Second Peter is the only letter among the CE to contain a parallel to Hebrews's conception that in a final shaking of the cosmic order, the temporal creation will be removed, leaving God's eternal kingdom remaining (Heb. 12:27-28; but see Rev. 20:11; 21:1). According to 2 Peter, the present cosmos will be dissolved in the fire of God's judgment (3:7, 10-12) and will give way to "new heavens and a new earth" (v. 13, NRSVUE; see Rev. 21:1, 5; both echoing Isa. 65:17 and 66:22).

Ecclesiology. Hebrews and all the CE understand Christian identity in ways that conceptually trade on the heritage of God's people, Israel. Underscoring this fact are references to "the people" (*ho laos*; Heb. 2:17; 4:9; 7:27; 10:30; 11:25; 13:12; 1 Pet. 2:9-10; 2 Pet. 2:1); Abraham as "our father" (James 2:21; see Heb. 2:16) and major exemplar of faith (Heb. 6:13, 15; 11:8, 17, 19; James 2:21, 23; see Rom. 4 and Gal. 3); and to fellow believers as "brothers" (43x in Hebrews and the CE). Examples of faithfulness and unfaithfulness are consistently drawn from the OT Scriptures (e.g., Heb. 3:7–4:13; 11:1-40; 12:16-17; James 2:20-26; 1 Pet. 3:6; 2 Pet. 2:1-22; 1 John 3:11-12; Jude vv. 5-7, 11). If Hebrews 10:25 and James 2:2 are referencing a synagogue meeting, then they both betray an early Jewish-Christian setting.[69]

Hebrews and 1 Peter have the most developed and explicit ecclesiology along the lines of the spiritual heritage of Israel, though we see traces in the other CE. There are two broad ways to illustrate this. First, Hebrews famously depicts the Christian life as a pilgrimage to the celestial city. The identity of the patriarchs as "foreigners and strangers on earth" (11:13) informs the way current believers see their own movement toward the heavenly city. First Peter grounds this notion of believers as "aliens and exiles" (2:11, NRSVUE) in the history of Judah's exile and subsequent Diaspora experience in Babylon (1:1; see 5:13). James also invokes this history in his address to his readers as "the twelve tribes in the dispersion" (1:1, NRSVUE). First Peter is distinctive by

---

68. Hebrews 1:14; 6:12, 17; 9:15 ("eternal inheritance"); 11:7; James 2:5 ("heirs of the kingdom," NRSVUE); 1 Pet. 1:4 ("an inheritance . . . kept in heaven"); 3:7 ("heirs . . . of the gracious gift of life").

69. James also refers to "the elders of the church" (5:14). The only other unambiguous references to an individual church in the CE are in 3 John vv. 6, 9-10.

comparison to both Hebrews and James because it applies Israel's alien status to Gentile converts rather than to Jewish Christians.

The broader notion of the Christian community being alienated from the world surfaces in the rest of the CE. James flatly states that friendship with the world is enmity with God (4:4). Second Peter describes believers as "having escaped the corruption in the world caused by evil desires" (1:4). First John repeatedly draws bold contrasts between the children of God and "the world" as a domain under diabolical control (more than 20x). Jude, too, contrasts the holiness of those who hold to true faith and possess the Holy Spirit over against the corrupt and defiling influence of certain interlopers (vv. 3-4, 19-20, 23).

Second, Hebrews describes the Christian community as a "house" over which Jesus Christ, their high priest, holds sway (3:1-6; 10:21). Likewise, 1 Peter identifies believers as a "spiritual house" (2:5), but this house is itself a temple, of whose foundation, Jesus Christ, is the cornerstone (vv. 6-7)—an image not foreign to Paul (1 Cor. 3:16; 6:19; Eph. 2:19-22). Hebrews treats the people of God and the heavenly sanctuary as separate entities instead of fusing them together. Noteworthy are the complementary emphases in Hebrews and 1 Peter. Hebrews spotlights the high priesthood of Jesus, while 1 Peter focuses on the "holy priesthood" or "royal priesthood" of believers (2:5, 9), as well as other features that hark back to God's covenant people in Exodus 19:5-6 and the LXX version of Exodus 23:22 ("chosen people," "holy nation," "God's special possession" [AT]). Thus the high priesthood of Jesus Christ is an explicit and developed theological construct in Hebrews, but present in 1 Peter only by inference. The obverse is true for the priesthood of believers, expressly stated in 1 Peter but implicit in Hebrews. In both epistles believers present "spiritual sacrifices acceptable to God through Jesus Christ" (1 Pet. 2:5; see Heb. 13:15-16), though the Hebrews passage particularizes these sacrifices as praise to God and deeds of service and generosity (cf. Rom. 12:1; Eph. 5:2; Phil. 2:17; 4:18).

The Christian Life. We discover the closest affinities between Hebrews and the CE when we look at their admonitions and encouragements concerning the normative Christian life. This closeness is due to their strikingly similar hortatory objectives. They encourage readers to trust in God so fully and commit themselves so wholeheartedly to his purposes that they enjoy an enduring covenant relationship with God—one that will prevent them from falling away from the living God.

The primary hortatory thrust of Hebrews, repeated again and again, consists of severe warnings about the dire consequences of apostasy (2:1-4; 3:7–4:13; 5:11–6:12; 10:19-39; 12:14-29) and strong exhortations to "hold fast to our confession" (4:14 and 10:23, NRSVUE; both being part of major transitional sections [4:14-16 and 10:19-23[70]]; see also 3:6, 14; 6:11, 18; 7:19; 11:1). A quick index of the importance of the same theme in the CE occurs at the conclusions to the collection's opening and closing books, James and Jude. Both epistles deliver parting words about restoring backsliders or apostates (James 5:19-20; Jude vv. 22-23). As well, a glance at key passages (some of them explicit purpose statements) in the CE shows the pervasive concern to encourage continued faithfulness in the face of challenges and to provide assurance of salvation (James 1:2-8; 4:7-8; 1 Pet. 1:3-9; 5:10, 12; 2 Pet. 1:10, 12; 3:15-17; 1 John 2:1; 5:13; 2 John v. 8; Jude vv. 3, 20-21).

Hebrews leads the way in delineating aspects of the victorious Christian life. Here we will discuss three: persevering faith, perfection (or holiness), and access to the divine presence.

1. *Persevering Faith.* Unquestionably, the showcase for persevering faith is Hebrews 11. This well-known "faith chapter" (containing twenty-five occurrences of "faith" vocabulary) is flanked by calls for readers "to endure" (*hypomenein, hypomonē*) in 10:19-39 (esp. vv. 32, 36) and 12:1-13 (esp. vv. 1-3, 7). Both "bookends" employ athletic imagery (10:32; 12:1, 4, 11; see 5:14). The preceding passage (10:35-39) introduces Hebrews 11 with a brief midrash on Habakkuk 2:3b-4, contrasting faith that leads to salvation with the action of shrinking back that leads to destruction. In the passage following the faith chapter (Heb. 12:1-13), the preacher invokes the "cloud of witnesses" from Hebrews 11 who exhibit the perseverance supremely exemplified in Jesus's endurance of the cross. Jesus is therefore "the pioneer and perfecter of faith" (12:2). There can be no dispute that Hebrews's primary hortatory aim, climaxing as one reaches the end of the sermon, is to encourage readers to

---

70. See Anderson 2013, 154.

persevere in faith and to discourage them from giving up their commitment and falling away in the midst of suffering. The sheer scope of his treatment of the topic of indomitable faith—utilizing the anaphoric "by faith" about twenty times in chapter 11—illustrates its importance for the overall message of Hebrews.

The teaching of James on faith dovetails nicely with the panoramic view of it in Hebrews. His letter opens with an exhortation to persevere through trials that test the mettle of one's faith. For James, it is the testing or proving of faith through trials that produces endurance (James uses the same vocabulary as Hebrews does for endurance: *hypomonē* [James 1:3, 4; 5:11]; *hypomenein* [v. 12]). The key trait of faith is trusting without doubting (v. 6), and the blessing that results from persevering, "having stood the test," is receiving the crown of life (v. 12). This characterization of faith is important to keep in mind when interpreting the discussion of faith and works in James 2:14-26. Faith issues in righteous action. It cannot be equated with a dead orthodoxy that thinks rightly but does not act accordingly.

First Peter parallels James's understanding of faith in the context of suffering trials (1 Pet. 1:6). The community's suffering on account of its faith in Christ is a pervasive theme in 1 Peter. While allusively present in James (1:3, 12), 1 Peter explicitly compares the trying of faith to the metallurgic testing and refinement of gold (1:7). The outcome of faith, as in James, is "the salvation of your souls" (1 Pet. 1:9; cf. Heb. 10:39). Significantly, 1 Peter's teaching is closer to Hebrews's future-oriented character of faith that is coordinated if not equated with hope (see Heb. 6:10-11; 10:22-23; 11:1; 1 Pet. 1:3, 5, 9, 13, and esp. 21 ["faith and hope"]).

First John regularly coordinates belief in Jesus Christ with believers' fulfillment of the love command (3:23; 5:1) and their confession of the true nature of Christ as the Son of God who has come in the flesh (4:1-4; 5:10). Believing in the Son of God fosters assurance that believers have eternal life (5:13). Faith is rarely the sole focus as a standalone concept. In fact, the nominal form "faith" (*pistis*) occurs only once in the Fourth Gospel and the Johannine Epistles—in 1 John 5:4: "This is the victory that has overcome the world, even our faith." Here faith is not an emblem of correct theological beliefs. It is *fidelity* to Christ that demonstrates believers' identity as persons

who are born of God and live in obedience to his commands.[71] This understanding, while fitting the wider theological concerns of the Johannine letters, coheres well with the kind of faith we have already sketched in Hebrews,
James, and 1 Peter.

In 2 Peter and Jude "faith" connotes a deposit or established set of beliefs
to which Christians are expected to adhere. Faith is "received" (2 Pet 1:1)
or "entrusted" (lit. "handed down" [Jude v. 3, NASB]). Yet faith cannot be
apprehended in these texts as a kind of dead orthodoxy such as James would
eschew. Faith is foundational for the cultivation of spiritual and moral virtues
(2 Pet. 1:5-8; Jude v. 20) that assures believers of their "calling and election"
(2 Pet. 1:10) and "eternal life" (Jude v. 21).

2. *Perfection and Holiness.* Perfection and holiness are central to the message of Hebrews. Holiness (or sanctification or cleansing) functions within a
cultic setting. Purification from the defilement of sin is the necessary preparation for worshippers to enter the presence of God. In Hebrews, Christ's obedient suffering and death constitute the definitive sacrifice for the sanctification
of God's people (10:10, 14, 29; 13:12). This sanctification is a once-for-all
past achievement of Christ's self-offering (10:10; see 7:27; 9:12, 26-27). At
the same time, holiness is an ongoing Christian pursuit (12:14). This is "practical holiness"[72] involving the ethical training of God's children under the
Father's providential hand of discipline (vv. 4-14). The aim of divine training
(*paideia*) is to bring believers into the enjoyment of God's own life and character of holiness (v. 10).

Perfection and holiness are not identical in Hebrews, but there is some
overlap between them (e.g., in 10:14). A lively debate continues concerning
the meaning of perfection in Hebrews.[73] In Hebrews there is a correlation
between the perfection of Jesus and the perfection of believers. This is possible because it was necessary for the Son to identify fully with human beings
so that he could be perfected (i.e., vocationally qualified as high priest)
through his suffering of death in obedience to God (2:10; 5:8-9; 7:28). Jesus
is therefore the source of salvation *and* the spiritual and ethical pattern for

---

71. Brown 1982, 572.
72. Bruce 1990, 348-49.
73. See Peterson 1982; Walters 1995, 83-153; McCruden 2013, 39-102; Simisi 2016.

the perfection of believers. Crucial to Jesus's perfection as high priest was his human life of reverent submission to God and obedience to God's will through suffering. For the Son, this was not a movement from sinfulness to righteousness, but a sinless life (4:15) that ethically expanded and matured in obedient response to every new vista requiring deliberate submission to God's will, culminating in his offering of himself as a sacrifice for sins.[74] This ethical dimension of Jesus's perfection vitally links his human life of obedience with the singular cultic and moral excellence of his priesthood (7:26; in contrast to the Levitical priesthood [5:3; 7:27]), as well as to his role as the supreme example of faithfulness that believers should follow (3:2, 5-6; 12:2).

As with holiness, perfection is a completed cultic achievement of Christ's death that qualifies believers to enter before God's holy presence—a perfection that was impossible under the first covenant (7:11, 19; 9:9; 10:1). However, in parallel to Jesus's own perfection, it also involves a divinely guided process of ethical maturation, the pinnacle of which is an acute moral sense of what is good and evil (5:11-14).[75] This is the "perfection" toward which the author of Hebrews calls his audience to advance, in reliance on God's active purpose in their lives (6:1). The initial ethical force in the perfection of believers comes to them in the cleansing of the conscience from the defilement of sins through Christ's sacrifice (9:9; see 9:14; 10:2, 22). This is not merely the forgiveness of sins (8:12; 10:18) but the vacating of sin's defilement and power (9:15, 26, 28; cf. 10:26; 12:1, 4). The cleansing of the conscience marks the complete religious orientation of worshippers toward God that opens up the "desire to live honorably in every way" (13:18). Christ's victory over temptation means he is able to help believers when they are tempted (2:18; 4:15).

Thus, like holiness or sanctification, perfection entails at once a finished achievement (the decisive purgation of the conscience from sin) and the divine education of believers in "reasoning about righteousness."[76] The aim is a mature Christian life that has the capacity to imitate the faithfulness of Jesus, resist the fatal sin of apostasy (3:12-13; 10:26-31; 12:1, 14-17), and sustain a lifestyle befitting those who are inheriting the coming kingdom

---

74. Walters 1995, 109-12, 126-29; Anderson 2013, 172-75.
75. Anderson 2013, 177-83.
76. See Koester 2001, 302, on Hebrews 5:13.

(13:1-6; see 12:28-29). The virtues that cohere with lives tending toward "salvation" (6:9) are love (in service and good works [6:10; 10:24]), hope (6:11; 10:23), and faith (involving endurance and the assurance that God will fulfill his promises [6:12; 10:22]).

Perfection and purity are integrally related in James. Second only to Hebrews (14x) is James in its employment of words for "perfect(ion)" with the Greek *telei-* stem (6x). The opening to James's discourse (1:2-27) announces perfection as "the overarching paraenetic aim" of the letter.[77] As in Hebrews, faithful endurance is essential to attaining perfection (James 1:2-4). However, James does not view perfection as the end point of a process of maturation (from childhood to adulthood) or learning (from elementary to advanced studies) but as the result of testing.[78] Perfection is the completeness or wholeness of believers who have become entirely devoted to God. Perhaps James would not object to the educational (Heb. 5:11-6:3) and parental (12:5-11) models for perfection and holiness, but he does not deploy them.

The goal of being "perfect" (*teleioi*) is allied with being "whole" or "complete" (*holoklēroi*) and "not lacking anything" (James 1:4). Perfection as wholehearted devotion to God is contrasted with lacking wisdom (v. 5), vacillating between believing and doubting (vv. 6-7), and hence being double-minded (v. 8; 4:8) and unstable in every way (1:8; 3:8, 16). Perfection or completeness originates in God's gift of wisdom (1:5, 17; 3:15, 17) and God's granting believers "birth through the word of truth" (1:18). It is manifested in those who are "doers of the word" (v. 22, NRSVUE) and who "speak and act" in accordance with the royal law of liberty (2:12; see vv. 8-12; see 1:25), particularly through performing good works on behalf of the needy (2:14-26; 3:17-18; 5:1-6).

James emphasizes the speaking and acting dimensions of true "religion" in the closing verses of the letter's introduction (1:26-27). First, persons whose devotion to God is empty and self-deceptive are those who "do not keep a tight rein on their tongues" (v. 26). The connection of the bridled tongue with perfection is spelled out in 3:1-12 (see esp. v. 2). Second, using the cultic language of purity, James states that "pure and faultless" (1:27) religion

---

77. Bauckham 1999, 148.
78. Ropes 1916, 138.

consists in caring for orphans and widows and keeping oneself "unstained" (v. 27, NRSVUE) by the world. Perfection or wholehearted devotion to God reveals itself in patterns of behavior that are pure (observe 3:17: the wisdom from above is "first of all pure") and result in harmonious and righteous relationships among God's people in contradistinction to the diabolical "wisdom" (vv. 15-16) that embraces a system of values aligned with "the world" and in enmity against God (4:4).[79]

Hebrews and James each have a unique "take" on the themes of perfection and purity. Hebrews explores them primarily in relationship to Christ's atoning sacrifice for sins. James relates perfection and purity to the religious and social life of communities of faith who need to draw careful boundaries of self-identity in contrast to "the world." Yet it is remarkable how many similarities exist between Hebrews and James. Both of them stress perfection (including the attainment of wisdom, though in different ways [contrast Heb. 5:14 and James 1:5, 17; 3:15, 17]), unwavering and persevering faith, doing good works as an index of true faith, radical commitment to God, and a scale of values that prioritizes "the crown of life" (James 1:12) or the heavenly kingdom more than earthly possessions (Heb. 10:34; 11:26; 13:5; James 2:5; 5:1-6).

We now turn to 1 John because it is next in line in the frequency of "perfection" (*telei-*) vocabulary (5x). First John utilizes this language exclusively to communicate the ways God's own love is perfected or made complete within the believing community. Being perfected in love means obeying the command to love one another (i.e., other believers; 2:5; 4:12). Mutual love in the Christian community completes the circuit of divine love enacted through Christ's atoning death (see 4:9-11). Perfect love casts out fear so that believers will have confidence at the final judgment (vv. 17-18). While the vocabulary of sanctification or purity is rare in 1 John (see the cognates "purify" [*hagnizein*] and "pure" [*hagnos*] in 3:3), the epistle could not be more adamant that the normative Christian life is one that avoids sinning (2:1; 3:4-10; 5:18) in imitation of Christ's righteousness (2:29; 3:7; see 2:1). Perfect divine likeness awaits manifestation at Christ's second coming (3:2), but in the meantime,

---

79. For a full discussion of perfection and purity in James, see Lockett 2008.

believers are expected to replicate Christ's purity (v. 3). This is accomplished by obeying the love command and fulfilling the obligation of living as Jesus did (2:6). The focal point of Christ's example for believers is the laying down of his life for us (3:16; see Heb. 12:2).

The letters of Peter and Jude do not employ the language of perfection, but they clearly map out the Christian life as one of holiness. First Peter invokes the repeated command from the Holiness Code (Lev. 11:44, 45; 19:2) as applicable to his Gentile readers who have become children of God: "You shall be holy, for I am holy" (1 Pet. 1:16, NRSVUE; see vv. 15-16). The Christian community takes on the characteristics of the historic people of God, Israel: "a holy priesthood" and "a holy nation" (2:5, 9). In 2 Peter, the eschatological teaching concerning the final conflagration and the expectation of new heavens and a new earth is accompanied by the exhortation "You ought to live holy and godly lives" (3:11). Second Peter begins with the reminder that God's divine power has provided believers with everything they need for "a godly life" (1:3). Both 2 Peter and Jude devote considerable space (proportionately) to the false teachers who are "ungodly" (2 Pet. 2:5-6; 3:7; Jude vv. 4, 15, 18), driven by their own "lusts" (2 Pet. 2:10; 3:3; Jude vv. 7, 16, 18), and therefore polluted or defiled (2 Pet. 2:20-22; Jude vv. 8, 23). By contrast, believers must strive to be found "spotless" and "blameless" at the coming of the Lord (2 Pet. 3:14; Jude v. 24).

Therefore, while each letter has its own distinctive emphases, the preceding review indicates that the themes of perfection and holiness/godliness span Hebrews and the CE.

3. *Access to the Divine Presence.* Hebrews sets forth a principal benefit of Christ's atoning sacrifice: Christ is the "forerunner" (6:20) and "new and living way" (10:20) into the very presence of God. This blessing is linked to Christ's work as our high priest and sin offering. In the two hinge points of the epistle, the exalted high-priestly status of the Son affords to believers "boldness" or "confidence" (*parrēsia*) to approach the throne of grace (4:16, NRSVUE) or have access to the heavenly sanctuary (10:19, NRSVUE). Hebrews conceives such access as a *present* privilege of believers to engage in full and meaningful worship. Hebrews uses the present tense of the verb "approach" or "come

near" (*proserchesthai*; 4:16; 7:25; 10:22; 11:6) and "draw near" (*engizein*; 7:19), as well as the perfect tense of "approach" (12:18, 22), to indicate this.

This theme is not strongly represented in the CE, but its introduction in Hebrews allows us to *see* it more distinctly when it appears in the CE. In James 4:8 the exhortation "Draw near to God, and he will draw near to you" (NRSVUE) and the cultically loaded commands for the double-minded to cleanse their hands and purify their hearts are surely enriched by the christological focus of Hebrews's understanding of the privilege of approaching God in worship (Heb. 10:22). First Peter 3:18 parallels the message of Hebrews: "For Christ also suffered once for sins, the righteous for the unrighteous, to bring [*prosagagē*] you to God" (the verb is a cognate of the noun used by Paul of the "access" [*prosagōgē*] believers have through God's grace in Christ [Rom. 5:2; Eph. 2:18; 3:12]; cf. Hebrews's repeated references to our "approach" to God). Second Peter refers to the "entrance" (*eisodos*) into the eternal kingdom as a future privilege (1:11, NASB), while Hebrews uses the same word to refer to present access for worship (10:19). Jude, too, looks to the future when God causes believers to "stand without blemish in the presence of his glory" (v. 24, NRSVUE).

First John shares both present and future emphases. The righteous conduct and perfection of love among God's children assure them that they will have "confidence" (*parrēsia*) at the final judgment (2:28; 4:17). But they also have "confidence" *now* in prayer to make any request of God, provided they are obeying God's commands and asking in accordance with his will (3:21-22; 5:14; cf. Heb. 3:6; 4:16; 10:19, 35). James essentially reflects the same reality when he mentions the "powerful and effective" prayer of the righteous for miraculous healing (5:16; see vv. 13-18).

Conclusion

This chapter has introduced Hebrews and the CE in their relationship to the NT canon as well as to each other. The way Hebrews and the CE are ordered within the NT is a helpful guide for interpretation. The church saw fit to place Hebrews within the Pauline collection of letters. Hebrews appeared in different positions within MS traditions—most often either at the end of Paul's ecclesiastical letters (after 2 Thessalonians) or at the end of the entire corpus (after Philemon). The final "received" order of Hebrews at the close of Paul's letters represents a consensus decision that Hebrews belongs among Paul's letters (a strong Eastern tradition since ca. AD 200) even though it was not written by the apostle (a strong Western position since the late second c.). This placement would allow Hebrews to come into its own as a unique and powerful voice among the NT letters.

The books of the CE are ordered primarily in conformity with the sequence of "the pillars"—James, Cephas, and John—as Paul lists them in Galatians 2:9. They also bear a symmetry in which letters by the brothers of the Lord Jesus (James and Jude) form an *inclusio* around the collection, and letters by the apostles Peter and John are at its heart. The CE collection is therefore the epistolary deposit of the earliest Jewish-Christian leaders and apostles who were eyewitnesses to Jesus in the flesh.

At one time or another, each of the NT letter collections (Pauline and CE) has occupied the first place after the Acts of the Apostles. The order Acts—CE—Paul attractively places the two letter collections into the chronological order of the respective apostolic missions in Acts. However, the church ultimately preferred the order Acts—Paul—CE. We discovered a number of features in the NT letters that commend this order, such as the Epistle to the Romans constituting a natural glide path after Acts's ending with Paul at Rome and the ways in which the CE themselves seem to assume a prior reading of the Pauline letters. We also argued that the placement of Hebrews at the end of the Pauline corpus facilitates a closer, albeit inverse, relationship to the narrative chronology in Acts. Just as Stephen and the Hellenists serve as a segue between the mission of the Jerusalem apostles and the mission of Paul, so also does Hebrews serve as a segue between the Pauline letters and the CE. Hebrews's transitional function is in evidence via a cluster of theological emphases shared between Hebrews and the Pauline letters and Hebrews and the CE.

The theologically rich Epistle to the Hebrews acts almost like a prolegomenon to the following seven CE. Its vision of the high-priestly Christ and eschatological salvation through the new-covenant sacrifice of Jesus forms a fitting backdrop for the letters from Jewish-Christian leaders that follow. Hebrews shares with the CE a strong emphasis on Christian discipleship that pursues perfection and holiness or, in a word, radical commitment to God through Jesus Christ. A key theme that binds them together is the call for authentic Christian devotion (in faithful, hopeful, and loving *action* and *behavior*, not just words) that trusts in God's stabilizing and keeping grace so that no believer will fall away from the living God but have assurance of salvation.

PART II

INTERPRETING HEBREWS AND THE CATHOLIC EPISTLES

We will now turn directly to the actual business of interpreting Hebrews and the CE. This part of the book is easy to introduce. We will set forth a simple and straightforward approach or method to interpreting these texts, followed by representative samples of such interpretation.

4

A Method for Studying Hebrews and the Catholic Epistles

At the outset we must emphasize that there is no one definitive or *right* method for studying the Bible. Sometimes hermeneutics is defined as the art and science of biblical interpretation. It is a science insofar as there are certain patterns of communication, such as syntactical relationships or figures of speech, which can be categorized, explained, and understood in a fairly routine manner. Yet it is also an art because no text can simply be analyzed in a mechanical fashion. Texts are like diamonds, each "cut" with similar tools (e.g., literary, historical, and ideological influences), but none in exactly the same way. Technical aspects of exegesis, then, are not enough. They must be accompanied by an almost intuitive sense of the text that comes from a personal encounter with it as a unique communication event. So we must banish from our minds the worn-out notion bestowed upon us by the historical critics that if we use the right critical method(s), we will arrive at *the* interpretation of any given text. This is not to say that good, rigorous, and consistent methodology is unhelpful. Indeed, it is necessary; but it is not *sufficient* for a faithful reading of the biblical text. Essential to a faithful reading of Scripture is a willingness to meet the biblical texts on their own terms (e.g., in their historical and canonical contexts) and with an attitude that is sympathetic to their theological and spiritual aims, that is to say, in a spirit of faith and obedience to their message.

A book of this short compass cannot presume to map out a complete method of exegesis or interpretation. There are many fine textbooks on hermeneutics and handbooks on exegesis available to students. In the latter category, Michael Gorman's *Elements of Biblical Exegesis* (2020) is helpful all around for serious students of the Bible, without requiring facility in biblical languages. One may also commend Gordon Fee and Douglas Stuart's *How to Read the Bible for All Its Worth* (2014) as an entry-level hermeneutics textbook (we would also recommend Jeannine Brown's *Scripture as Communication* [2021]). The method set forth here will keep things simple. Any biblical text needs to be studied through three lenses: historical, literary, and theological interpretation. Anyone who digs into the biblical text in any depth will notice the complexity that surfaces when pursuing any one of these three dimensions of biblical interpretation.

Historical Interpretation

Christianity embraces what is known as "the scandal of particularity." Both the Old and New Testaments of the Bible are comprised of texts that are situated in concrete historical contexts. (Like Gorman,[1] we are using the term "historical contexts" as a catchall for "historical, sociopolitical, and cultural contexts.") Neither Judaism nor Christianity is a philosophical system or mystical religion that stands apart from historical events. For many, it is scandalous that the God of the universe chose the shabby, nomadic descendants of Abraham to become the nation of Israel through whom the divine saving purposes would unfold. Yet more scandalous is the notion that a Jewish craftsman and self-styled rabbi would atone for sins and become the exclusive Savior of the world by running afoul of the Jewish authorities and getting crucified by the Romans. "Christ crucified" remains "a stumbling block to Jews and foolishness to Gentiles" (1 Cor. 1:23).

The first reason for applying historical analysis in interpretation is that the biblical texts themselves in myriad ways manifest a self-consciousness about their embeddedness in discrete historical contexts. This is true in Hebrews and the CE. Hebrews makes references to "Jesus' life on earth" (5:7) and to the importance of the apostolic witness to the gospel (2:3). Peter identifies himself as a witness to Christ's sufferings (1 Pet. 5:1) and to Christ's glory at the transfiguration (2 Pet. 1:16-18). The historical veracity of these events is crucial for Peter: "For we did not follow cleverly devised myths when we

---

1. Gorman 2020, 76n1.

made known to you the power and coming of our Lord Jesus Christ, but we had been eyewitnesses of his majesty" (v. 16, NRSVUE). First John 1:1-3 relates the multisensory experiences the apostles had of Jesus that stand behind their proclamation of "the Word of life" (v. 1, KJV).

A second reason to pursue historical interpretation is that it contributes to the validity of our readings of Scripture. Scriptural texts do not come to us as a series of propositional "timeless truths." Every text is "culturally located."[2] The author of every text (whether we are talking about the historical author, the implied author, or the divine author—God) communicates within and through culturally located times, places, events, social contexts, literary conventions, and so on. This cultural "situatedness" has a claim on how the communication is to be received. Cultural location is so pervasive and determinative for successful communication that authors hardly give a thought to certain cultural givens that they anticipate readers will assume even if left unexpressed in the text. Culture is like the air texts breathe, and its natural inhabitants never actually have to "see" it. As a quick example, scholars have long struggled with the import of the final admonition in 1 John 5:21: "Dear children, keep yourselves from idols." While it is helpful to search for deeper theological or metaphorical interpretations focused on any erroneous belief system that strays from "the true God" (v. 20), ancient readers would have immediately grasped the command. Modern readers too easily forget that the dominant religious context in which early Christians found themselves was polytheistic. It is unnecessary to run after metaphorical idols when ancient readers would have felt the lure of actual idols.

The communicative aims of texts are therefore best apprehended within their proper historical contexts. This is all the more important because readers reflexively interpret texts in accord with their native cultural assumptions. For modern readers this can lead to interpretations that are far off the mark. It can be like trying to use the wrong key to open a door. It might be like lifelong Anglicans attempting to understand Jesus as high priest in Hebrews by comparing his ministry to that of their parish priest or the archbishop of Canterbury. Responsible interpretation requires one to do some extra work to

---

2. See esp. Brown 2021, 94-97.

understand the religious and cultural backgrounds of priesthood (both Jewish and Hellenistic) in order to grasp this powerful image of Jesus's high priestly role on behalf of his people. Attempting to draw out understandings of a text that are true to its historical context is one of the primary operations of "exegesis" (from Greek *exēgeomai*, "lead out," "draw out"). Reading our own world into a text is the essential error of "eisegesis."

One does not have to be a professional historian or biblical scholar to engage in such responsible, contextual interpretation of the Bible. No one has done more to equip laypersons to understand the Scriptures in light of their ancient historical and cultural backgrounds than Craig Keener. *The IVP Bible Background Commentary* on the NT (Keener 2014) is a treasure trove of background material for virtually every verse in the NT (there is a companion volume for the OT: Walton, Matthews, and Chavalas 2000). The *NIV Cultural Backgrounds Study Bible* (2016) reflects much of the material in both of the IVP Bible Background Commentaries. There are numerous Bible dictionaries and specialized resources for students who want to dig even deeper into the historical contexts of the Bible.[3]

Postmodern interpreters are quick to criticize historical analysis because of its shortcomings. In chapter 1 we discussed how difficult it is to get a handle on the precise settings of Hebrews and the CE. However, while a biblical book (say, Ruth or Jude) may give us little in the way of information to attain a "GPS" sort of precision about its authorship and occasion, there are still many cultural traits embedded in the text to provide us a representation of the general historical and cultural conditions in which the authors and earliest readers lived. Historical and socioscientific methods are in themselves limited, especially when they fill in gaps through modeling or develop historical reconstructions that are measured in degrees of probability. Yet it would be foolish to reject the capability of gaining a somewhat clearer picture of a text's background just because crystal clear vision is impossible. There is no wrong in welcoming a method of analysis when it yields much fruit but humbly recognizing when it does not. In this life, we see through a glass darkly, so often we must be content with less than

---

3. See the bibliography in Gorman 2020, 227-32.

precise information or understanding. Even so, there are additional tools in our interpretive toolbox to attend to other features of the text that will satisfy our desire to understand it better.

Since interpretation involves the encounter between two horizons—the horizon of the text within its historical contexts and the horizon of our own modern cultural settings—it stands to reason that we cannot very well say that we understand a text if we neglect its horizon and replace it with our own. Interpretive solipsism requires no text or ancient context to express its own ideology. Indeed, such an approach does not need the Bible at all, except to hijack its authority for its own ends. Our contention is that we must attend to the horizon of the biblical text—"the strange new world within the Bible," as Karl Barth called it (see Barth 1957, 28). Critical distance between our horizon(s) and those of the Bible will help to bring our readings closer to the way the text was read in its "native" settings instead of being an image of what we want the text to mean within our contemporary context. Will our endeavor to read the text within its historical context be absolutely complete and accurate? Not always. But we must not let the perfect become the enemy of the good.

The study of a text's historical contexts works on two levels: book-level and passage-level historical contexts. In what follows we will briefly describe what is involved at both levels.

Book-Level Historical Context

Book-level historical context has to do with those matters that are often handled in NT introductions: authorship, date, the intended recipients, the locations of the author and recipients, and the occasion for the writing. As we noted in chapter 1, many of these historical data are difficult to ascertain with regard to Hebrews and the CE. For each book one must piece together as many parts of the puzzle as are available. Often our work is like that of a crime-scene investigator searching for every partial fingerprint and every nanogram of DNA to discover the historical background.

We must be careful not to read too much into the data we collect. Particularly with epistolary literature, we must be cautious about "mirror reading." This is when we attempt to discern facts *about* the readers based on what is written *to* them in the text. Thus Hebrews's command to show hospitality to strangers (13:2) and the elder's command not to be hospitable to false teachers (2 John vv. 10-11) tell us as much or more about the widespread ancient value of hospitality than about either Christian community's deficiency or undiscerning practice of being hospitable. The good news is that even when we cannot determine precise information about the time, place, and circumstances of a NT letter, there are features of the text that point to broader cultural factors important for interpretation. For instance, what Peter states as Christian behavior within the contemporary political environment (1 Pet. 2:13-17) or in the domestic sphere of slaves (vv. 18-25), wives (3:1-6), and husbands (v. 7) would have been applicable virtually anywhere within the ancient Mediterranean world within the reach of the Roman Empire. The cultural matrix in Rome would have varied little from that in the Roman provinces of Anatolia.

As we move to discussing passage-level historical context, it is also important to note that matters of book-level historical context are not all equally important. Sometimes beginning students obsess over book-level historical concerns that are not directly relevant to interpreting the passage at hand. The location of the author of Hebrews or the epistle's readers may be useful for orienting our reading of the book as a whole, but it is not crucial to our understanding of the book's central arguments in 4:14–10:18.

Passage-Level Historical Context

The study of passage-level historical context is focused on the historical, social, political, cultural, and religious elements represented in the particular passage being studied. Sometimes such features of the text will reveal further details about the author and readers in their specific historical contexts. More often we will need to explore the cultural backgrounds of the text in order to comprehend more clearly the communicative aims of the passage itself. We cannot emphasize enough the need for students of the Bible to attempt to encounter the text in its "otherness" from our own cultural settings. The goal is to interpret the text "on its own terms" insofar as this is possible. We want to "hear" the passage with an optimum of its cultural nuance and texture before we evaluate and recontextualize the text's message in our contemporary cultural settings.

Literary Interpretation

While historical interpretation seeks to understand the text in light of "behind the text" matters of cultural background, literary interpretation concerns "in the text" features that shape the way the text communicates its message. There is a great deal of truth in Marshall McLuhan's famous statement, "The medium is the message."[4] There is a symbiotic relationship between the content of a message and the media through which it is conveyed. An author's choice of literary genre results in the message both harnessing and being constrained by the literary conventions associated with that genre. The structure of an entire epistle or a given passage shapes the message in such a way as to have a designed rhetorical *effect* on readers. The employment of a literary style sets the mood for how readers are to receive the message.

Literary interpretation also has book-level and passage-level features. On the book level, a literary analysis concerns the literary genre of the biblical book along with the way that book is structured. On the passage level, a literary analysis concerns the literary form of the passage, along with its structure and content flow.

Book-Level Literary Interpretation: Genre and Structure

Genre

Hebrews and the CE are classified as NT letters. While every piece of literature is designed for a more or less specific audience (no work is unrealistically targeted to *everybody*), letters are unique because they are formally *addressed* to their audience. Letters always presume, often explicitly, some sort of relationship between the author (sender) and readers (recipients). Even the least letter-like books, Hebrews and 1 John, are expressive of a pastoral connection between the author and readers (see Heb. 13:18-19, 22-24 and, for 1 John, the frequent tender address ["little children" or "beloved"] and authoritative tone throughout [see NRSVUE]). By contrast, other NT genres (such as biography or history) have Christian readers in mind but are not necessarily directed to any particular community or local church.[5] Luke's

---

4. McLuhan 2001, 7.
5. Bauckham 1998.

address to "most excellent Theophilus" (Luke 1:3; see Acts 1:1) does not limit the audience but expands it by invoking the influence of the person named in the "dedicatory address." Most of the CE are addressed to more "general" audiences than are Paul's various letters (as we explored in ch. 3), which is why they are called "Catholic Letters."

The main body of an ancient letter usually takes on characteristics to suit the purpose(s) of the letter. There were letter-writing manuals in the ancient world that categorized nearly every possible type of letter, literally dozens of them.[6] For example, a commendatory letter was designed as a kind of "reference letter" written on behalf of another person. Third John bears the marks of a commendatory letter in its praise for Gaius and Demetrius. An advisory or paraenetic letter seeks to persuade and dissuade readers concerning certain actions or behaviors. This letter type applies to Hebrews, James, 1 Peter, 2 Peter, 1–2 John, and Jude. Often letters are of a mixed type. For instance, advice or paraenesis may be paired with consolation or encouragement, as we find in Hebrews, James, 1 Peter, 1 John, and Jude. Dissuasion can be sharpened to include elements of vituperation that comprise an attack on the character of persons who exercise a negative influence, such as we find in 2 Peter, 3 John, and Jude. There is an obvious interpretive advantage to identifying the epistolary subgenre or type and therefore the primary thrust of a NT letter.

Structure

Ancient letters have a straightforward structure:
1. *Letter opening*, usually with an address (sender to receiver) and greeting
2. *Letter body*, which sets forth the message of the letter
3. *Letter closing*, containing a variety of possible closing elements (a request, information about the letter carrier, travelogue, benediction, doxology, final greetings, and/or farewell)

The letter genre is pretty flexible. This is not unexpected for a form of writing designed for person-to-person(s) communication of an occasional nature. Letters are one side of a dialogue or even a speech couched in epistolary form.[7] This would explain why Hebrews and 1 John begin and proceed more

---

6. See Bateman 2013, 34-48, and the literature cited there.
7. Witherington 2007, 559.

like sermons than letters and why James and Jude follow some of the canons of ancient rhetorical practice. Yet students should refrain from squeezing letters into the kind of rhetorical structures laid out in ancient rhetorical handbooks. The flexibility of letter organization is evidenced in the very different arrangements pursued by Paul in Romans and 1 Corinthians. One may see a more standard letter form in 2–3 John and considerably more freedom in the pastoral address of 1 John.

The most important factor in devising a structural outline for any biblical book is to represent fairly the topics discussed and the work's flow of thought or argument. For some NT books there are practically as many structural outlines as there are commentators. This is the case for Hebrews, 1 John, and James. Bible students should not be anxious about trying to map out *the* outline for a given book. Structural outlines are heuristic devices meant to aid in approaching and discovering the contents of a writing. The vital function of an outline is to help the interpreter gain an understanding of the literary context (both broad and immediate) for any passage one is studying. The most beneficial structural outline is one that assists us in adequately situating a passage within the overall message of the letter and therefore aiding our understanding of how the passage itself contributes to the larger message or set of rhetorical aims for the letter as a whole.

Passage-Level Literary Interpretation: Form, Structure, and Movement

Form

Even as genre (or subgenre) identifies the literary function of a work as a whole, form identifies the literary function of smaller units of text. The parts of a letter are themselves forms, for they generally follow set formal patterns (e.g., the opening address in the form A → B, i.e., sender to receiver, followed by a greeting). A given form exercises its function in a specific context. The social or cultural environment in which a form operates is often called its *Sitz im Leben* (Ger., "setting in life"). Indeed, a form acts as a kind of cultural sign. Readers who share the same culture immediately recognize the social setting associated with well-known forms. When modern English speakers hear the words "Dearly beloved, we are gathered here today" or the simple two-word promise "I do," they recognize them as statements associated with a wedding ceremony. Or if we hear the question, "Do you swear to tell the truth, the whole truth, and nothing but the truth, so help you God?" we recognize this as the form by which someone is sworn in as a witness at a court of law. But forms do not simply evoke settings; they are performative. They *do* things. (According to speech-act theory, they have illocutionary force.) In the preceding examples a minister calls wedding guests to publicly witness a marriage, a bride and groom make vows, and a court official obliges a witness to testify truthfully.

Identifying forms in the Bible is interpretively significant, since it helps readers to understand what a passage (or part thereof) is intended to accomplish. As an obvious example, christological hymns (Heb. 1:1-3; 1 Pet. 2:21-25)—whether they have a preliterary existence or are originally crafted by the biblical authors—draw readers into acknowledging theological truths about Christ and participating in an act of worship. A similar function obtains for a benediction (Heb. 13:20-21) or doxology (Jude vv. 24-25). The use of *exempla* (in rhetoric, short stories or anecdotes that explain or model moral teaching) serves to amplify or illustrate a salient point either positively (Heb. 11:1-40; James 2:21, 23, 25; 5:11, 17) or negatively (Heb. 12:16; 2 Pet. 2:15; 1 John 3:12; Jude v. 11). Among the many forms found in Hebrews and the CE are creeds or confessions, paraenetic sections, virtue (or vice) lists, household codes (Ger., *Haustafeln*), wisdom sayings, diatribes, personal testimony, formulaic citations of Scripture (including the *catena* or "chain" of scriptural quotations in Heb. 1:5-13), prophetic woes (riffing on a form used by OT prophets), and apocalyptic material. Identifying the forms in a passage, along with their accompanying functions, goes a long way toward leading interpreters to a passage's meaning and/or designed effect.

Structure and Movement

Book-level and passage-level structures involve discerning the organization or arrangement of material in texts, but on different scales. Many of the same patterns of organization apply broadly (at the book level) and narrowly (at the passage level). Michael Gorman defines structure and movement as follows: "The *structure* of a passage refers to its parts, its main divisions and subdivisions, while the *movement* of a passage refers to the progression of the text, through its parts, from beginning to end."[8] The structure and movement of a text represent the organization of an author's thoughts in order to shape an argument, emphasize a point, elicit emotion, or achieve some other rhetorical effect. A variety of organizational patterns assist authors in ordering a text: repetition, comparison, contrast, catalogues (or lists), cause and effect, working from the general to the specific (or vice versa), questions and answers (or problem and solution), dialogue, conditions, emotional terms (or tone), intercalation, chiasm, and *inclusio*, among others.[9]

Consider the structure and movement of 1 John 1:5–2:2 as an example. This passage begins with the declaration that "God is light" (1:5), announcing the overarching theme for the first major division of the letter (1:5–3:10). It is followed by three pairs of contrasting statements: three matching claims and counterclaims.[10] Each claim and counterclaim has a consistent form (the example is from 1:6):

Condition: "If we claim to have fellowship with him and yet walk in darkness,"
Consequence: "we lie"
Explanation or second consequence: "and do not live out the truth."

We can outline the passage like this:
   I. Opening Declaration: "God is light" (1:5).
   II. Three Claims and Counterclaims (1:6–2:2).
      A. First Claim and Counterclaim (1:6-7)
         1. Claim: Denial of the Fact of Sin (v. 6)
         2. Counterclaim: Cleansing from Sin (v. 7)
      B. Second Claim and Counterclaim (1:8-9)
         1. Claim: Denial of the Effect of Sin (v. 8)
         2. Counterclaim: Forgiveness of Sins, Cleansing from Unrighteousness (v. 9)

---

8. Gorman 2020, 95.
9. For full discussions of these structural devices, see Gorman 2020, 97-104, and esp. Bauer and Traina 2011, 79-158.
10. Brown 1982.

C. Third Claim and Counterclaim (1:10–2:2)
    1. Claim: Denial of the Act of Sin (1:10).
    2. Pastoral Interjection: "I write . . . so that you will not sin"
       (2:1*a*).
    3. Counterclaim: Jesus Christ Atones for Sins (vv. 1*b*-2).

A careful look at the structure of this text reveals a dual movement. First, one observes an intensification of the consequences for each of the three claims. The author characterizes the opposing position as incoherent and inconsistent. There is a disconnect between claiming fellowship with God (and concomitantly claiming to be untouched by sin) and continuing to engage in sinful behavior. The consequences of this incongruity intensify in the passage: deception ("we lie" [1:6]) progresses to self-deception ("we deceive ourselves" [v. 8]) and finally to the practical effect of making God out to be a liar (v. 10)!

Second, a parallel movement emphasizes the cleansing and forgiveness of sins available to those who walk in the light (v. 7), confess their sins (v. 9), and avail themselves of the effects of Christ's sacrifice for sins. This movement climaxes in a threefold description of Christ's work of salvation: he is our "advocate," "the Righteous One," and "the atoning sacrifice" (2:1-2). The pastoral interjection in 2:1*a* breaks the symmetry of the structure but thereby underscores the author's insistence that he is most certainly not advocating a position that covenant relationship with God through Christ's atonement is compatible with a sinful lifestyle. The atonement is not the pretext for an ongoing cycle of sinning and forgiveness/cleansing. Rather, it is a safeguard in the eventuality that believers fall into sin as they continue to have fellowship with God and walk in the light. Notice how this careful structure orders the content of this passage so that it conveys the author's message methodically and with proper nuance and emphasis.

A Word about Detailed Textual Study

There are many things to be said about analyzing a passage in detail. Here we can mention only two.

First, analysis of a passage must attend to the syntactical relationships in the text. This involves observing variations in verb tense, antecedents for pronouns, the presence of conditional clauses, and other grammatical or syntactical features that appear to have interpretive significance. The discovery of syntactical relationships complements the detection of the organizational patterns listed above.

Second, the interpreter should take note of key words in the passage that require in-depth study. Words requiring further investigation are usually theologically significant, used rarely in the NT, are difficult to translate adequately into English, or are notoriously difficult to define. Obviously, both interpretive tasks (syntactical and semantic analyses) are performed optimally by working with the Greek NT. If the interpreter is confined to English versions, it is advisable to utilize several Bible translations and consult appropriate tools for biblical study to delve into these matters to the best of one's ability.[11]

Theological Interpretation

Historical and literary analyses of texts are the stock-in-trade of what we call *exegesis*. As we have already noted, these are essential building blocks of faithful and informed interpretation of the Scriptures. They help to develop crucial skills for reading the text with a degree of critical distance that provides space for the text to speak for itself rather than our foisting preformed ideas upon it. Nevertheless, we must acknowledge that there is no such thing as an entirely neutral reading of any text. In fact, historical critics who claim to approach the biblical texts objectively and neutrally have often espoused interpretive presuppositions that run counter to the fundamental claims of the biblical texts themselves, such as when they deny that the Scriptures are constitutive of divine revelation in any way. Feminist or postcolonial critics are no different when they apply a "hermeneutic of suspicion" with the primary goal of unmasking the ideological structures of power and oppression that they believe are latent in any text. In either extreme (modern or postmodern), whether we are dealing with pseudoneutrality or the abandonment of neutrality altogether, the approach to the text involves a posture of doubt or

---

11. For further guidance concerning detailed analysis, see Gorman 2020, ch. 6.

unbelief. This is antithetical to reading the Bible as Christian Scripture, which involves a posture of faith and obedience to the Scripture as God's Word.

Exegesis is a helpful set of tools, not an end in itself. It is part of a larger project of interpreting the Old and New Testaments as Scripture known as *theological interpretation*. Bare exegesis is primarily concerned with elucidating the meaning of texts on their own terms, but this can lead to an antiquarian interest in what the biblical texts *meant* "back then" without any connection to how they function as God's Word *today*. This, mind you, is assuming that exegesis can be carried out perfectly. Even still, most Christians are not and *should not* be interested in reading the Bible for the sole reason of comprehending facts about ancient history or cultural anthropology. The interest of theology is precisely at the intersection of what the Scriptures have to say about God and creation in engagement with the complicated issues and questions that exist in our complex contemporary world. To use a musical metaphor, theological interpretation seeks to hear the ancient melodies of the Scriptures and then provide instructions for performing them in our contemporary context, transposing them into a different key when necessary.

Theological interpretation seemed like second nature in previous eras of church history, before it was choked out by the rise of academic approaches to Scripture. But in the wake of the post-Enlightenment scholarship of the past three and one-half centuries, it has made a resurgence in the last few decades. Since in many respects theological interpretation remains a burgeoning movement, there is no generally agreed-upon approach.[12] In what follows we will explore the most basic elements of theological interpretation without delving deeper into theoretical discussions that readers may pursue elsewhere. My own understanding of theological interpretation has been informed by the work of Treier.[13]

The Purpose of Biblical Interpretation: Christian Formation

Augustine (354–430) clearly set forth the purpose of biblical interpretation in book 1 of his *On Christian Teaching*, which became the Western church's textbook on hermeneutics for many succeeding centuries. According

---

12. See Klink and Lockett 2012.
13. Treier 2008; see also Vanhoozer 2005; Billings 2010.

to Augustine, interpreters should make every effort to understand precisely what the biblical authors meant by what they wrote down. To do otherwise would be mendacious. However, the overarching purpose of interpreting any biblical text is to promote the double love articulated in Jesus's two great commandments: love of God and love of neighbor. If one inadvertently interpreted a passage in ways that do not cohere with the author's intended meaning, yet the interpretation stimulates the double love of God and neighbor, the interpreter is not to be condemned as unethical. In one sense, the interpreter has been self-deceived and should be corrected. Yet the interpreter has not willfully perpetrated a falsehood. Thus, for Augustine, valid interpretation involves being true not only to factual information about a passage's meaning but more importantly to the divine purposes for Scripture as a whole to nourish and support discipleship.

In theological interpretation, the goal of reading the Bible is not solely the rational, cognitive operation of intellectually grasping the meaning of a text. It is not enough to understand Scripture. Scripture makes a claim on its readers, pointing to the divine Author, who is to be believed and obeyed. Vanhoozer has helpfully described the interpretive enterprise as a drama.[14] The Scriptures are the script. Believers are the actors on the stage. Theology (or doctrine) supplies the stage instructions to assist us in enacting or performing what the divine Playwright has written. We look to the canon of Scripture itself, as well as to the tradition of past interpreters in the church, for interpretive cues. Even more importantly, we rely on the power of the Spirit for the inspiration and wisdom to perform the divine script improvisationally yet faithfully in our present contexts.

The interpretation of Scripture has as its aim the joining together of human beings into fellowship with the triune God so that they reflect the divine image and character. Theological interpretation should result in "actors" who exhibit the "character" traits (i.e., virtues, holiness) that are appropriate to their "roles" in the divine drama. Paradoxically, the virtuous life is both the prerequisite and goal of faithful interpretation. As interpreters are increasingly conformed to the divine image, they are able to do more than

---

14. Vanhoozer 2005.

just act out a part; they are able to *inhabit* the roles marked out for them by God. In turn, they become better interpreters—and "performers"—of Scripture. Christian formation, then, is the primary aim of biblical interpretation. The Father, through the Word and Spirit, transforms believers into the holy and godly inhabitants of the future new creation "where righteousness dwells" (2 Pet. 3:13).

The Three Contexts of Theological Interpretation

Theological interpretation seeks to facilitate the interaction of two horizons: that of the ancient biblical text and that of the contemporary reader. It does so by working within three contexts: canon, church, and culture.

The Context of the Canon

The most determinative context for theological interpretation is the biblical canon. More than just the context for theological reflection, it is the form and content of divine teaching against which all other cultural contexts and theological formulations must be compared, tested, and (when necessary) reformed. The canonical context for theological interpretation is expressed in two fundamental principles of biblical interpretation, particularly within the Protestant tradition. The first is *sola Scriptura*, which embraces the Holy Scriptures as our sole rule and guide for faith and practice. For John Wesley, this meant being *homo unius libri*, "a man of one book."[15] Corollaries to this principle are the clarity and sufficiency of Scripture. Taken as a whole, Scripture clearly communicates everything we need to know about the divine purposes for our salvation—for life and godliness. The second principle flows from the first: Scripture interprets Scripture. The canon is itself a guide for how we can apprehend God's Word.

There are two aspects to using the canonical context for theological interpretation. The first is a *tiered* approach to interpreting the canon. This is simply taking into consideration all the layers of the canonical context for reading any given passage of Scripture (see fig. 4.1). One needs to interpret a passage in light of its immediate context, as well as in connection with the

---

15. Wesley 1984, 5:3.

major discourse unit and the entire book in which it resides (see also our discussion of literary interpretation, p. 101). One must then explore the passage in relation to the canonical collection to which it belongs (e.g., Gospels, Paul's letters, the CE), the requisite testament that it is in (OT or NT), and then the other testament. In brief, one needs to take into account the entire Bible in relation to the passage one is studying.

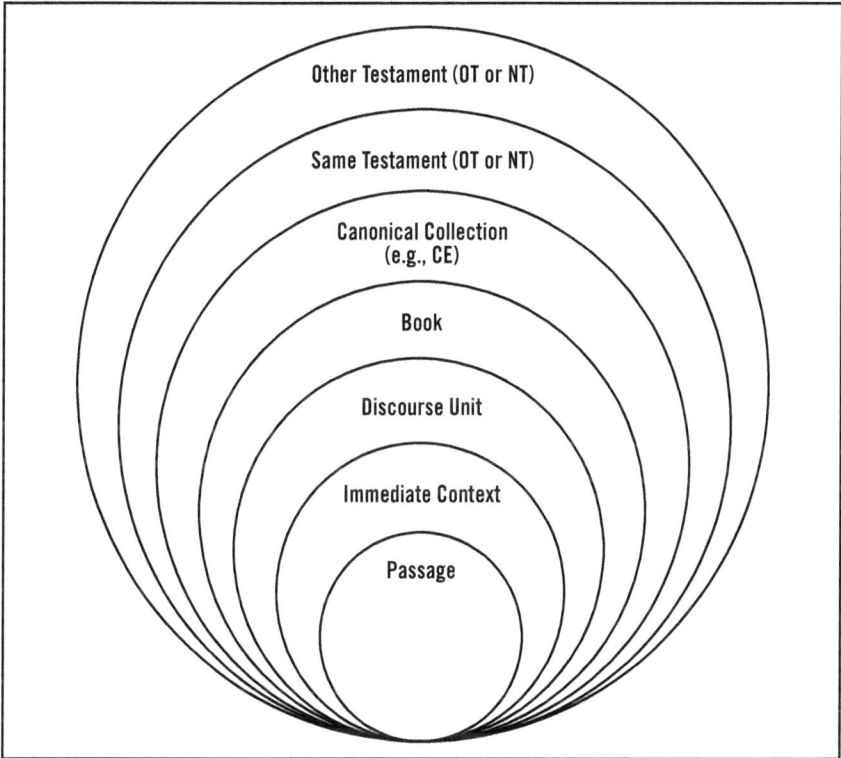

Fig. 4.1. Tiers of canonical context

A second, complementary operation is the exploration of *topical* connections within the canon. We have already modeled this with respect to material within and between canonical collections (see ch. 3). If one is to interpret Scripture with Scripture, it stands to reason that one must compare like with like (or contrast like with unlike). This should be undertaken in tandem with the tiered approach described above. When pursuing a topic within the entire canon, it is essential for the interpreter *not* to assume that there is a one-to-one correspondence between relevant biblical passages.

Every passage must be understood within its matrix of literary and canonical contexts. One should also consider how differing literary genres bear upon interpretation. For example, how do the epistolary instructions to submit to governmental authorities in 1 Peter 2:13-17 compare to those in Paul (esp. Rom. 13:1-7)? What about the narrative instances when figures in the NT (e.g., Peter and John in Acts 5:17-42) or the OT (e.g., Daniel in Dan. 6:1-28) engage in civil disobedience? And how does one assess the thoroughly negative depiction of world regimes in apocalyptic literature, especially in the book of Revelation? One should also be attuned to progressive revelation or historical developments that explain the differences between Old and New Testament teachings. An example would be Hebrews's discussion of the superiority of Christ's sacrifice in comparison to the Levitical sacrifices of the OT. Both the correlations and tensions within the biblical canon contribute to a full and faithful hearing of the Bible's teaching on a topic raised by the passage one is studying.

The Context of the Church

In Presbyterian and Methodist settings, one will hear a lector close the reading of a biblical lesson with the words "The word of God for the people of God." One of the crucial aspects of theological interpretation is that it is performed in an ecclesial context. The reading and interpretation of Scripture is done by and for the church. This context is by no means confined to our contemporary setting. It includes the voices of saints, past and present, who are "experienced in the things of God."[16] According to Anglican (and Wesleyan) tradition, the church fathers of the first five centuries should be consulted for their theological and interpretive insights, since they are "closer to the fountain." Resources such as Thomas Oden's Ancient Christian Commentary on Scripture series are an entrée to rich veins of ancient interpretive tradition.

The historic Christian church exercises its influence on our interpretation of Scripture particularly through "the rule of faith" (*regula fidei*). The rule of faith is a concise summary of the biblical story and authoritative Christian teachings in the form of a creedal statement. It began as a statement of faith recited by those who were receiving the sacrament of baptism and eventually

---

16. Ibid.

developed into the Apostles' Creed and the Nicene Creed. It has a Trinitarian shape and highlights the work of the triune God in creation and redemption. Since no one encounters the Bible without any presuppositions or preunderstandings, the rule of faith provides a handy and sure framework for reading in a way that is not alien to the Bible's contents and purposes. Irenaeus used the example of a mosaic whose accompanying key depicts how the tiles are to be placed in order to assemble the image of a king. Gnostic teachers took the same mosaic tiles and arranged them into the form of a dog or fox, all the while claiming that it was that of a king. The rule of faith is such a key to interpreting the Scriptures in their proper "order" and "connection."[17]

It is important to note a couple of points about the rule of faith or the Christian creeds as a presuppositional starting point for scriptural interpretation. First, the rule of faith is not extraneous to the Scriptures but rather derived from them.[18] In Irenaeus's example, it is the Gnostics who are imposing their own configuration of tiles to compose the likeness of a fox or dog. The mosaic is *intended* to be that of a king. Second, the rule of faith is not exhaustive. It only supplies a basic theological framework for interpretation. It does not fully represent the epic sweep of the whole Bible or its rich tapestry of genres. As N. T. Wright points out, the creeds do not adequately situate the good news of God's kingship via Messiah Jesus within the whole story of Israel. They therefore potentially contribute to a chronic neglect of the OT.[19] Neither do the creeds tell us much about ethics. They are focused on Christian *faith*, not practice. If the larger, detailed body of scripturally based Christian teaching is like a full instruction manual for engaging Scripture, then the rule of faith is a quick-start guide. It is not meant to replace ongoing substantive theological reflection relevant within cultural contexts. Our understanding and practice of biblical faith must continually return to the Scriptures for fullness, refinement, and correction (2 Tim. 3:16-17). The rule of faith, as an accurate summary of genuine Christian faith, functions as the nonnegotiable starting point and guide for theological interpretation.

---

17. Irenaeus, *Haer.* 1.8.1 (*ANF* 1:326).
18. See Cyril of Jerusalem, *Catech.* 5.12 (*NPNF*[2] 7:32).
19. Wright 2012, 256-57.

The ecclesial context of theological interpretation does not mean that our interpretive practice insulates itself from the approaches and methodologies associated with the academic study of the Bible. Even the most radical approaches that invoke a "hermeneutic of suspicion" can alert us to errors or dangers in interpretation, keep us honest in our interpretive endeavors, and push us to work harder at validating our interpretations. Nevertheless, the ecclesial context for interpretation behooves us to read the Bible with the church's interests in mind. This means we are not focused on the latest scholarly ideologies or fads but on God's mission through Christ and his church to bring salvation and holiness and joyous fellowship with God to fallen men and women.

The Context of Culture

One of the main tasks of theology is to engage Scripture in such a way as to translate the biblical messages from their ancient settings into the cultural milieux of later Christian contexts. At its heart, then, theological interpretation is *cross-cultural*. Every culture has a default set of conceptual and linguistic "equipment" that assists participants of that culture in making sense of the world around them. No culture can maximally and coherently grasp the vast complexities of reality and truth in divine revelation or in creation. Every culture has weaknesses, blind spots, brokenness—fallenness. So interpreters will do well to avail themselves of interpretive sources that will give them the greatest number of cross-cultural perspectives as possible. Every source should be used critically, out of an awareness of the distinctive cultural interests that color interpretations. As well, other aspects of historical, literary, and theological interpretation can cross-check the relative faithfulness of interpretations.

There are two ways to expand our cross-cultural horizons. The first is to drink deeply from the great traditions of the Christian church in all its major branches, whether Protestant, Catholic, or Orthodox. Study of the church fathers (both Greek and Latin) will open our eyes to theological and practical concerns that we might not have considered in our own context. We should also be cognizant and self-critical of our own distinctive Christian tradition (e.g., the Wesleyan-Holiness tradition) and its cultural roots. Churches in the

Reformed tradition are right to hold to the motto *ecclesia reformata, semper reformanda* —that is, "the church reformed and always reforming."

The second involves learning from the global church today.[20] The contemporary church in places such as Latin America, China, India, Africa, and the Middle East provide cultural perspectives that illuminate the Scriptures and foster genuine discipleship on levels not readily available to Western interpreters. For instance, honor-shame cultures in Asia, the Middle East, and Latin America draw readers closer to quite similar social dynamics reflected in the Mediterranean culture in which the biblical texts were produced. Asian and African Christians live in cultures where polytheistic and idolatrous practices are real options, so they can read many passages of Scripture with an immediacy not shared by Westerners. Many Christians in the global church undergo severe persecution, so they find themselves identifying directly with the motif of the suffering righteous ones throughout the Bible.

Most significantly, across the global church one finds cultural perspectives that strongly affirm the reality of the supernatural. Global Christians are "Pentecostal" in the broad sense that they believe and experience the power of God to heal, provide spiritual guidance, and banish demonic spirits. This is in stark contrast to the Western tendency, especially among the well-educated, to discount or provide natural explanations for supernatural phenomena that global Christians take for granted as all too real. Openness to cross-cultural perspectives from the global church has the potential to break Western Christians free from their besetting sin of disbelief in divine power. We can then take seriously James's exhortation to resist the devil (4:7; also 1 Pet. 5:8-9) and to call upon the elders of the church to anoint the sick for healing (James 5:15-16) or Hebrews's invocation of the divine witness to the gospel through gifts of the Spirit (2:4). The continuationist (as opposed to cessationist) embrace of the Spirit's work attested in Scripture *and* realized among believers in the global church today is a dominant theme running through Craig Keener's fine monograph on biblical interpretation, *Spirit Hermeneutics* (2016).

---

20. See Treier 2008, 157-86.

The Total Theological Program

Finally, when we talk about the *theological* interpretation of Scripture, we are referring to the full complement of subdisciplines that comprise theological study and practice. These include the following:

1. *Exegesis*, which aims to explore the texts "on their own terms" within their ancient historical, cultural, and literary contexts.

2. *Biblical theology*, which pulls together the theological threads of the whole Bible, synthesizing (where there is discernible unity or consistency) the coherent biblical perspective on relevant theological topics.

3. *Historical theology*, which canvasses what past divines have preached, commented, and sung concerning Holy Scripture. It also includes the normative symbols of faith that we find in the Apostles' Creed, Nicene Creed, and Definition of Chalcedon.

4. *Systematic or constructive theology*, which brings a self-consciously philosophical outlook to the theological material of the Bible in order to fashion a system of Christian belief in which the various parts fit into a coherent whole.

5. *Pastoral or practical theology*, which appropriates Christian doctrine for the ministries of the church. It is multifaceted, involving not only homiletics, liturgy, pastoral care, counseling, and spiritual direction but also Christian education, evangelism, missions, compassionate ministries, and matters of social ethics and responsibility.

Ideally, the theological enterprise is a linear process from exegesis to practical ministry. In truth, all five of the subdisciplines are portals to theological reflection. All five must keep in close contact with careful readings of the Scripture so that every facet of theological formulation and practice remains genuinely *biblical*. In practice, interpreters usually do not have the time or expertise to work across the whole panoply of theological subdisciplines. Nevertheless, interpreters must be willing to engage whatever theological lens will help them put an individual text into proper focus and clarity. In the sample interpretations of the following chapters, my employment of the theological subdisciplines is selective. I will focus on exegesis, biblical theology, and (when appropriate) historical theology. Systematic and pastoral theologies deserve a larger scope than is manageable in this small book.

The subdisciplines correspond to the parts of the so-called Wesleyan quadrilateral: Scripture (exegesis and biblical theology), tradition (historical theology), reason (systematic theology), and experience (pastoral theology).[21] In the ecclesial context of theological interpretation, understanding and appropriating Scripture is paramount. Scripture is the foundation for all theological formulation and practice. But legitimate understanding is ultimately gauged by the salutary *uses* and *abilities* that our interpretations of Scripture foster.[22] Valid interpretations are not just contemplated between someone's ears, in the mind, but urged by Spirit-filled Christian ministers and enacted in the real world by sincere believers who are hungry to know and love God and to love their neighbors as themselves. Therefore, theological interpretation begins with Scripture but must always issue in the responses of the church to the Word of God in worship and mission. All the hard work of exegesis, biblical theologizing, historical theology, and systematics comes to naught if it is not put to good use in the church for our service to God's kingdom.

Conclusion

In this chapter we have briefly sketched a threefold approach to interpreting Scripture. Reading and interpreting Hebrews and the CE, or any biblical text, will be enriched by employing the lenses of historical, literary, and theological interpretation. In the chapters to follow we will provide representative examples of this basic method.

---

21. On the Wesleyan quadrilateral, see Thorsen 2005 and 2018 and Gunter et al. 1997.
22. On understanding as ability and usage, see Wood 1993, 16-20.

5

Go On to Perfection

(HEB. 5:11-6:3)

To demonstrate the interpretive process, we have selected Hebrews 5:11–6:3 because of its connection to the two primary discursive functions in Hebrews: exposition and exhortation. On the one hand, the passage makes direct reference to the doctrinal burden of the entire epistle concerning Christ's high priesthood (5:11, referring back to vv. 5-10). On the other hand, it is partly constitutive of the "preacher's"[1] hortatory agenda to rouse his audience to a determined commitment to a life of faith and righteousness.

Historical Interpretation

In the interest of being concise, book-level historical-background information about Hebrews appears in sidebar 5.1. The remaining discussion in this section will focus on passage-level historical background. The reader is encouraged to read Hebrews 5:11–6:3 before proceeding.

SIDEBAR 5.1. HEBREWS AT A GLANCE

Author: Anonymous. The epistle is traditionally attributed to the apostle Paul, but it was likely written by an unknown Christian connected to the circle of Paul's coworkers (see Heb. 13:23). Numerous figures have been proposed as the author, but many modern scholars have tentatively followed Luther's suggestion of Apollos (see Acts 18:24-28).

---

1. We refer to the author of Hebrews as the "preacher" because the book bears the marks of a sermon, albeit sent as a letter (see "Literary Interpretation" section that follows on p. 123).

Addressees: In accord with the title, "To the Hebrews," it was addressed to Jewish Christians somewhere in the Roman Empire. Ancient interpreters identified the readers as Hebrew Christians in Jerusalem. The consensus today is that Hebrews was written to a small Jewish-Christian community in Rome.

Date: The book's apparent assumption that the temple cult is still functioning in Jerusalem, as well as its failure to mention the fall of Jerusalem in AD 70 or the martyrdoms that occurred during Nero's persecution in the mid-60s, support the view that it was written in the early 60s.

Occasion and Purpose: The readers were becoming discouraged in their Christian faith due to social pressure or the threat of persecution (perhaps potential martyrdom). The preacher warns them about the danger of lapsing into their preconversion (non-Christian) Jewish faith and impresses upon them the superiority of the new covenant.

Message/Argument: God's final and definitive revelation has occurred in the eschatological appearance of the Son—Jesus Christ—in his incarnation, reverent and obedient life, and sacrificial death. Christ's self-offering provided decisive cleansing of the conscience from sins and inaugurated his new-covenant ministry as high priest so that believers have bold access to God's presence in worship now and the hope of life in God's unshakable kingdom in the future (i.e., God's rest, the heavenly homeland, the new Jerusalem).

Significance: The two foci of the Christian life are (a) persevering faith in God modeled after Christ's own faithfulness and (b) a life of worship and gratitude to God and loving service to others within the Christian community. Abandoning one's loyalty to Christ and association with the church in order to reconnect with one's past religious commitments in (nonmessianic) Judaism results in the loss of salvation. The "first covenant," with its repeated priestly offices and sacrifices in an earthly sanctuary, does not provide for a thorough purgation of sins; it stands as a fading shadow and prefiguration of Christ's superior "new covenant," final sacrifice, and high priestly ministry in the heavenly sanctuary.

This passage in Hebrews is about believers going on to perfection. It follows on the heels of the author's statement that the Son was made perfect through his obedient suffering to become "the source of eternal salvation" and the high priest like Melchizedek (5:9; see vv. 8-10). This is admittedly a difficult message to grasp (v. 11), and one which takes most of the epistle to unfold. The real difficulty, though, is not the subject matter. It is the readers' dangerous attitude of nonchalance and unresponsiveness to the fullness of the gospel that impedes Christian growth toward maturity—and could even wipe out the benefits and identity of their Christian life altogether (6:4-8; see 3:6, 14). The preacher has been hammering at this problem from the beginning of the sermon. However, at this point he not only addresses his audience in the second person (which he has done in previous exhortations [3:12-13, 15; 4:1, 7]) but also places his finger directly on their problem: "You have become sluggish in hearing" (5:11, NRSVUE).

The preacher pursues a two-sided strategy to jar his readers into responding. First, he chides them for becoming spiritually immature (vv. 11-14). Second, he urges them to move on toward perfection (6:1-3). Beyond our passage, this carrot-and-stick approach intensifies as the preacher sets forth the worst case scenario for those who apostatize (vv. 4-8) and then assures his readers that he is more optimistic about their prospects for salvation (vv. 9-12) provided they continue to imitate the faith and hope of those who inherit God's sure promise (vv. 13-20).

This passage is saturated with tropes and images commonly associated with Greco-Roman education. A fundamental aspect of ancient pedagogy remains with us today. Teachers introduce students to simple, rudimentary elements before leading them onward to more complex and difficult matters (e.g., from the alphabet to grammar to literary criticism to philosophy and rhetoric).[2] Teachers, then and now, also complain about their pupils' slowness or resistance to learning.[3] In 5:11 the preacher shames his readers by telling them that by now they ought to be teachers (a position of status and honor

---

2. See the classic study by Marrou 1982 and the synopsis of ancient education in Anderson 2013, 178-79.
3. Keener 2014, 646.

in ancient society) but that they are acting like babies or little children (with little or no status) who still must *be* instructed.

Ancient philosophers frequently describe educational progress by drawing analogies to human growth (from childhood to adulthood), corresponding diet (from milk to solid food), and moral development (culminating in the discernment of good and evil). For example, Epictetus identifies the uneducated as childish in their ignorant and unaccomplished lives.[4] Like in Hebrews 5:12c ("You need milk, not solid food!"), Epictetus scolds his students, "Are you not willing, at this late date, like children, to be weaned and to partake of more solid food."[5] Philo contrasts milk with solid food, infants with full-grown adults, and the inexperienced with the perfect—compare "inexperienced" (Heb. 5:13, NET) and "perfect" (v. 14, AT; "mature" [NIV]). Philo compares baby food or milk with the branches of general education (*ta enkyklia*, or what would later become known as "the liberal arts") and advanced knowledge with the virtues, whose province of study is philosophy.[6]

Hebrews uses identical imagery, but his application is somewhat different. Rudimentary teachings, or "milk," correspond to "the elementary truths of God's word" (5:12; "the ABC of God's oracles" [REB]). In 6:1 he uses another common metaphor employed by philosophers to refer to elementary instruction: a "foundation."[7] He calls the foundation "the elementary teachings about Christ" (v. 1a) and enumerates its six elements in verses 1b-2. Though the three pairs of elements ("faith" and "repentance," "cleansing rites" and "laying on of hands," "resurrection" and "eternal judgment") are preparatory for the Christian life, there is nothing about them that is distinctively Christian. The preacher has already alluded to the advanced teaching or "solid food" that he thinks his readers should be able to digest: the truths about Jesus's incarnation, obedient suffering, and perfection as high priest (5:7-10)—about which "we have much to say" (v. 11).

Hebrews incorporates another kind of metaphor—athletic training (*gegymnasmena* [v. 14])—that was often used by ancient authors to speak

---

4. Epictetus, *Diatr.* 2.1.16; 3.19.6.

5. Ibid., 2.16.39; see 3.24.9.

6. See the brief summary of Philo's images of educational progress in Anderson 2013, 180-81, as well as Thompson's (2008, 119-22) more wide-ranging discussion of ancient educational theory in correlation to this passage in Hebrews.

7. deSilva 2000, 216.

about intellectual, rhetorical, or ethical training.[8] The result of such training also sounds a lot like that proposed by ancient thinkers: mental faculties that have been conditioned to discern good from evil. Such ability is a textbook definition of *wisdom* among ancient philosophers.[9] However, when we take the broader message of Hebrews into consideration, this is only a proximate goal. The ultimate goal is to reach a spiritual "perfection" (KJV, NRSVUE) or "maturity" (6:1, NIV) that is only attainable through Christ's sacrifice.

Unlike the Levitical sacrifices under the old covenant, Christ's sacrifice cleanses the conscience from the defilement of sins (9:9; 10:22). It imparts "the full assurance that faith brings" (10:22) and the full assurance of "hope" (6:11) that strengthen believers to be steadfast in their commitment to Christ. Consequently, they are unlikely to turn away from the living God or have their hearts hardened by the deceit of sin (3:12-13). This is why the preacher sees no use in simply going over the rudimentary elements of the faith. The alternative to spiritual maturity is apostasy. He has no choice but to urge his readers toward maturity (with God's providential help [6:3]) by serving them the "solid food" of teaching concerning Christ's Melchizedekian priesthood.

Literary Interpretation

Genre and Overall Structure of Hebrews

Hebrews is a homily or sermon that was sent as a letter. The preacher refers to both of these genres in Hebrews 13:22. He identifies his work as a "word of exhortation," the same expression used to designate a synagogue sermon in Acts 13:15.[10] He also states, "I've only written a short letter to you" (CEB; see GW; translating a form of *epistellō*, "inform/instruct by letter" [BDAG]).

The structure of Hebrews is a subject of considerable disagreement among scholars,[11] and we are unlikely to resolve the debate here. The question of whether patterns of ancient rhetoric contributed to Hebrews's

---

8. See the extensive references in Anderson 2013, 182.
9. Ibid., 183.
10. For additional pointers to Hebrews's sermonic form, see Anderson 2013, 45.
11. See Guthrie 1998.

structure has elicited further differences of opinion.[12] A key to the book's structure consists of the "bookends" to the central arguments of the letter in 4:14-16 and 10:19-23.[13] What emerges is a tripartite structure expressed in the following outline:[14]

I. Hearing the Apostle and High Priest of Our Confession (1:1–4:13)

   A. Hearing God's Son in These Last Days: Jesus the Merciful and Faithful High Priest (1:1–2:18)

   B. Hearing God's Word Today: Jesus the Apostle and High Priest of Our Confession (3:1–4:13)

II. Jesus's Superior High Priesthood (4:14–10:18)

   A. The Qualifications of the Great High Priest (4:14–5:10)

   B. Preparing for Advanced Teaching on Christ's High Priesthood (5:11–6:20)

   C. The High Priesthood like Melchizedek: The Son Perfected Forever (7:1-28)

   D. The Superior Ministry of the Son's High Priesthood (8:1–10:18)

III. Call to Persevering Faith and Acceptable Worship (10:19–13:25)

   A. Exhortations to Persevere in Faith (10:19–12:13)

   B. Exhortations to Offer Acceptable Worship (12:14–13:25)

The first part of Hebrews introduces the Son's incarnation and suffering as God's definitive revelation in the last days. The appropriate human response to God's speaking is hearing, believing, and obeying the divine voice rather than turning away with a hardened heart, disbelieving, and disobeying. The preacher's pastoral concern is sounded in 2:1 ("We must pay the most careful attention"), pursued at length in the midrash of 3:1–4:13, and culminates in the sermon's final warning (12:25). All of 5:11–6:20 is another version of the same concern, structurally signaled by the *inclusio* involving the Greek word for "sluggish" (*nōthros*) in 5:11 ("sluggish in hearing" [NET, LEB]) and 6:12 ("sluggish" [NET, LEB]).

---

12. See Thompson 2008, 16.
13. Anderson 2013, 154.
14. As per ibid., 5-6.

The second part of Hebrews comprises the central arguments for the entire sermon, centering on Jesus Christ's high priesthood, perfect sacrifice, and new-covenant ministry in the heavenly sanctuary. This subject matter is introduced in 4:14–5:10, but it is strategically interrupted in 5:11–6:20 before being developed at length in 7:1–10:18. The digression in 5:11–6:20 is not really a digression at all. The preacher knows that he must confront the arrested spiritual development of his listeners before he can profitably set forth the meaty christological doctrine of his sermon. Our passage (5:11–6:3), then, is part of a section of the letter designed to prepare readers to embrace the full message of the gospel according to Hebrews.

The hortatory aims of 5:11–6:20 are resumed in the third major part. In the closing chapters of Hebrews (10:19–12:13), the preacher exhorts listeners to persevere in faith and respond to God's kingdom with the receptivity of gratitude, as well as in worship that shows forth in lives of holiness, love, and trust.

Form, Structure, and Movement

Form

Rhetorically, 5:11–6:3 is part of a "digression" (5:11–6:20), much like 3:1–4:13. A digression is a part of a speech that veers from the logical order and yet tackles a topic or theme that is crucial for readers to heed the case being presented.[15] As we have already noted, 5:11–6:20 is an indispensable preparation for the weighty central arguments of the sermon. It sharply confronts the listeners' condition of arrested spiritual development, calling them to go on to perfection rather than fall away from the faith. The character of 5:11–6:20 as a digression is evident in how it interrupts the topic of Christ as the high priest according to the order of Melchizedek (5:10) and then smoothly segues back to it in 6:20.

---

15. Quintilian, *Inst.* 4.3.

Structure and Movement

The preacher's pastoral concern for his listeners comes to expression in five subsections in 5:11–6:20, with the first two composing the passage we are considering:

1. Reproof (5:11-14). The preacher chides his listeners for their stunted spiritual and moral growth.

2. Exhortation (6:1-3). The preacher invites his listeners to "go on to perfection"—that is, progressing to the fullness of the gospel as it is embodied in Christ instead of standing pat with those elements of the faith that are continuous with the nonmessianic commitments of their former lives in Judaism.

3. Warning (vv. 4-8). This passage comprises one of the most terrifying warnings in Hebrews. It asserts that one cannot recover from final apostasy.

4. Reassurance (vv. 9-12). The preacher expresses his confidence that the community's love and service are positive signs that its situation is not as dire as the preceding warning might suggest. He is optimistic about their salvation, provided they are diligent in imitating those who through faith and patience inherit God's promises.

5. Powerful encouragement (vv. 13-20). The preacher provides strong encouragement by pointing to Abraham's faith and patience in receiving God's promise in light of God's demonstration of his utter trustworthiness.

The movement of this entire section is pretty straightforward. Our passage (5:11–6:3) encloses the beginning twofold action of reproving the readers for their deficient spiritual development (5:11-14) and exhorting them to progress toward maturity in Christ (6:1-3). The remaining subsections reinforce this exhortation by appealing to the fearful prospect of falling away (vv. 4-8), assuring them of their ultimate salvation (vv. 9-12), and inspiring confidence in the rock-solid dependability of God (vv. 13-20).

Significant Details

Three expressions in this passage are critical to understanding its primary thrust. We will mention the last of them first because its meaning is circumscribed by the previous two expressions.

What does the preacher mean by the exhortation "Let us . . . be taken forward to maturity" (6:1)? The Greek word for "maturity" or "perfection" (NRSVUE) is the noun form (*teleiotētēs*) of the verb *teleioun*, "to perfect," "to make perfect" (occurring 9x in Hebrews). The word is also a cognate of the adjective for "mature" or "perfect" (AT) (*teleios*) found in 5:14. This last connection is important, since the "perfection" of 6:1 is directly related to the preceding description of what is entailed in being "perfect." All of these cognate words have to do with reaching an end or goal (*telos*) and hence convey the idea of completion. The educational context of 5:11–6:3 (which we explored above), with its concomitant images of human development from infancy to adulthood, warrants the NIV's rendering of these terms as "mature" (5:14) and "maturity" (6:1). Education begins with rudimentary instruction ("milk") for infants until they are full grown and can handle advanced teaching ("solid food"). But what is the state or condition that is constitutive of maturity? Two other expressions address this question.

The two expressions we wish to explore are like two sides of the same coin. The first is "not acquainted with the teaching about righteousness" (5:13); the second is "who by constant use have trained themselves to distinguish good from evil" (v. 14). In verse 13, the preacher identifies his readers as infant-like because they are "not acquainted"—or, rather, "inexperienced" (CSB, NET), "unschooled,"[16] or "not proficient"[17]—with "the teaching about righteousness" (lit. "the word of righteousness" [*logou dikaiosynēs*]). Walters understands "the word of righteousness" to mean "the matter or subject of what is right."[18] However, among Hellenistic moral philosophers the expression means "reasoning about what is right,"[19] taking both terms (*logos* and

---

16. Walters 1995, 111, 125.
17. Koester 2001, 302.
18. Walters 1995, 125.
19. See examples in Koester 2001, 302, and Johnson 2006, 156.

dikaiosynē) in an active sense. The preacher is referring to a developed capacity "to discern and follow a correct course of action."[20]

The second expression states the same basic idea positively. Whereas infants are ethically inexperienced (5:13), "the mature . . . by constant use have trained themselves to distinguish good from evil" (v. 14). The translations "by constant use" (NIV) and "by practice" (NRSVUE) do not capture the sense of the Greek phrase *dia tēn hexin*. "The term *hexis* does not refer to the process of training, but to the proficiency, mastery, character, or habit resulting from practice."[21] "Practice makes perfect," as we say. The preacher is referring to the perfection of proficiency that the mature possess. The ethical capacity of the mature has been developed by their "being trained" (*gegymnasmena*) or—to translate the athletic metaphor into modern parlance—"being conditioned." That which is being conditioned is one's inner "faculties" (NRSVUE) of ethical and spiritual discernment. What they are being conditioned *for* is "to distinguish good from evil."

The notion of going on to perfection, then, most certainly involves the development or maturation of one's ethical or spiritual sensibilities. The shorthand term for the capability of discerning the right course of action is *wisdom*. While this is stated using the broadest philosophical—and biblical (Num. 14:23; Deut. 1:39; Isa. 7:15-16)—categories of discerning good and evil, in the context of Hebrews the right course of action is more particularly a determined faith in God (good) rather than apostasy (evil).

Theological Interpretation

Biblical Theology

The theological interpretation of our passage raises the question of how we are to understand what it means for a follower of Christ to "go on to perfection." In chapter 3 (beginning on p. 84), we compared Hebrews's teachings on perfection and holiness with the same themes in the CE, so we need not go over that ground again. In summary, we may say that "perfection" for believers (according to Hebrews and the CE) is to be established in a

---

20. Cockerill 2012, 258.
21. Anderson 2013, 182.

new-covenant relationship of steadfast faith in and stable obedience to God. By contrast, an infantile level of spirituality is marked by inconsistent, vacillating commitment and often sinful lifestyle choices that cause one to teeter on the edge of apostasy.

For further canonical exploration of the topic of perfection, the most important OT instances are when the Greek adjective *teleios* in the LXX modifies "heart" (Gk., *kardia* = Hebr., *lēb*). A "perfect" (*teleios* = Hebr., *shāmēl*, "complete," "perfect") heart means that one's covenant loyalty to God is complete and unwavering (1 Kings 8:61; 11:4; 15:3, 14; 1 Chron. 28:9). Similarly, persons (like Noah [Gen. 6:9]) or things are described as or commanded to be "perfect" (= Hebr., *tāmîm*, "complete," "blameless") before God (Exod. 12:5; Deut. 18:13; 2 Sam. 22:26; Ezra 2:63). God commanded Abraham to be pleasing before him and become "perfect" or "blameless" (*tāmîm*, Gen. 17:1). This OT conception of perfection as constancy in one's covenant loyalty to God also seems to have informed James's understanding of perfection (1:4).

In the NT, this OT background illuminates Jesus's command in the Sermon on the Mount: "Be perfect, therefore, as your heavenly Father is perfect" (Matt. 5:48). This saying also echoes the refrain from the Holiness Code: "Be holy, because I am holy" (Lev. 11:44, 45; see 19:2; 20:7). The preceding context of Jesus's saying shows that the quality of divine perfection the disciples are called upon to imitate is the undifferentiated love the Father bestows on all his creatures, "the righteous and the unrighteous" (Matt. 5:45). On one occasion, Jesus confronted a rich young man concerning the fatal deficiency in his devotion to God: his wealth. Jesus said to him, "If you want to be perfect (*teleios*), go, sell your possessions and give to the poor, and you will have treasure in heaven. Then come, follow me" (19:21).

Apart from Hebrews and the CE, Paul's letters have the most references to perfection. In 1 Corinthians 14:20, Paul's teaching coheres with Hebrews 5:13-14 insofar as infants have an innocent mindset toward evil, while "adults" (NIV) or "the mature" (ESV) have a power of discernment concerning good and evil. In 1 Corinthians 3:1-3, although the language of perfection is absent, the associated images of infancy (and milk) and adulthood (and solid food) are clearly present. Paul identifies the Corinthian Christians' infantile behavior in verse 1 as "fleshly" (NRSVUE) or "worldly" (NIV; Gk., *sarkikos*) rather than "spiritual" (NRSVUE) or "by the Spirit" (NIV; Gk., *pneumatikos*). Elsewhere Paul uses perfection language to indicate a level of Christian discipleship in which believers are "perfect in their relationship to Christ" (Col. 1:28, NLT) or fully aligned with God's will (4:12). In Ephesians 4:13-16, Christian perfection is expressly described as growth from infancy to adulthood, in which Christ is the model of the mature person (lit. "perfect man," *andra teleion*), comprised of the entire church growing into Christ, its head. Here maturity involves unity of faith, knowledge of the Son of God, growth in love, and truth—all of which guard against the destabilizing effects of devious false teachings (v. 14). Crucially, this text conceives of perfection with respect to "the whole body" of Christ (v. 16; i.e., the church as a corporate whole), while Colossians 1:28 would indicate that Paul views such spiritual development as applicable to every individual believer too.

Paul's teaching on perfection in Philippians 3:12, 15 is perhaps the most instructive for our purposes. Here Paul speaks of perfection in two ways. In verse 12, Paul denies having "already arrived at my goal" (lit. "have already been perfected" [*teteleiōmai*]). He is referring to attaining the resurrection of the dead (v. 11), which is the goal or prize of the upward call of God in Christ Jesus (v. 14). Paul is undoubtedly referring to a future, *eschatological* perfection in which disciples will experience ultimate Christlikeness in immortal, embodied existence. It is when Christ "will transform our lowly bodies so that they are like his glorious body" (v. 21). Paul also speaks of a *present* perfection in verse 15: "All of us, then, who are mature [*teleioi*] should take such a view of things." Paul's use of perfection language here is consonant with the OT background we reviewed above. However, within the context of Philippians, Paul is more narrowly speaking of the spiritually mature who share "the same mindset as Christ Jesus" that he commended earlier in the letter (2:5).[22]

Hebrews shares with Paul both realized and eschatological conceptions of perfection, as well as Christ's incarnation, suffering, and exaltation as the pattern for and source of Christian perfection. Christ's whole life of reverence and submission to God—culminating in his decisive act of obedience in the

---

22. See Flemming 2009, 193.

suffering of the cross—perfected him to be the great high priest (Heb. 2:10; 5:9). His sacrifice and high priestly ministry make it possible for believers to have bold access to the divine presence. The perfection of worshippers is due to an inward spiritual transformation—the definitive cleansing of the heart from a defiled conscience (9:9; 10:1, 22)—so that we can enter the most holy place in worship through the new and living way prepared by Christ's death and exaltation (10:19-22). But this is the starting point for a deeper perfection, which is the concern of our passage (5:11–6:3). Following on the heels of the description of Christ's perfection (i.e., his learning obedience through suffering [5:7-10]), this perfection is nothing short of ethical and spiritual growth into Christlike obedience. It is living into the new-covenant blessings, which include the release from sin's defiling grip and the divine enablement for new obedience (10:16-17). This is the kind of obedience that holds fast to the confession of Christ Jesus, even if it means sharing in the same sort of suffering and abuse that Christ endured (13:13).

Thus the perfecting of believers means their access into God's presence now (realized aspect) and their ultimate entrance into rest and salvation (4:1, 3, 6, 10, 11; 9:28; eschatological aspect). Eschatological perfection is what the author points to when he speaks of all of the OT worthies of faith dying without receiving God's promise, "since God had planned something better for us so that only together with us would they be made perfect" (11:40). However, the author does not understand perfection solely as reaching a heavenly destination (vv. 10, 16; 12:22; 13:14). Perfection also means being made fit in our present life for our future life with God. Both realized and eschatological perfection converge in God's divine training of his sons and daughters (12:5-13) to become the obedient children who not only produce a harvest of righteousness (v. 11) but also will ultimately share in God's own holiness (v. 10). Growth in virtue and ever-increasing obedience with every new step in God's gracious training is not an end in itself. The goal is to be drawn into God's own life and blessedness, which we may only enjoy by being perfected like God's Son. "Without holiness," the preacher states, "no one will see the Lord" (v. 14).

Historical and Systematic Theology

Ancient Christians held to Christian perfection as a possible attainment in this life. At baptism one is sanctified, sealed, and empowered for growth in grace and virtues. Indeed, baptism was viewed as the starting point on a journey toward perfection. However, by the late fourth century this sacramental significance was abraded, especially in the Western (Latin) church. Gradually the second step in the baptismal ritual (confirmation or chrismation) was practiced as a separate sacrament in the West, signifying the Holy Spirit's strengthening of the believer; but the idea of sanctification or perfection was deemphasized in both the East and West. As Paul Bassett writes,

> Baptism-confirmation was seen as entry into the Church. And the Church, now much more institutional than ever before, makes way in its theology and in its disciplinary processes for believers who are self-consciously both saints and sinners. The Church admits its sinfulness as it had not earlier. That is, it comes to confess it as a matter of course.[23]

The fine balance in the New Testament between the "already" and the "not yet" of the victorious Christian life increasingly tilted toward the "not yet." Yet the biblical promise of Christian perfection did not completely die out.[24]

Two figures from the Eastern church of the late fourth century are of particular interest: (Psuedo-)Macarius the Egyptian and Gregory of Nyssa. Both wrote extensively concerning Christian perfection and were a formative influence on John Wesley.[25] Our purpose is to explore three facets of their teaching that seem either to correlate with or to shed light on the doctrine of perfection in Hebrews.

First, what is Christian perfection? In short, according to Gregory of Nyssa, it is to embody and reflect everything connoted by the identifying title "Christian." Gregory explains,

> If, therefore, someone puts on the name of Christ, but does not exhibit in his life what is indicated by the term, such a person belies the name and puts on a lifeless mask in accordance with the model proposed to

---

23. Bassett and Greathouse 1985, 72.
24. For historical surveys of the doctrine of Christian perfection, see Bassett and Greathouse 1985; Flew 1934.
25. Merritt 1987.

us. For it is not possible for Christ not to be justice and purity and truth and estrangement from all evil, nor is it possible to be a Christian (that is, truly a Christian) without displaying in oneself participation in these virtues.[26]

Thus perfection is Christlikeness. It is "imitation of the divine nature," or the restoration of the likeness of God in which human beings were originally created.[27] In *On Perfection*, Gregory expounds upon nearly thirty qualities or descriptions of Christ that are intended to shape the Christian life, either through the imitation of them or through worship.[28] For Macarius, too, Christlikeness,[29] or "the image of the virtues of the Spirit,"[30] marks out what Christian perfection is. But for the sanctified, the original image of God in Adam is not merely restored, but surpassed:

I have already said that sin is eradicated, and man recovers the primal fashioning of the pure Adam. Man, however, by the power of the Spirit and the spiritual regeneration, not only comes to the measure of the first Adam, but is made greater than he. Man is deified.[31]

In its own way, Hebrews expresses the perfection of Christ as the goal of the Christian life. Christ, "the radiance of God's glory and the exact representation of his being" (Heb. 1:3), was perfected through his humiliation, incarnation, suffering, and exaltation to become the agent through whom God is "bringing many sons and daughters to glory" (2:10; see 2:5-18). The perfection of Jesus in reverent submission and obedience to God (5:7-8) is the pattern for God's children who are being instructed in virtue (vv. 12-14; 12:3-13). The focus of Christian commitment is on Jesus, "the pioneer and perfecter of faith" (12:2). Provided that believers hold on to their confession of faith (3:6, 14), they are "partners" (NRSVUE) or "sharers" (LEB) of a heavenly calling (v. 1), of Christ (v. 14), and of the Holy Spirit (6:4).[32]

---

26. Gregory of Nyssa 1967, 85.
27. Ibid.
28. Ibid., 9, 101.
29. Macarius, *Homilies* 15.38; 18.10 (Macarius 1921, 125, 155-56).
30. Ibid., 46.5 (Macarius 1921, 289).
31. Ibid., 26.2 (Macarius 1921, 185).
32. On the association of these expressions with the doctrine of theosis, see 2 Pet 1:4 and Long 2011, 101-11.

Second, there is the question of whether Christian perfection is attainable in this life. We have already pointed out the existence in Hebrews of both a realized perfection (as spiritual and ethical maturation) and eschatological perfection (in the heavenly Jerusalem). Hebrews envisions the whole Christian life as a journey to the heavenly city. Believers are encouraged to "approach" or "draw near" to the divine presence (4:16; 10:22; see 7:25; 11:6 [present tense forms of *proserchomai*]) while also being told that they have *already come* to Mount Zion (12:18, 22 [perfect forms of *proserchomai*]). Both the realized and eschatological dimensions of perfection are expressed in the claim that believers "are entering" (present tense) into God's final, eschatological rest (4:3, AT). Thus Hebrews holds in tension both the present and future attainment of perfection for worshippers both through Jesus's atoning sacrifice (10:14) and the Father's training (*paideia*; see 12:5, 7-8, 11) in holiness.

Gregory of Nyssa approaches this question in a more philosophical mode. In his *Life of Moses*, he states that perfection of the divine nature (which is the Good itself) is not circumscribed or limited. So it is impossible for finite human beings ever to attain to divine perfection. Yet we cannot ignore Jesus's command to be perfect (Matt. 5:48). While we can never attain to God's unbounded virtue, we may nevertheless *participate* in it.[33] In *On Perfection*, he writes,

> This, therefore, is perfection in the Christian life in my judgment, namely, the participation of one's soul and speech and activities in all the names by which Christ is signified, so that the perfect holiness, according to the eulogy of Paul [1 Thess. 5:23-24], is taken upon oneself in "the whole body and soul and spirit," continually safeguarded against being mixed with evil.[34]

Gregory also turns on its head the argument that changeable human nature could never achieve the good of the divine, immutable nature. While this is true, the very fact that human nature is changeable means that one may *grow* in goodness. The human capacity for change is "a kind of wing of flight to

---

33. Gregory of Nyssa, *Life of Moses* 1.3-10 (Gregory of Nyssa 1978, 30-31).
34. Gregory of Nyssa 1967, 121.

greater things." Gregory concludes, "For this is truly perfection: never to stop growing towards what is better and never placing any limit on perfection."[35]

Macarius writes of entering into the "measures of perfection" or "perfect measures,"[36] or what he also calls "measures of the Spirit."[37] There are twelve steps leading to perfection, though Macarius does not describe them.[38] He relates how a person might reach the twelfth, highest step of perfection at one moment or season, being "pure and free from sin," but then end up a step down at the eleventh step, or even at "the first and lowest step of perfection."[39] He confesses that he has never encountered a perfect Christian who is entirely free from sin.[40] When asked about what measure of perfection he has attained, Macarius responds with a description of a mystical experience in which he beholds almost unending, unspeakable wonders opened up before him.[41]

The problem is not that the measures of perfection are impossible to reach; it is that Macarius is aware of the "large range of wickedness" within us, requiring repeated tests of our resolve, even though divine grace could cleanse and perfect us "in the turn of an hour."[42] It is no easy task to arrive at the purity and singleness of heart that relinquishes egocentrism and embraces the perfect love of God. Yet even if someone thinks he or she has attained perfection, Macarius cautions (in a way similar to Gregory of Nyssa) that "the Lord has no end, and there is no comprehending Him."[43] A theme that saturates Macarius's *Homilies* is the indispensable recognition of one's human limitation, since perfection can only occur through complete and utter dependence upon divine grace.[44]

This leads to the third and final question, regarding the role of both the human will and God's grace in perfection. Theologians from the Eastern church have always stressed the importance of human free agency in

---

35. Ibid., 122; for the same thought, see Gregory of Nyssa, *Life of Moses* 1.10 (Gregory of Nyssa 1978, 31).
36. Marcarius, *Homilies* 8.3-4, 6; 17.1-2; 27.20; 38.4.
37. Ibid., 15.7, 35.
38. Ibid., 8.4.
39. Ibid., 8.3-4.
40. Ibid., 8.5.
41. Ibid., 8.6.
42. Ibid., 41.2.
43. Ibid., 26.17.
44. See Bassett and Greathouse 1985, 77-78.

cooperation with divine grace. Gregory of Nyssa writes of spiritual progress under the analogy of birth: "We are in some manner our own parents, giving birth to ourselves by our own free choice in accordance with whatever we wish to be, . . . moulding ourselves to the teaching of virtue or vice."[45] Between the dual nature of human beings—the one intelligent and light (= reason), the other material and heavy (= flesh, passions)—lies the power of choice; and the strength or weakness of either side is proportionate to the choice that one makes.[46] Yet we must bear in mind that spiritual progress toward perfection applies only to those in whom God's grace is already operative. Gregory addresses himself to persons who have "'taken off' the old humanity" (Col. 3:9) and have "'put on' our Lord Jesus Christ himself" (Gal. 3:27)[47] and have therefore "opened an entrance for the Word."[48] The power of agency is itself a gift of divine grace, which Gregory likens to the recovery of wings that had been robbed from humanity through "the downward impulse of evil."[49] Thus even the desire to ascend higher and higher in goodness and perfection is not something of our own making, but rather an acquiescence to and participation in the divine life.

For Macarius, too, human free will is sacrosanct. God does not coerce anyone to pursue the path to perfection. God did not make the human being "a creature of necessity."[50] "[F]reedom of choice remains even in perfect Christians," who can fall from grace through the use of their free will.[51] Homily 19 describes the exertions that must be made by those who desire to be indwelt by Christ, filled with the Holy Spirit, and released from inward sin.[52] They must force themselves to be humble, to be compassionate, to obey the commandments, and to persevere in prayer ("the topmost of right actions"[53]), even when they are disinclined to do so. They must compel themselves to do these things until the Lord has fully tested their resolve.[54] Then the Lord

---

45. Gregory of Nyssa, *Life of Moses* 2.3 (Gregory of Nyssa 1978, 55-56).
46. Gregory of Nyssa, *Homilies* 12.19-27 (Gregory of Nyssa 2012).
47. Ibid., 1.13-18 (Gregory of Nyssa 2012).
48. Ibid., 11.14-23 (Gregory of Nyssa 2012).
49. Ibid., 15.17-29 (Gregory of Nyssa 2012).
50. Macarius, *Homilies* 27.21.
51. Ibid., 27.9.
52. Ibid., 19.
53. Ibid., 40.2.
54. Ibid., 9.1.

himself will enter in and, through the Holy Spirit, produce the fruits of righteousness so that trusting, obeying, showing mercy, and walking in humility are second nature.

Although Macarius insists that there can be no spiritual progress without such intentionality, he is no Pelagian (or semi-Pelagian). He makes it clear that human efforts cannot avail for life in the kingdom without "the co-operation of the Spirit" and "God's power and the efficacy of grace."[55] The Lord "secretly helps" people who have taken their stand to serve the Lord.[56] Righteousness and obedience occur only "by means of the invisible wealth of grace that is in them."[57] Indeed, God's own work precedes human virtue, for "it is He that worketh in you both to will and to do"[58] (see Phil. 2:13). The success of our endeavors "is His own work in us."[59] No one emphasizes more than Macarius the distinguishing trademark of Christianity: absolute humility and dependence upon God.[60]

The burden of the Epistle to the Hebrews is expressed well in the title of William Lane's commentary *Call to Commitment*.[61] The entire letter is devoted to encouraging its readers to become authentic disciples of Jesus. The author intentionally provokes a crisis of decision. The readers must choose to persevere in faith or abandon all hope of salvation. In 10:39, the preacher sets forth the binary choice: shrinking back to destruction or having faith that leads to salvation. Readers may stand still or go backward at their own peril. The sole, viable alternative for believers is to "be taken forward to maturity" (6:1). This can happen only if, in the first place, they *heed* God's word—especially God's speaking through his Son (1:2). This theme is prominent in the first third of the letter (2:1, 3; 3:7, 15-16; 4:2, 7)—including our passage (5:11)—and ascends to a climax in 12:25-29.

Perseverance in faith means, negatively, avoiding a fall from grace (v. 15) or apostasy. This involves repudiating the deceitfulness of sin that hardens

---

55. Ibid., 24.5.
56. Ibid., 21.5.
57. Ibid., 18.1.
58. Ibid., 37.9.
59. Ibid., 4:17.
60. Ibid., 15.37-38, and all throughout the *Homilies*.
61. Lane 1985a.

the heart and wickedly steers it away from the living God (3:12-13). It means struggling against sin (12:4): refraining from willful sins (10:26), including "every hindrance and the sin that so easily ensnares us" (12:1, CSB). Positively, it means being strengthened by God's grace (13:9) and fixing our attention on Jesus's supreme example of faithfulness (3:1; 12:2) in the full assurance of faith and hope in the new-covenant blessings provided by our Great High Priest. The chief of these blessings are Christ's once-for-all sacrifice for sins and his ongoing intercession to aid us when we are tempted, with the goal of our being saved "completely" (7:25). Perseverance issues in lives that exhibit faith, hope, and love (6:10-12; 10:22-24). Thus, in Hebrews, too, we see the delicate balance between human agency and God's gracious provision. Yet, as we have seen in Gregory of Nyssa and Macarius, God is the ultimate source of salvation and goodness:

> Now may the God of peace, who through the blood of the eternal covenant brought back from the dead our Lord Jesus, that great Shepherd of the sheep, equip you with everything good for doing his will, and may he work in us what is pleasing to him, through Jesus Christ, to whom be glory for ever and ever. Amen. (Heb. 13:20-21)

6

Faith Perfected by Works

(JAMES 2:14-26)

James 2:14-26 is a *crux interpretum*. In other words, it is a passage whose interpretation has proved difficult and/or crucial to the exposition of a scriptural doctrine. This passage is a *crux* in both ways: it is difficult to interpret in various particulars and crucial to what the Bible says about the relationship between faith and works. Luther relegated James to the periphery of the canon, in large part because he judged this passage to contradict Paul's preaching of the gospel: salvation by faith and *not* by works. Contemporary interpreters are not similarly scandalized by James's teaching in this passage. The more carefully we read both Paul *and* James, the more we come to realize that these two towering figures in the early church were not contradicting each other. Rather, their messages are complementary.

Historical Interpretation

We cover book-level historical matters in sidebar 6.1. The remaining discussion in this section will concern passage-level historical background for James 2:14-26.

SIDEBAR 6.1. JAMES AT A GLANCE

Author: Most scholars identify James as one of four brothers of Jesus born to Joseph and Mary (Mark 6:3 // Matt. 13:55) and the leading figure of the early church in Jerusalem (Acts 12:17; 15:13; 21:18; Gal. 1:19; 2:9, 12). Scholars who hold to pseudonymous authorship usually believe that this figure is the implied author. The traditional Roman Catholic (Hieronymian) view is that the siblings of Jesus in Mark 6:3 // Matt. 13:55 were really cousins, born to a sister of the Virgin Mary by the same name. The traditional Eastern Orthodox (Epiphanian) view is that a widowed, octogenarian Joseph had children by a previous marriage, and so the brothers listed in Mark 6:3 // Matt. 13:55 are stepsiblings of Jesus.

Addressees: "To the twelve tribes scattered among the nations" (James 1:1) is an allusion to the Diaspora: the "scattering" of the Jewish people because of their sins, associated especially with the exile to Babylon in the sixth c. BC. The reference is likely metaphorical, making James an encyclical letter to Jewish Christians who had been "scattered" from Jerusalem at the time of Stephen's martyrdom (Acts 8:1, 4; 11:19). As the head of the Jerusalem church, and one of "the pillars" of the Jewish-Christian mission (Gal. 2:7-9), James might have addressed himself to Jewish Christians as far away from Jerusalem as "Antioch, Syria and Cilicia" (the locales addressed in the letter issuing from the Jerusalem Council [Acts 15:23]) and perhaps Asia Minor, if not the entire Roman Empire.

Date: Some conservative scholars date James as the earliest book in the NT, written prior to the Jerusalem Council in AD 49. Many date the letter to sometime in the 50s or just before James's death in AD 62. The religious, socioeconomic, and political strife experienced by Jews in Syria-Palestine during this time frame is consistent with problems addressed in James (e.g., oppression of the poor by Jewish aristocrats and increasing recourse to violence in opposing Roman rule). Those who hold to pseudepigraphal authorship date James to sometime in the late first century.

Occasion and Purpose: While this letter was not written to a specific church with unique challenges, but as an encyclical to a wider audience, James wrote it to deal with common challenges facing Jewish Christians in the Greco-Roman world. The goal of the letter is to promote genuine faith and unwavering commitment to the ethical demands of the kingdom ("the royal law") in the face of temptations to compromise with—or be "polluted" by—the world's values and priorities. In short, James wants his readers to

develop integrity or wholeness of character rather than have divided loyalties or inconsistency between one's speech and actions
(being "double-minded"). Spiritual devotion and ethical purity are
essential to maintaining a vibrant covenant community that lives
under the glory and lordship of Jesus Christ.

Message/Argument: James writes in the Jewish wisdom tradition—indebted to Ben Sirach, the Wisdom of Solomon, Proverbs,
and (not least) Jesus. Yet he also employs Greek style and rhetorical devices, such as the diatribe form, that would have been familiar to a Greek-speaking audience. In his exhortations to become
"perfect" or "mature" in faith and conduct, the fulcrum of James's
message is an appeal for listeners to align their lives with "the
wisdom that comes from above" (James 3:17, KJV) rather than
with worldly wisdom that is "earthly, unspiritual, demonic" (v. 15).
Earthly wisdom cultivates strife, instability, and wicked acts in the
community. Heavenly wisdom produces peace and righteousness
and thus shapes the attitudes and behaviors of God's people to
meet with divine approval in the final judgment.

Significance: All the CE, with James at its head, represent the
apostolic witnesses to the gospel identified with the early Jerusalem church. James draws from the wisdom of Jesus to urge
us to live according to the kingdom expectations for disciples.
The spiritual topics addressed in this epistle are just as profitable
today as they were in James's time: perseverance of faith in trials,
humility, attitudes and actions toward the rich and poor, consistency of speech and action, dangers of the uncontrolled tongue,
accountability to the Judge under the "royal law," submission to
God rather than to human passions, the power of prayer, confession of sins, among others. James is an antidote to antinomian
misreadings of Paul's letters. Faith not resulting in a transformed
life that performs good deeds is not saving faith.

Wealth and Poverty in the Greco-Roman World

The first point of historical background important for the interpretation of James 2:14-26 concerns its socioeconomic backdrop. Below, under
"Literary Interpretation" (p. 148), we will consider the relationship of this

passage to the preceding one (vv. 1-14), in which James condemns the practice of favoring the rich over the poor. James's first illustration of faith without works (v. 18) has to do with the neglect of the needy and thus ties back to the preceding discussion of partiality. All of this epistle needs to be interpreted in light of the massive socioeconomic inequity that existed in the ancient Roman world.

The socioeconomic pyramid of the Roman Empire had three major "orders" of society at the top. In Rome the senatorial and equestrian orders occupied the summit of political and economic power but represented only .002 percent and less than .10 percent of the empire's population respectively.[1] The decurion order (like senators, only on the municipal level) held wealth and power in cities and regions throughout the empire and yet accounted for only 2 to 3 percent of the population. Just below them was a small class of retainers and religious figures (such as the priestly class in Jerusalem) who benefited as clients of the upper echelons, as well as a small merchant class. Most of the populace consisted of peasants: some were artisans—others tenant farmers; many were day laborers scarcely earning subsistence wages. At the bottom of the social pyramid were slaves and other undesirables.[2] In sum, 85 to 90 percent of the Roman population lived in grinding poverty, while a tiny minority (about 3 percent) lived in the lap of luxury as the possessors of nearly all the wealth and political power in the empire.

James's community surely ranked among the poor and powerless in society. They experienced economic hardship and oppression at the hands of the wealthy (James 2:6-7; 5:1-6). Yet even they needed to be reminded of how fleeting wealth is (1:9-11), especially when compared to the crown of life promised to God's beloved who bear up under trials (v. 12). The world's scale of values is alluring. It is easy to fall into the pursuit of moneymaking and pleasures, taking no thought of the Lord's will (4:1-3, 13-17). It is easy to overlook the plight of the orphan and the widow (1:27). Selfish ambition and boasting in it (3:14; 4:16), as well as preferential treatment for the well-heeled in society (2:1-4), were natural and honorable things in the competitive,

---

1. MacMullen 1974, 88-89, cited in Nystrom 1997, 125n35.
2. Lenski 1966.

status-seeking environment of the ancient world. James's message is counter-cultural. Resisting such tendencies is what it means to have "pure and unde-filed religion" (CSB) that is not "polluted by the world" (1:27). God has chosen the poor in the world to be rich in faith and heirs of the kingdom (2:5), so being on friendly terms with the world's way of doing things is to be at odds with God (4:4).

James and Paul

A second historical question concerns whether James 2:14-26 is a response to the teaching of the apostle Paul on faith and works. There are essentially three views of the matter. The first, identified with F. C. Baur and the Tübingen School (nineteenth c.), envisions the early church as locked in a battle between a Jewish-Christian faction (led by "the pillars") and a Helle-nistic-Christian faction (championed by Paul). The two factions vehemently opposed each other on the issue of whether Torah observance was necessary for salvation. According to this view, James 2:14-26 mounts a frontal attack on Paul's law-free gospel.

The second view, of which J. B. Mayor is representative,[3] argues that James is not responding to Paul at all. The fact that James utilizes some of the same vocabulary as Paul does ("faith," "works," "justify"), as well as the key Abrahamic text (Gen. 15:6), may be accounted for by a shared Jewish tradi-tion of discussion about faith and works (e.g., Sir. 44:19-20; 1 Macc. 2:52; *4 Ezra* 5:1; 6:28; 7:34; 9:7-8; 13:23) rather than James's purported famil-iarity with Paul's letters. Furthermore, if indeed James had Galatians and/or Romans at hand, he failed to make any real attempt at refuting the *arguments* Paul uses in his letters.

A third, mediating position is that James and Paul are "talking past each other."[4] While the two apostles did not likely interact with each other's writ-ten correspondence, and had met personally on only a few occasions, they responded to many of the same live issues in the early Christian movement. They were working in separate spheres (as Paul asserts [Gal. 2:7-9]) and with somewhat different interests. At least in some instances the one may have

---

3. J. B. Mayor 1910, xci-xcix; see Plummer 1907, 135-48.
4. Brosend 2004, 79-82; see deSilva 2018, 729-30; Dowd 2000, 196.

reacted to the other with the knowledge that secondhand reports were not free from distortion. One may reasonably suppose that "certain men . . . from James" (Gal. 2:12) were not at pains to convey a fair accounting of Paul's gospel to James. Paul himself recognized the difference between Judaizing partisans ("false believers") who opposed him and "the pillars" who gave him the right hand of fellowship (Gal. 2:4, 9). James surely knew that Pharisaic Jewish Christians were exaggerating Paul's teaching about circumcision (Acts 21:20-21; see 15:1, 5). Neither might have been able to filter out all of the interference from third-party communications. Thus it is not impossible that James 2:14-26 corrects a confused version of Paul's teaching based on certain slogans (such as "justified by faith and not works") misquoted apart from Paul's carefully textured arguments.

The final, mediating position has the most to commend it. The first view has been almost completely abandoned in contemporary scholarship. F. C. Baur's picture of early Christian history based on a Hegelian dialectic (thesis [Judaic Christianity] → antithesis [Hellenistic Christianity] → synthesis [Early Catholicism]) was discredited over a century ago. The second view is correct insofar as it rejects the first view. Clearly, if James had intended to confront Paul's teaching head-on, he could have stated Paul's position with greater clarity and attacked Paul's arguments with greater specificity. At the same time, James's phrasing often matches Paul's much too closely to have originated in a common stock of Jewish tradition rather than to have derived ultimately from Paul's own mouth or pen. In any case, regardless of the elusive *historical* reality (i.e., James's intended target for his criticisms of "dead" faith), the *canonical* juxtaposition of the Pauline and Catholic Epistles (and, hence, James) behooves us to negotiate between the teachings of the two apostles.

Abraham and Rahab

James sets forth two historical examples of active or saving faith. He selects "the most stellar example" (Abraham) and probably "the most scandalous example" (Rahab the harlot) from Israel's history.[5] The two represent

---

5. Witherington 2007, 477.

the opposite ends of the scale in reputation, moral standing, economic status, gender, and ethnic extraction (the father of the covenant people of Israel versus a Canaanite).[6]

Abraham was an obvious choice as the example par excellence of faith. According to Jewish tradition, the so-called Akedah (= "binding [of Isaac]") in Genesis 22 was the supreme demonstration of Abraham's faith. At first glance, it might appear that this incident does not completely fit James's argument. The Akedah depicts an act of obedience to God, but not an act of mercy, which would be called for by the context (James 2:15-16). "At this point there is some slippage in developing an understanding of the nature and function of justifying works."[7] However, there are a couple of reasons why there is likely no "slippage" at all in the development of James's thought.

First, it is true that in Jewish tradition Abraham's offering of Isaac was, in the words of Philo, the patriarch's "most important action of all."[8] Yet in the tradition it is frequently denominated as the culmination of ten trials.[9] What's more, even at the moment Abraham is poised to plunge the knife into his son Isaac, rabbinic tradition often attaches significance to Abraham's practice of hospitality as central to his covenant righteousness (focused on Gen. 18).[10] The Akedah was a seal and sign of Abraham's lifelong faithfulness to God.

Second, James's interpretation resembles the midrashic precedent of pairing the Akedah with Genesis 15:6. First Maccabees 2:51-52 is strikingly similar to James:

> Remember the deeds [*ta erga*] of the ancestors, which they did in their generations, and you will receive great honor and an everlasting name. Was not Abraham found faithful when tested [*en peirasmō*; cf. James 1:2-4, 12], and it was reckoned to him as righteousness [*elogisthē autō eis dikaiosynēn*, alluding to Gen. 15:6; cf. James 2:21]? (NRSVUE)

---

6. Blomberg and Kamell 2008, 140.
7. Painter and deSilva 2012, 108.
8. Philo, *Abr.* 167.
9. For example, *Jub.* 19:9 (cf. 17:17); *'Abot* 5:4; *'Abot R. Nat.* 33:2; *Pirqe R. El.* 26-31.
10. See Davids 1982, 127.

Notice even the parallel use of a rhetorical question in James 2:21 and 1 Maccabees 2:52).[11] James appears to be following a line of Jewish exegesis in which Genesis 15:6 (along with the Akedah) was "a timeless sentence" (or "motto")[12] inscribed over Abraham's entire life.[13]

So James has in mind the cumulative effect of Abraham's righteous conduct (culminating in the Akedah) as the fulfilment of Genesis 15:6 (James 2:23). This is evident from James 2:22: "You see that faith was active together with [synērgei] his works, and by works, faith was made complete" (CSB). Observe that James twice refers to Abraham's "works" (pl., not sg.; NIV translates "actions" and "what he did" respectively). More importantly, the verb rendered "active together with" (CSB) or "working together" (NIV) is in the imperfect tense in Greek, denoting either repeated (iterative) or customary (habitual) action in the past (CEB: "See, his faith *was at work along with* his actions"; italics added). The cooperation or synergy of Abraham's faith and works continued over the course of his life—especially since the day he trusted in God's covenant promises (Gen. 15:1-21).

The reason for Rahab's inclusion as a biblical example is more difficult to determine. Perhaps James's introduction of Rahab alongside Abraham is designed to shock. What he says about them is directly parallel:

Abraham (James 2:21, AT)	Rahab (James 2:25, AT)
our father	the prostitute
was justified	was justified
by works	by works
when he offered his son Isaac on the altar	when she welcomed the spies and sent them out by another way

The parallelism is further signaled in verse 25 by the word *homoiōs* ("in the same way" [NIV]; "likewise" [NRSV]). But the glaring point of contrast is the identification of Rahab as a harlot. The NIV best captures James's sentiment: "In the same way, was not *even* Rahab the prostitute considered righteous . . . ?" (italics added).

---

11. Moo 2000, 133.
12. Ibid., 139.
13. Davids 1982, 129.

The portrait of Rahab in Jewish and Christian tradition is complex. This is largely due to wrestling with the ethical problems of the Old Testament's account: Rahab as a Canaanite woman of ill repute aiding the Israelite spies. According to A. T. Hanson, "In the rabbinic material extant Rahab appears in four characters, as a profligate, as a proselyte, as the wife of Joshua and ancestress of prophets, and as herself a prophetess."[14] The first of these "characters" is held in tension with the other three. Two main strategies were used to handle the tension.

One was the attempt to obfuscate or eliminate Rahab's identity as a prostitute. Josephus identified Rahab as an innkeeper.[15] He likely inherited the targumic translation of the Hebrew word for "prostitute" by the Aramaic word for "hostess" or "innkeeper,"[16] which was in turn followed by later rabbinic tradition. Additional linguistic creativity among some rabbis transformed Rahab the harlot into a worker of linen (in connection with the flax she used to conceal the spies [Josh. 2:2]) or a perfumer.[17] Thus any shame that could have attached to Rahab's purported Israelite descendants (which included the prophets Jeremiah and Ezekiel) was sponged clean. The Christian tradition has not usually taken this tack, beginning with the NT texts that show an awareness of (Matt. 1:5) or that explicitly label Rahab as a harlot (Heb. 11:31; James 2:5), as we also see in one of the earliest apostolic fathers, Clement of Rome.[18]

Another approach was to intensify Rahab's sexual vice, only to magnify her as the prototypical proselyte. The Talmud lists Rahab among the four most alluring women in the world (Sarah, Abigail, Rahab, and Esther).[19] She was a prostitute since age ten and plied her trade over the forty years that Israel wandered in the wilderness.[20] Other rabbinic traditions accentuate Rahab's notorious ability to ravish men.[21] But Rahab's conversion became more complete than that of other model proselytes, Jethro and Naaman. The rabbis

---

14. A. T. Hanson 1978, 58.
15. Josephus, *Ant.* 5.2.8.
16. *Tg. Ps.-J.* on Josh. 2:1.
17. Baskin 1979, 150-51.
18. Clement of Rome, *1 Clem.* 12:1; see Lyons.
19. *Meg.* 15a.
20. *Zebaḥ.* 116b.
21. *Meg.* 15a; *Ta 'an.* 5b; *Zebaḥ.* 116a-b.

claimed that Rahab swore off idolatry entirely, acknowledging Yahweh as the only God in heaven and on earth (Josh. 2:11).[22] Rahab repented of her sins, asking forgiveness in exchange for having endangered herself with the cord, window, and flax.[23]

James's characterization of Rahab is more in keeping with the latter set of traditions, but his matter-of-fact reference to her harlotry does not betray any knowledge of the more lurid speculations of the rabbis. James makes no mention of Rahab's faith (as does Hebrews [11:31]), though it is implicit in the context (see James 2:14, 17-18, 20, 22, 26). James emphasizes two of Rahab's "works": her hospitality and her diversionary tactic to protect the spies. Davids[24] thinks that both James and *1 Clement* (12:4) are drawing on a Jewish tradition that cited Abraham and Rahab as examples of charity (= hospitality; see *1 Clem.* 12:1, 3). This is a possible explanation for James's choice of these two OT figures. But the Venerable Bede may have hit upon the rhetorical function of Rahab in James's argument:

> There must have been some people who would have argued that Abraham was a special case, since nobody would now be asked to make such a sacrifice, and that therefore his example does not really count. To answer this objection, James looks through the Scriptures and refers to the case of Rahab, a wicked woman and a foreigner to boot, who nevertheless was justified by her faith because she performed works of mercy and showed hospitality to members of God's people, even though her life was thereby put in danger.[25]

Literary Interpretation

Genre and Overall Structure of James

By virtue of its inclusion in the collection of the Catholic Epistles, James is acknowledged as a letter. Its opening bears the customary marks of an ancient letter with its address and greeting. It does not contain the features

---

22. See Hirsch and Seligsohn 1906.
23. *Zebaḥ. 116b*; see Baskin 1979, 144-46.
24. Davids 1982, 133; following Chadwick 1961, 281.
25. Bray 2000, 33-34.

of an epistolary closing such as we encounter in other NT letters: greetings, a request, news about fellow ministers, travelogue, benediction/doxology.[26] However, the letter genre is highly flexible. The lack of a more complete epistolary "fingerprint" is due to the letter's character as a pastoral address circulated to Jewish Christians of the "Diaspora" within the orbit of James's influence. In short, James is a catholic letter. As to its contents, James is a paraenetic letter. It is designed to encourage and admonish listeners to live by God's righteous wisdom. An index for this identification is the incidence of no fewer than fifty-nine imperatives within the span of its five short chapters (or 108 verses).

The question of James's structure has generated considerable disagreement among scholars. Three main approaches predominate.[27] The first is the older view of the form critics (particularly Martin Dibelius) that James does not possess any overarching plan. Various topical segments are merely strung together—like pearls on a string—using "catchwords." Stephen Travis likens James's method to someone who has a set number of colored balls in a bag and who pulls out and puts back balls one by one in random order.[28]

The second view takes a thematic approach. Scholars divide up sections of James based upon the discernment of numerous themes. However, there is no agreement about how many themes shape the letter. Luke Timothy Johnson sets out seven sections;[29] Kistemaker, five;[30] and Ralph Martin, three.[31] This approach is marginally superior to simply listing the eleven discreet pericopae that are easily demarcated in the letter.

The third approach detects chiastic patterning in James. Peter Davids, building on the earlier work of F. O. Francis, discerns a double overture to James in chapter 1.[32] There are two panels (1:2-11, 12-27) that repeat the same three themes: testing (vv. 2-4, 12-18), wisdom/pure speech (vv. 5-8, 19-21), and wealth/poverty (vv. 9-11, 22-25). Then the letter takes up the

---

26. See Attridge 1989, 405.
27. Blomberg and Kamell 2008, 23-27.
28. Marshall, Travis, and Paul 2016, 263.
29. Johnson 1995, 11-16.
30. Kistemaker 1986, 21-22.
31. Martin 1988, xcviii-civ.
32. Davids 1982, 22-28.

same three themes (A B C) in reverse (chiastic) order (C′ B′ A′) in the body of the letter: poverty/wealth (2:1-26); pure speech (3:1–4:12); and testing (4:13–5:6). Blomberg and Kamell substantially agree with Davids's structural analysis.[33]

George Guthrie follows in the tradition of Davids with regard to the double overture of James.[34] However, drawing on the discourse analysis by Mark Taylor, Guthrie builds out the remainder of James's structure differently—and more defensibly. The body of the letter is organized through an elaborate chiasm:[35]

A Violating the Royal Law through Judging the Poor: Wrong Speaking and Acting in Community (2:1-11).

B *So Speak and So Act as One Being Judged by the Law of Liberty* (vv. 12-13).

C Wrong Actions toward the Poor (Need for an Active Faith) (vv. 14-26).

D Wrong Speaking to One Another in Principle (3:1-12).

E **RIGHTEOUS VS. WORLDLY WISDOM** (vv. 13-18).

D′ Wrong Actions and Speaking toward One Another in Practice (4:1-5).

C′ A Call to Humility and Repentance (vv. 6-10).

B′ *Do the Law; Do Not Judge It* (vv. 11-12).

A′ Twin Calls to the Arrogant Rich (4:13–5:6).

The letter closes in 5:7-20 with two movements that mirror the double introduction to the letter.

If this outline is a faithful guide for our interpretation of James, we can make several observations about the literary context for our passage in 2:14-26. First, the central point or pivot for the main body of James's message is the contrast between "earthly, unspiritual, demonic" wisdom and God's righteous wisdom "that comes from heaven [lit. "from above"]" (3:15, 17; see vv. 13-18). This segment has many lexical parallels that tie back to chapter 1: the request for divine wisdom (1:5-8) and the acknowledgment that "every good and perfect gift is from above" (v. 17; see vv. 17-21).

---

33. Blomberg and Kamell 2008, 26-27.
34. Guthrie 2006, 203-9.
35. Adapted from ibid., 206.

Second, the *inclusio* of 2:12-13 and 4:11-12 frames James's message in terms of speaking and acting under the rule of "the law that gives freedom" (2:12) rather than autonomously judging others and the law (4:11-12).

Third, in addition to 2:12-13 marking an *inclusio* with 4:11-12, it forms a climactic statement on the heels of 2:1-11, as well as a transition to verses 14-26. Indeed, verses 14-26 complements and builds upon verses 1-11. The opening verse to the body of the letter (v. 1) may well articulate the main theme in each of these two pericopae respectively: admonition against showing partiality to the rich (vv. 1-11) and active "faith" in our glorious Lord Jesus Christ (vv. 14-26). Whereas verses 1-11 show how favoritism toward the wealthy is a violation of "the royal law" ("Love your neighbor as yourself" [Lev. 19:18]), James 2:14-26 argues that inaction toward the plight of the poor is indicative of a dead, worthless faith.[36]

James 2:14-26 does not possess the close ties with 3:1-12 that it does with 2:1-11 (revolving around the treatment of the rich and poor). This is because 3:1-12 directs one's attention to the next theme: the dangers of the tongue. However, there is a linkage with the pivotal passage in the entire letter (vv. 13-18). In the opening verse to that passage (v. 13), a wise person's "works" are a demonstration of that person's "good life," which springs from wisdom.

Notes sounded in 2:14-26 are also paralleled elsewhere in James: "pure and faultless" versus "worthless" religion (1:26-27), the high position of those who are in "humble circumstances" (v. 9), the Lord's judgment on those who store up treasure and defraud the poor (5:1-6), and the incompatibility between "friendship with the world" (4:4) and friendship with God (cf. Abraham as God's friend [2:23][37]).

Form, Structure, and Movement

Form

There is practically universal agreement that James 2:14-26 employs an ancient rhetorical form known as the diatribe. According to Sharyn Dowd, the diatribe form is "characterized by rhetorical questions, irony, the setting

---

36. For the numerous links between verses 1-11 and 14-26 of James 2, see Martin 1988, 77-79.
37. So Blomberg and Kammell 2008, 125.

up and destruction of arguments attributed to opponents, and invective apostrophe."[38] Confronting an imaginary interlocutor ("someone" [*tis*]; 2:14, 18) is a signature feature of the diatribe.[39]

Structure and Movement

The key to discerning the structure of James 2:14-26 is the fourfold repetition of the central contention of the passage (in bold in the outline below). In each instance the statement functions as a concluding summary (vv. 17, 24, 26) or transition (v. 20):

    I. Faith without Works Is Not Beneficial (2:14-17)[40]

        A. Opening Question: What Is the Benefit of Faith without Works? (v. 14).

        B. Example of Neglecting the Poor (vv. 15-16).

        C. Conclusion: "In the same way, **faith by itself, if it is not accompanied by action, is dead**" (v. 17).

    II. Dueling Views: Faith *or* Works (2:18-19)

        A. An Objection: Faith, Not Works (v. 18*a*)

        B. Initial Refutation (vv. 18*b*-19)

            1. Counterpoint: Faith Must Be Demonstrated through Works (v. 18*b*).

            2. Example: Monotheistic Faith (Shared Even by Demons) Is Insufficient (v. 19).

    III. Scriptural Case for Faith plus Works (2:20-26)

        A. Opening Address (transition from previous paragraph): "You foolish person, **do you want evidence that faith without deeds is useless**?" (v. 20).

        B. Exhibit A: Abraham (2:21-24)

            1. Abraham Was Justified by Works: The Akedah (v. 21).

            2. Explanation of the Example: Abraham's Faith Was Perfected by His works (v. 22).

            3. Scriptural Support from Genesis 15:6 (v. 23).

---

38. Dowd 2000, 198.

39. For more elements of the diatribe form in 2:14-26, see Witherington 2007, 471.

40. Observe the *inclusio* "What good is it?" (*Ti ophelos*) in verses 14 and 16.

    4. Conclusion: "**You see that a person is considered righteous by what they do and not by faith alone**" (v. 24).

  C. Exhibit B: Rahab (2:25-26)

    1. Rahab the Prostitute Was Justified by Works (v. 25).

    2. Conclusion by Way of Analogy: "**As the body without the spirit is dead, so faith without deeds is dead**" (v. 26).

The repeated statement helps to shape the four paragraphs in James's argument (2:14-17, 18-19, 20-23, 24-26) and hammers home the point he is making: faith is not saving or justifying—but is ineffective, imperfect, dead—if it is not accompanied by corresponding actions.

The flow of James's argument begins with an opening proposition that questions the saving benefit of faith without works. This point is supported by an illustration of a believer who turns a blind eye to someone in need. James then engages with an objector who asserts that faith and works are mutually exclusive and implies that faith is superior to works. James counters that faith must be demonstrated *through* actions. Furthermore, holding to the orthodox faith that there is only one God does not in and of itself accomplish anything, since even demons believe thusly—out of fear. The movement of the argument reaches its climax in verses 20-26. It opens with invective in verse 20 ("foolish person" [NIV]; "you ignoramus" [NABRE]) and centers on two biblical examples (Abraham and Rahab).

So, we can see that James moves from a practical scenario (vv. 14-17) to a theological dispute (vv. 18-19) to the scriptural foundations (vv. 20-26) that support his contention that faith without works is dead.

Significant Details

The meaning of three terms are crucial for the interpretation of James 2:14-26: "faith," "works," and "justify." There is a concentration of this vocabulary in our passage:

	"faith" (pistis)	"believe" (pisteuō)	"work" (sg.) (ergon)	"works" (pl.) (erga)	"justify" (dikaioō)
Total Times in James	16x	3x	2x	13x	3x
Times in James 2:14-26	11x	3x	0x	11x	3x

Faith

The word "faith" stands prominently at the beginning of the body of the letter (2:1). Faith is associated with "our glorious Lord Jesus Christ" (as its object) and is introduced as a key topic in chapter 2 (esp. vv. 14-26). But what does "faith" mean for James? The authoritative Greek lexicon BDAG supplies three primary definitions for *pistis*: (1) "that which provokes trust and faith," hence, *"faithfulness, reliability, fidelity, commitment"*; (2) "state of believing on the basis of the reliability of the one trusted, *trust, confidence, faith*"; and (3) "that which is believed, *body of faith/belief/teaching*."[41] Throughout James, "faith" (and the word for "believe" [*pisteuō*] in 2:18, 23) fits best under the second definition, but in verses 2:14-26 one must pay careful attention to context and usage in order to apprehend its precise meaning.

We may delineate several features of James's usage in verses 14-26 that narrow its sense. (1) James differentiates between two kinds of faith: one that is beneficial (vv. 14, 16), saving (v. 14), and an important factor in justification (vv. 23-24), and another that is useless (v. 20) and dead (vv. 17, 26). (2) The sort of faith that is inert is "by itself" (v. 17) or "alone" (v. 24)—that is, "without works" (vv. 18, 20, 26, NASB). It is imperfect or incomplete. Saving faith is a faith that cooperates with works and is thereby perfected or brought to completion (v. 22). (3) Crucially, James characterizes useless faith as a form of dead orthodoxy. James 2:19 describes such "faith" as belief in monotheism (clearly alluding to the Shema in Deut. 6:4). To shock readers, James asserts, "Even demons believe that—and shudder." So, by implication, such defective faith is demonic, like the false "wisdom" that does not come down from above (3:15). To exhibit true faith or true wisdom involves reflecting the character of God (see v. 17).

Works

The basic sense of "work" (*ergon*) is expressed in the first chapter of James. The "doer of the work" (1:25, KJV; *poiētēs ergou*) is someone who does not merely hear God's word (v. 23) but carries out "the perfect law that gives freedom" (v. 25). Likewise, in 3:13 "works" refer to *actions* that

---

41. BDAG, 818-21.

demonstrate a person's "good conduct" (CSB). James's specific examples in 2:14-26 show that the works in view concern acts of compassion toward the needy (vv. 15-16), Abraham's obedience in offering up his son on the altar (v. 21), and Rahab's actions as a saboteur in loyalty to God's people (v. 25).

Although such works fall under the umbrella of "the royal law" (v. 8), they are not "works of the law." James does not advocate for Torah observance through Sabbath keeping, kosher diet, or circumcision. (James could leave unsaid the fact that these practices are characteristic of *Jewish*-Christian identity, even if they are not any more determinative of salvation than a bare confession of monotheism.) Undoubtedly, the NIV distinguishes the works in James from "the works of the law" in Paul by translating James's use of the Greek word *erga* as "deeds" (vv. 14, 18, 20), "action(s)" (vv. 17, 22), or variations of "what he did" (vv. 21-22, 24-25) rather than the traditional rendering "works."

Deeds of compassion toward the down-and-out conform well to the royal law of love toward one's neighbor. On one level, so do the Akedah and Rahab's actions on behalf of God's people, insofar as Abraham's obedience was the culmination of his faithfulness to God, and Rahab exercised hospitality to the Israelite spies and active allegiance to Yahweh (see the rabbinic interpretations above under "Historical Interpretation," p. 139).

On another level, the actions of both Abraham and Rahab run counter to the Mosaic law. Abraham's testing pressed him to commit murder, though he was hindered from carrying out the deed. Rahab's practice of the world's oldest profession exposed her as an adulteress. Both actions are condemned under the law, as James himself attests (2:11). Rahab's deceit violated the commandment against bearing false witness. Such ethical enigmas were of no concern to James. The point is that James is not promoting legalistic adherence to the Mosaic law, but fulfilment of God's will as expressed in both the law and the gospel. Taking James 2 as a whole, the "works" that believers are urged to perform consist largely of charity or generosity that foreswears all partiality.

Justify

The language of justification in James was suggested by the key Abrahamic text in Genesis 15:6 (James 2:23) and perhaps by Paul's discussion of this topic (see under "Historical Interpretation" above, p. 139). But what does James mean by being justified? Two possibilities commend themselves based upon the use of "righteousness" vocabulary (*dikaioō, dikaiosynē*, etc.) in the OT, in Second Temple Judaism, and by Jesus.[42]

The first is "justify" in the ethical sense of "shown to be right" (2:21, NLT) or "vindicate." This does not mean that one is set right with God through works but that one's works are a *"demonstration* of one's deepest commitments."[43] This is akin to Jesus's meaning in Matthew 11:19: "Wisdom is proved right [*edikaiōthē*] by her deeds." According to this meaning, Abraham's (or the believer's) works constitute proof of ethical "rightness."

The second possible meaning is "vindicate in the final judgment," as attested in the LXX (1 Kings 8:31-32; Mic. 6:11) and Jesus (Matt. 12:36-37). In theology this is called "final justification." According to this interpretation, as Moo explains, "Abraham was granted a positive verdict in the judgment by God on the basis of his pious acts."[44]

The choice between these two readings is difficult, but the scales tip in favor of the second. First, James is concerned with faith that endures testing, is perfected, and receives the crown of life (1:2-4, 12) and true religion that results in salvation (vv. 21-27) or survives divine judgment (2:12-13). Second, in 2:14 James poses the question of whether a faith without works can "save" a person. Consequently, James is speaking of God's final verdict on a person's righteous life as it has played out in his or her *deeds* or *actions* that have been animated by vital faith in God.

Theological Interpretation

The burning question raised by James 2:14-26 concerns the role that works play in salvation. The precise terms of the theological debate—"faith" and "works"—have been stipulated almost exclusively by Paul and James

---

42. See Martin 1988, 91-92; Moo 2000, 133-36.
43. Crowe 2015, 172.
44. Moo 2000, 135.

in their writings. In chapter 1 we introduced the apparent contradiction between Paul and James on faith and works (under "The Challenge of Theological Difficulties," p. 23), as well as Luther's estimate of James as "an epistle of straw." Here we will lay out the problem in more detail, along with its solution. The tension between James and Paul is twofold.

First, a "verbal contradiction is unavoidable" between James and Paul,[45] evident in a comparison of the following texts (boldface added):

> Know that a person is not justified by the **works** of the law, but by **faith** in Jesus Christ. So we, too, have put our **faith** in Christ Jesus that we may be **justified** by **faith** in Christ and not by the **works** of the law, because by the **works** of the law no one will be **justified**. (Gal. 2:16)

> For we maintain that a person is **justified** by **faith** apart from the **works** of the law. (Rom. 3:28)

> If, in fact, **Abraham** was **justified** by **works**, he had something to boast about—but not before God. (Rom. 4:2)

> Was not our father **Abraham** considered righteous [= **justified** (CSB)] for what he did [= by **works** (CSB)] when he offered his son Isaac on the altar? (James 2:21)

> You see that a person is considered righteous [= **justified** (CSB)] by what they do [= by **works** (CSB)] and not by **faith** alone. (James 2:24)

When one reads both James and Paul in Greek, one is struck by the fact that they use precisely the same terminology: "Abraham" (*Abraam*), "faith" (*pistis*), "works" (*erga*), and "justified" (*dikaioō*). Paul asserts that no one is justified by works of the law but by faith. James asserts that a person is justified by works and *not* by faith alone.

Second, both James and Paul employ the same key text (Gen. 15:6) to bolster their respective arguments. Paul cites this text (in Rom. 4:3) to support his contention that Abraham was justified by faith and not by works of the law. James cites the same text (in 2:23) as part of his argument that faith without cooperating works is useless.

---

45. Ladd 1993, 639.

A surface reading of James and Paul seems to lead inexorably to the conclusion that the two authors flatly contradict each other. However, a more careful comparison shows that the two apostles are not discoursing about exactly the same things. They express complementary rather than contradictory teachings. We may enumerate the *differences* between James and Paul as follows.

First, James and Paul are not concerned with the same kind of works. We have already noted above that in James 2 the "works" that accompany true faith are primarily acts of compassion or generosity to the needy. They are not "works of the law," by which Paul meant those rituals or practices that were badges of Jewish ethnic and religious identity: circumcision, kosher diet, and the observance of Jewish feasts and Sabbaths. That Paul thought of "works of the law" in this way is evident in Romans 3:28-30: "For we maintain that a person is justified by faith apart from the works of the law. Or is God the God of Jews only? Is he not the God of Gentiles too? Yes, of Gentiles too, since there is only one God, who will justify the circumcised by faith and the uncircumcised through that same faith." Thus, in James the lack of "works" indicates partiality toward the rich over against the poor, while in Paul "works of the law" express favoritism of Jews over Gentiles. The concerns of James and Paul about "works" could not be more different.

Second, one must carefully understand what James and Paul mean by "faith." We may safely say that both understand faith as trust, confidence, or even allegiance to God and his promises. Paul emphatically and repeatedly stresses Jesus Christ (in his death and resurrection) as the object of the believer's faith, compared to James's sole reference in 2:1. In James 2:14-26, James speaks of a deficient faith—something that Paul never does. (Paul, however, envisions a hierarchy of the theological virtues in which love takes priority over faith [1 Cor. 13:13], even over faith that can move mountains [v. 2]!) For James, nonsaving faith is nothing more than an empty confession of the Shema—that God is one—which even demons grant, but in defiance and fear rather than in relational trust and service. For Paul, confession of Jesus as Lord and belief in one's heart that God raised Jesus from the dead results in righteousness or justification (Rom. 10:9-10). James and Paul look at faith from different, complementary angles.

Third, James and Paul do not refer to justification in the same sense. In the texts in which Paul speaks of justification by faith, he is referring to what systematic theologians call "initial justification." Faith in Jesus Christ and in his atoning death is the reception of God's reconciling work. Faith receives divine pardon for sins and the restoration of a right relationship with God. This justification is a legal, proleptic righteousness: because of divine grace, the one who has faith in Jesus is reckoned as righteous in anticipation of coming before the bar of God's final judgment. James, however, is referring to one's whole life of faith coming under scrutiny at the final judgment. James has "final justification" in mind. At the final judgment God will render the verdict about whether the person's deeds are the righteous fruit of true, saving faith.

This opens up a theological issue that is too vast for us to address adequately here: the role of works in the final judgment.[46] Suffice it to say, while Paul is adamant that salvation is procured by God's grace through Jesus Christ and received by faith, he also asserts that everyone will appear at the final judgment to give an account of what he or she has done in the body (Rom. 14:10; 2 Cor. 5:10; see Rom. 2:6-11, 16). This accords with the teaching of Jesus (esp. Matt. 25:31-46) and other NT texts (1 Pet. 1:17; 4:5; Rev. 20:12-13). Without fully explaining the relationship between initial justification and judgment according to works at the final judgment, Paul nevertheless sees sanctification and living according to the Spirit (rather than living according to the flesh) as an indispensable step toward attaining eternal life (Rom. 6:15-23; 8:6-13).

In this same vein, Paul is opposed to antinomianism: the notion that believers in Jesus are assured of salvation regardless of whether they exhibit a righteous lifestyle (see Rom. 6:1-23). Paul rejects an "easy believism" that divorces faith from the transformation of one's ethical life. Indeed, Paul brackets all of Romans with a statement of his commitment to advance "the obedience of faith" (1:5; 16:26). Paul would wholeheartedly agree with James that Christians are obligated to conduct themselves in accordance with "the royal law"—or Jesus's second greatest commandment (Matt. 22:39 // Mark

---

46. See Stanley 2013.

12:31), "the law of Christ" (Gal. 6:2; 1 Cor. 9:21)—to love one's neighbor as oneself (Rom. 13:9; Gal. 5:13-14). "Love is the fulfillment of the law" (Rom. 13:10). Paul would have likely had serious reservations about James's formulation, "You see that a person is justified by works and not by faith alone" (2:24, CSB). But James's understanding of faith "working together" with and being perfected by one's deeds (2:22) is not far removed from Paul's assertion that what matters is "faith working through love" (Gal. 5:6, CSB).

We may conclude, then, that James and Paul are not in hopeless conflict with each other. Importantly, James does not say that anyone is saved by works. Works of mercy are a sign that faith is genuine, alive, and operative. A loose parallel may be seen in Ephesians 2:8-10, where Paul declares that we are saved by grace through faith in Jesus Christ, not by works, but that we are also created "to do good works" (v. 10).

7

Everyone Who Has Been Born of God Does Not Sin

(1 JOHN 3:4-10)

In his journal entry for Thursday, 1 September 1763, John Wesley wrote glowingly about the First Epistle of John: "How plain, how full, and how deep a compendium of genuine Christianity!"[1] First John 3:4-10 was a key passage for Wesley. In his sermon "The Marks of the New Birth" one of the marks of being born again is expressed in 1 John 3:6: "Everyone who remains in him does not sin" (CSB).[2] Because of the new birth, Wesley asserts, the believer has "power over outward sin."[3] Wesley's well-known definition of sin—"a voluntary transgression of a known law [of God]"[4]—was inspired by the statement in 1 John 3:4, "sin is lawlessness."

Wesley's interpretation continues to be controversial. Regardless of one's stance toward Wesley's theology, this passage (in conversation with others in 1 John) presents unique challenges. The difficulties concern not only Greek grammar and attempts to grasp the thought worlds of both the author and his opponents but also what ought to be the day-to-day experience of Christ followers. In what way is it true that genuine believers in Jesus not only do not sin (3:6, 9*a*) but *cannot* sin (v. 9*b*) because they are born of God?

---

1. Wesley 1984, 3:146.
2. Ibid., 5:215.
3. Ibid., 5:214.
4. Ibid., 11:396.

Historical Interpretation

In sidebar 7.1, we deal with book-level historical background. What follows are aspects of passage-level historical background for 1 John 3:4-10:

SIDEBAR 7.1. FIRST JOHN AT A GLANCE

Author: First John is formally anonymous, and 2–3 John are addressed from "the elder." The traditional view is that the apostle John is the author of these letters, as well as the Gospel of John.

Addressees: The author frequently addresses his audience with the affectionate term "beloved" (*agapētoi*; "dear friends" [NIV]). In 2 John, the address to "the lady chosen by God and her children" (v. 1) and the greeting from "the children of your sister, who is chosen by God" (v. 13) suggest that the author exercised oversight over a network of churches. In accordance with church tradition, one may surmise that the apostle John wrote from Ephesus to Christian communities in the Roman province of Asia.

Date: The Johannine Epistles were probably written in the late first century, sometime between AD 80–100.

Occasion and Purpose: The author wrote in response to "antichrists" (1 John 2:18, 22; 4:3; 2 John v. 7) who had caused unrest in the churches before withdrawing from them (1 John 2:19). The false teachers were likely proto-Gnostics who denied the incarnation and disregarded the ethical teachings of Jesus. First John opposes these false teachings and seeks to neutralize the unsettling effects of the schism. Its primary purpose is to assure believers in the Son of God that they belong to the truth and have eternal life (5:13).

Message/Argument: First John is a pastoral address bearing witness to the truth that God grants us eternal life through the incarnation of his Son. That Jesus Christ has come in the flesh is foundational to his sacrifice of atonement for sins and his life example for how his followers should live self-sacrificially and righteously in the love of God.

Significance: According to 1 John, the love of God is central to the Christian life. God's love for us was the motive-force behind the atoning death of his Son. Obedience to Christ's new command-ment of mutual love is the evidence for true knowledge of God and the way that God's love is perfected or "brought to full expression" among believers (4:12, NLT).

Two areas of historical investigation shed light on our passage. The first relates to the thought world of the false teachers who have disrupted the faith of John's community. The second relates to the eschatological background that is essential for understanding the teaching in 1 John 3:4-10.

The Thought World of "the Antichrists" in 1 John

The identity of the false teachers in the Johannine letters (esp. 1–2 John) is a topic of debate.[5] The author uses three labels for them. First, he calls them "false prophets" (1 John 4:1) because they claimed to possess super-natural power to speak truth from God. However, they really had a spirit of "falsehood," "error," or "deception" (4:6, NIV, NRSVUE, CSB respectively). Second, he calls them "deceivers" (2 John v. 7). In 1 John 2:26, he writes, "I am writing these things to you about those who are trying to lead you astray," and in 3:7, he cautions, "Dear children, do not let anyone lead you astray." Third, he calls them collectively "antichrists" (2:18) and any one of them an "antichrist" (v. 22; 2 John v. 7). They are harbingers of the end-time coming of *the* "Antichrist" (1 John 2:18, NKJV, NLT). They are possessed by "the spirit of antichrist" (4:3). This name was doubtless chosen because of their false and disastrous Christology.

It is difficult to render a full and clear portrait of the opponents. This is partly because the author has primarily offered pastoral assurance to his readers instead of writing a full-scale polemic against adversaries. There are many things left unsaid about the false teachers because the original read-ers knew them firsthand. It is not likely that the lines of attack against the opponents constituted a rhetorical overinflation of a minor squabble.[6] This

---

5. See Brown 1982, 49-68, 71-86; Kruse 2000, 15-27; Marshall 1978, 14-22; Painter 2002, 88-93; Stott 1988, 43-54.

6. Against Perkins 1979, xxi-xxiii.

was no tempest in a teapot, but a deadly serious issue about truth and error that resulted in schism (2:19). It would be rhetorical overkill, indeed, for the author to counsel his flock not even to pray for those who had committed the sin of apostasy (5:16) and to withhold any hospitality from them (2 John vv. 10-11).[7]

It is impossible to align the false teachers with other known heretical groups that plagued the early church. Scholars have identified the opponents with the licentious and idolatrous Nicolaitans (Rev. 2:6, 15), Jews who believed in Jesus as Messiah but not as divine Son (Ebionites), or some form of Gnosticism such as Docetism or Cerinthianism. The difficulties lie in the fact that the Johannine Epistles do not provide a complete profile of the opponents. The "tenets" of the false teachers hinted at in John's letters do not match up exactly with any of the known Gnostic schemes, and later heretical groups postdate the Johannine setting by decades or even a century or more. Our own view is that the false teachers held to an embryonic, proto-Gnosticism that most closely resembles the later teachings of Cerinthus.[8]

The author exposes the antichrists' errors on two main counts: Christology and ethics.

Christology of the Antichrists

The false teachers denied that Jesus is the Christ (1 John 2:22; see 5:1). They repudiated the personal identity of the human Jesus as the Messiah. It appears that they understood the Christ as a purely divine figure who either could not become human or would not join himself permanently to bodily human existence. Therefore, in 1–2 John the full title "Jesus Christ" is used deliberately to indicate his identity as both a human being and the Messiah, God's Son (1 John 1:3; 2:1; 3:23; 5:6, 20; 2 John v. 3).

Particularly, the false teachers rejected the claim that "Jesus Christ has come in the flesh" (1 John 4:2; see 2 John v. 7). The perfect tense "has come" (*elēlythota*) indicates the permanence of the Son's incarnate existence.[9]

---

7. Brown 1982, 48-49; Painter 2002, 89.
8. Similarly, Stott 2009, 54, and tentatively Marshall 1978, 21.
9. Williamson 2010, 136-37.

This passage is consistent with a polemic against Docetism, the Gnostic understanding that the Son never actually became a flesh-and-blood human being but only *seemed* or *appeared* to be so (the word "docetism" comes from Gk. *dokeō*, "to seem," "to appear"). Docetism was a threat in Asia Minor during the early second century and was opposed by Ignatius, bishop of Antioch.[10]

However, another passage may indicate opposition to an aberrant Christology more akin to Cerinthianism. Cerinthus taught that the divine Christ descended upon the merely human Jesus at his baptism but then departed from him before his crucifixion.[11] By using the symbolism of water for baptism and blood for the crucifixion, 1 John 5:6 may counter a similar false teaching: "This is the one who came by water and blood—Jesus Christ. He did not come by water only, but by water and blood."

Even if we do not know the trajectory of this proto-Gnosticism (Docetic or Cerinthian), its negative implications are clear. Its faulty Christology was dangerous because it denied the reality or permanence of the incarnation and thus vacated the possibility or significance of Christ's death on the cross. According to 1 John, Christ's sacrifice was the demonstration of God's love (4:10), the atonement and cleansing for sins (1:7; 2:2), and the supreme example for how believers should love one another self-sacrificially (3:16). But John's opponents presented a further problem: they did not think they needed either atonement or an example of sacrificial love. This leads us to the ethics of the false teachers.

Ethics of the Antichrists

First John attaches an ethic (or lack thereof) to the false teachers that is the mirror image of the new-covenant ethic for those who have been born of God. The Johannine ethic may be summed up in three points: avoiding sin, practicing righteousness, and loving fellow believers. Note incidentally that all three elements congregate in 1 John 3:4-10.

First John's method of attacking the error of the opponents has created some confusion among interpreters. Rather than calling them out directly,

---

10. Ign. *Smyrn.* 1:1-2; 2:1; 3:1-3; 4:1-2; 5:1-3; 6:1–7:1; Ign. *Trall.* 9:1-2; 10:1.
11. Irenaeus, *Haer.* 1.26.1 (*ANF* 1:351-52).

the author criticizes seven of their slogan-like claims.[12] He cites them formulaically with a threefold "If we say . . ." (1:6, 8, 10, NASB), a threefold "The one who says . . ." (2:4, 6, 9, NASB), and the equally indefinite "If someone says . . ." (4:20). This indirect approach has led some scholars to think that the ethical thrust belongs to the pastoral aims of our author but is unrelated to the christological error of the false teachers. However, the author equally warns his readers about *being* deceived by false notions concerning Christ (2:26) and ethical righteousness (3:7). He uses the same label for those who mislead on either count: "liar" (2:4, 22; 4:20; see 1:6, 10; 5:10). The ethical obligation of believers is inextricably linked to the person and work of Christ, especially his incarnate life of obedience (2:6; 4:17) and substitutionary death (3:16; 4:9-10). Indeed, both Christology and ethics are encapsulated in the dual command: "to believe in the name of his Son, Jesus Christ, and to love one another as he commanded us" (3:23).

The extent of the false teachers' ethical depravity is unknown. Were they libertines whose lifestyle was driven by the world's lusts (2:15-17; see 4:5)? Did they compromise with the ubiquitous idolatry in the pagan culture around them (5:21)? Perhaps. What we know for certain is that they were not concerned about their ethical behavior (1:6-10; 2:3-6). At the very least, they were "moral indifferentists."[13] Their fundamental ethical lapse was a lack of love for fellow believers (2:4-5; 3:10, 14; 4:8, 20). A concrete example of this is the callous, greedy disregard for the material needs of poor believers (3:17; cf. 2:16). An intriguing suggestion is that "the antichrists" were well-heeled people who, by seceding (2:19), left the poor members of the Christian community in the lurch by depriving them of house churches to meet in and the provision of hospitality for itinerant missionaries.[14]

Both the author of 1 John and his opponents promoted a doctrine of perfection. They both held that believers are in some sense without sin, but there is a vast difference in how they understood this perfection. The false teachers believed that a sinful lifestyle cannot detract from the perfection they enjoyed in their fellowship with and knowledge of God. The author of 1 John held

---

12. Painter 2002, 90.
13. Brown 1982, 55.
14. Klauck 1988, 56-57.

that Jesus Christ's righteousness and love are the source and pattern for genuine Christian life. Believers find deliverance from the defilement and power of sin through Jesus's cleansing blood and by being born of God.

The Eschatological Background of 1 John 3:4-10

The eschatological backdrop for the teaching in 1 John 3:4-10 is indispensable to its interpretation. This cannot be overemphasized. The teaching in 1 John fits within a matrix of Jewish and Christian traditions that envisioned the eschatological age as marked by both the intensification of evil and the manifestation of incomparable holiness among the saints.

First John 3:4 draws an equation between sin and "lawlessness" (*anomia*), or better, "a lawless spirit"[15] or "rebellion" (CEB). In an important study, Ignace de la Potterie shows that the word *anomia* does not mean "transgression of law"—as often used in classical texts and in keeping with its etymology. Instead, it refers to the end-time satanic antagonism against the messianic kingdom and its Christ.[16] Parallel texts from the OT, Dead Sea Scrolls, OT Pseudepigrapha, and the NT attest to this usage.[17] Possibly the most striking parallels are Paul's description of the wicked eschatological figure, "the man of lawlessness [*anomia*]" (2 Thess. 2:3; see 2:8), and of "the secret power of lawlessness [*anomia*] . . . already at work" (v. 7).

Alongside the theme of increased wickedness in the last days, we find the expectation of the holiness of God's people. In another study, Ignace de la Potterie provides a description of this teaching:

> At the end of time, the chosen people will be a holy people, a people without sin; this sanctity, this impeccability, will be due to the active presence of the Spirit, wisdom, and law within the hearts of the chosen ones. From their relationship with God they will receive strength to sin no longer and the gift of life.[18]

---

15. Williamson 2010, 114.
16. de la Potterie 1971a.
17. See Brown 1982, 400; Williamson 2010, 113-14.
18. de la Potterie 1971b, 178.

Again, numerous texts in the Bible, Dead Sea Scrolls, and OT Pseudepigrapha bear witness to this hope.[19] The prophet Isaiah foresaw a messianic age in which "all your people will be righteous" (Isa. 60:21). Daniel called future Israel "the holy people of the Most High" (Dan. 7:18, 27; 8:24). The Lord promised through Ezekiel, "I will put my Spirit in you and move you to follow my decrees and be careful to keep my laws" and "I will save you from all your uncleanness" and "cleanse you from all your sins" (Ezek. 36:29, 33; see v. 27). Jeremiah's prophecy about the new covenant (Jer. 31:31-34) promised that the law would be inscribed on people's minds and hearts (v. 33) and that they would know the Lord and experience decisive release from sins (v. 34). We find even more explicit references to the future sinlessness of God's people in the Pseudepigrapha[20] and the Dead Sea Scrolls.[21] We could multiply texts from the NT, too, some of which we will cite below under "Theological Interpretation" (p. 173).

The prevalence of such an eschatological background is evident in 1 John itself. The author uses the symbolism of darkness and light to express the ethical revolution that is already happening. The new age of obedience and Christlikeness is overtaking the old age of disobedience and sin: "the darkness is passing away and the true light is already shining" (2:8, CSB). In the context preceding 3:4-10, the author concludes that it is "the last hour" (2:18). This is evidenced by "many antichrists" appearing (v. 18). He also anticipates the coming of Christ (v. 28), when the perfection of God's children will be fully revealed (3:2). Our passage, then, is manifestly set within an eschatological context.

Literary Interpretation

Genre and Overall Structure of 1 John

Genre

Scholars have long debated the genre of 1 John. It is obviously a personal communication from an important church leader, addressed tenderly to the

---

19. de la Potterie 1971a, 178-82.
20. See *T. Levi* 18:9; *Jub.* 5:12; *1 En.* 3:8.
21. Especially 1QS IV, 20-23.

"little children" under his care. The four most common identifications of genre have been a universal religious tract, an encyclical or circular letter, a pastoral address or homily, or an exposition or clarification of the Gospel of John.

The chief difficulty is 1 John's lack of clear genre indicators. Although we call it a letter, 1 John has the least letter-like format of any of the twenty-one NT letters,[22] while 2 and 3 John are nearly "textbook examples of the Greco-Roman letter form."[23] An attractive proposal is to understand 1 John as an encyclical address sent to a network of churches in the wake of the schism (2:19), with 2 John as a cover letter. Third John is a letter responding to further fallout from the schism.[24] A precise identification of the genre of 1 John is out of reach, as is any reconstruction of its relationship to 2 and 3 John and the historical situation for all three documents. Since the church saw fit to classify them as Catholic Epistles, we will do well to attempt to discern not only their historical particularity as best we can but also their universal application to the church catholic.

Structure of 1 John

It is just as challenging to determine the structure of 1 John. There are three primary approaches: a three-part structure, a two-part structure, and no structure.[25] A three-part structure discerns a spiraling pattern in which several themes are cyclically repeated in 1:5–2:28 and 2:29–4:6 and 4:7–5:21.[26] A two-part structure is grounded in a repeated declaration (see below) and a resemblance between the structure of 1 John and the Fourth Gospel. Many scholars have given up all hope of tracing an overarching structural pattern in 1 John.

We find a two-part structure to be persuasive. Brown argues that the two-part structure for both the Fourth Gospel and 1 John—a prologue, two major parts, and an epilogue—indicates that 1 John proceeds in imitation

---

22. Brown 1982, 86-87.
23. deSilva 2018, 394.
24. Painter 2002, 51-57.
25. For an accessible overview, see Pate 2011, 241-42.
26. The classic expression is Law 1968.

of the Fourth Gospel.[27] This may or may not be so. More convincing is the appearance of nearly identical declarations that forge hinge points for 1 John:

This is the message we have heard from him and declare to you: God is light. (1:5)
For this is the message you heard from the beginning: We should love one another. (3:11)

Significantly, these are the only two places where the expression "this is the message [*angelia*]" occurs in 1 John. This facilitates the following outline:[28]

The Prologue (1:1-4):   Witness to the life-Giving Word

Part I (1:5–3:10):   The gospel that God is light, and we must walk in the light as Jesus walked.

Part II (3:11–5:12):   The gospel that we must love one another as God has loved us in Christ.

Conclusion (5:13-21):   A statement of the author's purpose

Our passage (3:4-10) is the final paragraph in part I. Part I opens with an announcement of its theme: "God is light" (1:5). The figures of light and darkness dominate 1:5–2:11 but set the tone for all of part I. Light represents God's righteousness and truth in contrast to the darkness of sin and deception. In 2:12-17, the author encourages the "little children" on the basis of their release from sins, knowledge of God, and victory over the evil one (vv. 12-14) and discourages them from loving the world (vv. 15-17). Verses 18-27 introduce the apocalyptic themes of the community's exposure to "many antichrists" and its possession of the eschatological "anointing" of the Holy Spirit. The final unit in part I (2:28–3:10) is a sustained contrast between the children of God and the children of the devil.

Form, Structure, and Movement

First John 3:4-10 is the final paragraph in 2:28–3:10. We have selected the subunit 3:4-10 to narrow the focus of our study, but in what follows we will look at the form and flow of all of 2:28–3:10.

---

27. Brown 1982, 123-29.
28. Adapted from Brown 1982, 124.

First John 2:28–3:10 forms a unit. It begins with the expression, "And now, dear children" (2:28). The unit is marked off by *inclusio* (or "bookends") in 2:29 and 3:10. That the Son is righteous and "that everyone who does what is right has been born of him" (2:29) sets the premise for what follows. In 3:10 the purpose for the whole unit is expressed (distinguishing the children of God from the children of the devil), citing the premise of 2:29 stated in the negative: "Anyone who does not do what is right is not God's child."

There are three subunits in 2:28–3:10. The first (2:28-29) consists of an exhortation to abide in Christ in order to meet him with confidence at the second coming and a description of the righteous conduct of those who are born of God. The second (3:1-3) describes the twofold aspect of divine sonship or filiation (i.e., being children of God): it is real "now" in present purity like Christ's own purity, but it will be fully manifested in the future as perfect likeness with God. The third (3:4-10) details a series of contrasts that differentiate the children of God from the children of the devil.

Our subunit (3:4-10) divides into two parts that are parallel to each other (vv. 4-6 and 8-9). Verse 7 functions as a transition or fulcrum: it restates the premise of 2:29, resembles the form and content of 3:3, and anticipates the conclusion in verse 10. Here is a summary of the parallels in verses 4-6 and 8-10:

3:4-6	3:8-9
Committing sin and the end-time satanic rebellion (v. 4)	Committing sin and belonging to the devil (v. 8*a*)
Purpose of Christ's appearance: To take away sins (v. 5)	Purpose of Christ's appearance: To destroy the devil's works (v. 8*b*)
Sinlessness of the one who abides in Christ (v. 6)	Sinlessness of everyone who is born of God (v. 9)

Significant Details

First John 3:4-10 abounds with exegetical challenges. We have selected a couple of key issues that impinge upon the central theme of this passage: the impeccability or sinlessness of the children of God.

Sin and Rebellion

Having already articulated the righteousness and purity of the children of God in 2:28–3:3, the author introduces the wicked conduct of those who are not God's children in 3:4: "Everyone who commits sin also commits rebellion, and sin is rebellion" (AT). Under "Historical Interpretation" above (p. 162), we discussed the eschatological import of *anomia* ("rebellion") as the end-time satanic opposition to God's kingdom. This interpretation is confirmed by the parallel in verse 8: "The one who commits sin is of the devil" (AT).

It is tempting to regard "*the* sin" (Gk. includes the definite article [*hē hamartia*] in vv. 4 and 8) as a specific sin, such as the principal sin of not believing in Jesus (see John 3:18; 8:24; 16:9). This sin fits with the identification of the antichrists by their repudiation of Jesus as the Christ (1 John 2:22) and may constitute "a sin that leads to death" (5:16). However, the expression "everyone who commits the sin" is in parallel contrast to "everyone who commits the righteousness" (2:29; 3:7, AT). The author uses similar expressions with "sin" (3:9) and "righteousness" (v. 10) without the definite article. In verse 5, he states the purpose of the Son's coming as a removal of "sins" (plural). Both "sin" and "righteousness" are therefore meant in a more general sense. Nevertheless, sin in this context is associated with the eschatological rebellion, and righteousness, with Christ's eschatological victory over sin and the devil through his atoning death (3:5, 8*b*; see 2:2; 4:10).

"God's Seed" (3:9)

First John 3:9 contains some startling statements. Among them is the claim that "God's seed" resides in the one who has been born of God. J. du Preez enumerates six interpretations of *sperma autou* (lit. "his seed," i.e., "God's seed"): children of God; the proclaimed word of God; Christ; the Holy Spirit; new life from God; and the new nature.[29] The two most commonly held views are that "God's seed" is either the word of God or the Holy Spirit. Elsewhere in 1 John, it is "the word of God" (or "what you have heard") that abides (*menō*) in believers (2:14, 24). In the Gospel of John, it is Jesus's "word" that makes his disciples

---

29. J. du Preez (1975); see also Brown 1982, 408-11.

clean (15:3) and abides in them (8:31; 15:7; see 17:17). But in the Gospel of John, the new birth occurs through the action of the Holy Spirit (3:5-8), and in 1 John, the truth of the word abides in believers through the "anointing" (= Holy Spirit?) that abides in them (2:20, 27).

Perhaps the expression "God's seed" does not have a precise reference but is another way of expressing the metaphor of being "born of God"—a metaphor making its first appearance in John 1:13. The anthropomorphic image of "God's seed" is no less shocking than the repeated claim that *God* abides in the believer (1 John 3:24; 4:12, 15-16). In 2:28–3:10, the focus is not on the means (e.g., the word) or the agent (e.g., the Holy Spirit) of the divine indwelling, but rather on the inward, generative source of divine sonship and the character of the divine likeness. Those who have been born of God do not and cannot sin because their spiritual life has been engendered by God so that it reflects his character, will, or nature. The CEB inventively translates, "God's DNA remains in them" (3:9). As long as readers apprehend this as a contemporary *metaphor* for "God's seed," this is a superb rendering. Neither metaphor refers to begetting or genetics in a physical, biological sense. "God's seed" or "God's DNA" conveys how the sonship granted by God bears the stamp of the divine likeness—a likeness that is currently hidden but will be fully revealed at Christ's coming (3:1-2).

Theological Interpretation

Depending upon one's perspective, the impeccability or sinlessness of the believer is a sublime, daring, impossible, or even blasphemous notion. We find some of the most forceful expressions of this doctrine in 1 John. There are four declarative statements (AT):

> Everyone who abides in him does not sin (3:6a).
> Everyone who has been born of God does not commit sin (3:9a).
> He is not able to sin, because he has been born of God (3:9c).
> We know that the one who has been born of God does not sin (5:18a).

These texts prompt theological struggles that are at once exegetical, historical, pastoral, and personal. This would not be so if the claims were not so absolute.

Before we attempt to make sense of John's teaching about the impeccability of believers, it will be helpful to note that he is not alone among NT authors. We begin with the CE.[30] James concedes that we all stumble in many ways (i.e., make mistakes or commit inadvertent sins) but then declares, "Anyone who is never at fault in what they say is perfect, able to keep their whole body in check" (3:2). This perfection (see 1:4)—keeping a tight rein on one's tongue (v. 26)—is one of the defining characteristics of true religion (v. 26) and follows from actively attending to and obeying "the perfect law that gives freedom" (v. 25). First Peter states that believers have purified themselves through "obedience to the truth" (1:22, NRSVUE); they have been reborn "not of perishable seed, but of imperishable" (v. 23). Second Peter reminds believers that they "participate in the divine nature" (1:4) and that by cultivating virtues they may confirm their calling and election and thus "will never stumble" (v. 10). Similarly, Jude praises God "who is able to keep you from stumbling and to present you before his glorious presence without fault" (v. 24).

None of the other CE quite approaches 1 John's claims of sinlessness, but Hebrews does so in 10:26: "If we deliberately keep on sinning after we have received the knowledge of the truth, no sacrifice for sins is left." Hebrews also urges readers to throw off "the sin that so easily entangles" (12:1). It is possible that Hebrews is referring to the deliberate sin of apostasy in these passages (see, e.g., 10:29; 12:15-17). Paul provides a parallel in Galatians 5:16: "I say, then, walk by the Spirit and you will certainly not carry out the desire of the flesh" (CSB). In Romans 6:1-2, Paul insists that believers have "died to sin" (v. 2) and should no longer "live in it" (v. 2). Our old self is crucified with Christ so that "the body ruled by sin might be done away with" (6:6; see Col. 2:11-14) and sin is no longer our master (Rom. 6:7, 14). We could further multiply examples (e.g., Matt. 5:48; John 8:34, 36).

The claims of impeccability for believers in 1 John 3:6, 9 seem inconsistent with the author's argument in 1:6–2:2. The author challenges the false teachers' claims of sinlessness (1:8, 10) and commends the remedy for sins

---

30. See also our discussion of "The Christian Life" under "Hebrews as a Segue to the Catholic Epistles" in chapter 3 (p. 81).

through confession (v. 9) and Christ's atonement that brings cleansing and forgiveness (vv. 7, 9; 2:1*b*-2). The slippage between 1 John 1:6–2:2 and 3:4-10 is even more puzzling in light of 5:16-18. Here an absolute statement about the sinlessness of the children of God (v. 18) immediately follows an example of interceding for a fellow Christian who has committed "a sin that does not lead to death" (v. 16)—but *not* "a sin that leads to death" (v. 16). Furthermore, our author asserts, "All wrongdoing is sin, and there is sin that does not lead to death" (v. 17). All sin entails danger, which is avoidable through personal confession or the intercession of others and Christ's atonement for sins.[31] But some sins are lethal—possibly the sort of christological and moral evils committed by the false teachers (e.g., denial of the incarnation of Jesus Christ, not loving fellow Christians, etc.[32]).

How, then, are we to understand 1 John's absolute claims of impeccability (3:6, 9; 5:18)? How may we square them with 1:6–2:2 and 5:16-17? Brown evaluates no fewer than seven attempted solutions to the problem.[33] The most common solution is to propose that the present-tense verbs in these absolute claims denote habitual sinning, as in the NIV's "No one who lives in him *keeps on sinning*" (3:6; italics added). But this grammatical explanation is overly subtle and only compounds the difficulty, since in 5:16 the believer's sinning is in the present tense.[34] As well, in 2:1 the author expressly states that he has written "so that you will not sin," using the aorist tense for action that is undefined (i.e., with no respect to whether it is an ongoing or simple act).

John Wesley's solution is to restrict the definition of sin. The true children of God do not commit sins that are willful and knowing transgressions of God's law. They may err or make mistakes unknowingly or due to infirmities, but they will not deliberately contravene God's revealed will. This idea is theologically useful and pastorally conducive to spiritual direction, but there is no indication that 1 John is operating with such a refined definition of sin. In 5:17 he states, "All wrongdoing is sin." The same objection stands against the Latin exegesis, largely influenced by Augustine, which defined the

---

31. See Rainbow 2014, 338-42.
32. See Marshall 1978, 247.
33. Brown 1982, 412-16; see also Kruse 2000, 126-32.
34. Marshall 1978, 180.

impossible sin for true Christians as the deliberate violation of the love command.[35] Neither solution provides an explanation for 1 John's assertion that the one who is born of God "*cannot* sin" (3:9*a*).

We believe that the ancient Greek church's interpretation gives a more satisfying resolution to the problem.[36] According to this view, the seed of God is divine grace or power that enables believers to cease from orienting their lives toward sin. Insofar as believers keep the grace of new birth and yield themselves to the Holy Spirit, they are unable to sin. This interpretation is encapsulated in Oecumenius's statement, "When someone who is born of God gives himself to Christ, who dwells within him by filiation, he remains beyond the attacks of sin."[37] Augustine expresses the thought more concisely: "To the extent God's seed abides in him, to that extent he does not sin."[38]

What is lacking in this view is the recognition that 1 John envisions the Christian life on two planes: the eschatological and the experiential.[39] We have already shown that the background for the stark dualism in 1 John 3:4-10—between the children of God and the children of the devil and between righteousness and sin—is the in-breaking of "the last hour" (2:18). The impeccability of the Christian operates on this eschatological plane. Believers possess an anointing, are born of God, and have the seed of God abiding in them—all benefits of life in the dawning new age. The potency of the new birth renders the believer incapable of sinning. However, on the experiential plane the impeccability of the Christian is jeopardized by the allurements of the world (vv. 15-16) and the deceptions of antichrists or false prophets (vv. 18-23; 4:1). The latter belong to the world (4:1, 3, 5; 2 John v. 7), and the world is dominated by the devil (1 John 5:19). Though the world and its lusts are passing away (2:17; see v. 8) and the Son came to destroy the devil's works (3:8), these evil forces still pose a threat to believers prior to Christ's second coming.

---

35. de la Potterie 1971b, 176.

36. The best representatives of the Eastern view are Severus of Antioch, Didymus the Blind, Maximus the Confessor, and Photius (ibid.).

37. PG 119:684.

38. Augustine, *Tract. ep. Jo.* 4.8, cited in de la Potterie 1971b, 177.

39. I am indebted to Dr. Alex R. G. Deasley (Epistles of John course at Nazarene Theological Seminary) for this formulation of eschatological and experiential (or, in his words, "experimental").

Therefore, a tension exists between the eschatological and experiential planes. It is easy to see how lust and pride and love for the world (2:15-16) can lead someone to walk in the darkness rather than the light. Failure to act in love pulls us back from walking just as Jesus walked (v. 6) or being like him in the world (4:17). The remedy for wrongdoing is confession of sin (1:9) or the intercession of fellow believers (5:16), but above all the forgiveness and cleansing of sins through the atoning death of Jesus (1:7, 9; 2:1*b*-2; 4:10). At the same time, one of the express purposes for which 1 John was written is "so that you will not sin" (2:1*a*). But how is this possible? How may Christians exist on the eschatological plane where the potency of the divine likeness ("God's seed") is prevailingly active so that we not only do not but *cannot* sin (3:9)? How is it even possible to purify ourselves even as Jesus is pure (v. 3)?

First John devotes little space to exhorting his readers not to sin (2:1*a*) or to refrain from loving the world (v. 15). He rather *describes* believers as not sinning and as not being from the world. The key to the impeccability of the Christian is found in the positive exhortation that begins 2:28–3:10: "Continue [or "remain" or "abide" (*menete*)] in him" (2:28). Believers do not avoid sin by sheer willpower, but through their union with Christ. "Everyone who remains (*ho menōn*) in him does not sin" (3:6*a*, CSB). Remaining in Christ is crucial to benefiting from his redemptive accomplishments. He appeared to take away sins and is himself sinless (v. 5). He appeared to destroy the works of the primal sinner, the devil (v. 8). The fact that God's seed "remains" (*menei*) in believers is the cause of their sinlessness (v. 9), but impeccability is not automatic. As Bultmann comments, "The 'abiding' of the 'seed' is freedom from sin, just as 'abiding in him' is the condition of this freedom."[40]

The believer's impeccability is an eschatological gift, enjoyed through abiding in Christ. We may see this more clearly by comparing the eschatological gift par excellence in the writings of John: eternal life. Providing assurance of eternal life is a main purpose for 1 John (5:13; see 1:2; 2:25). Eternal life, like Christian impeccability, is a present possession of believers because of their relationship to Christ (5:11-12). "We know that we have passed from death to life" (3:14; see John 5:24). But eternal life is present through faith

---

40. Bultmann 1973, 53.

in the Son of God (1 John 5:13) and by being in him (v. 20). Moreover, the presence of eternal life is manifested through believers' mutual love for one another, even as the presence of death is made apparent by hate (3:14-16). So whether we look at eternal life or Christian impeccability, we are dealing with divine gifts. Both are revealed and embodied in the incarnate Christ. Both are received by believing in Christ. Both are made manifest in the mutual love and practices of righteousness within the Christian community. Faithfulness to Christ (i.e., "remaining in him") and obedience to the divine commands are the conditions for retaining either gift.

Pastorally, believers should be encouraged to deepen their relationship with Christ and to commit themselves fully to him. They may expect to exhibit the character of Jesus in their lives now, even to the extent of living without sin as they follow in his steps. If they do fall into sin, Christ's atonement is a safety net. When Christ returns, they will fully share in God's likeness, "for we shall see him as he is" (3:2).

Reference List

Aland, Kurt, and Barbara Aland. 1989. *The Text of the New Testament.* Translated by Erroll F. Rhodes. 2nd ed. Grand Rapids: Eerdmans.

Althaus, Paul. 1966. *The Theology of Martin Luther.* Translated by Robert C. Schultz. Philadelphia: Fortress Press.

Anderson, Kevin L. 2013. *Hebrews: A Commentary in the Wesleyan Tradition.* New Beacon Bible Commentary. Kansas City: Beacon Hill Press of Kansas City.

Attridge, Harold W. 1989. *Hebrews.* Hermeneia. Philadelphia: Fortress Press.

Barns, Thomas. 1903. "The Catholic Epistles of Themison: A Study in 1 and 2 Peter." *Expositor* 8 (1): 40-62.

———. 1904. "The Catholic Epistles of Themison. II." *Expositor* 9 (5): 369-93.

Barth, Karl. 1957. *The Word of God and the Word of Man.* Translated by Douglas Horton. New York: Harper and Row.

Baskin, Judith. 1979. "The Rabbinic Transformation of Rahab the Harlot." *Notre Dame English Journal* 11 (2): 141-57.

Bassett, Paul M., and William M. Greathouse. 1985. *The Historical Development.* Vol. 2 of *Exploring Christian Holiness.* Kansas City: Beacon Hill Press of Kansas City.

Bateman, Herbert W., IV. 2007. *Four Views on the Warning Passages in Hebrews.* Grand Rapids: Kregel.

———. 2013. *Interpreting the General Letters: An Exegetical Handbook.* Handbooks for New Testament Exegesis. Grand Rapids: Kregel.

Bauckham, Richard. 1983. *Jude, 2 Peter.* Word Biblical Commentary 50. Waco, TX: Word Books.

———, ed. 1998. *The Gospels for All Christians: Rethinking the Gospel Audiences.* Grand Rapids: Eerdmans.

———. 1999. *James: Wisdom of James, Disciple of Jesus the Sage.* London: Routledge.

Bauckham, Richard, James R. Davila, and Alexander Panayotov. 2013. *Old Testament Pseudepigrapha: More Noncanonical Scriptures.* Grand Rapids: Eerdmans.

Bauer, David R., and Robert A. Traina. 2011. *Inductive Bible Study: A Comprehensive Guide to the Practice of Hermeneutics.* Grand Rapids: Baker Academic.

Bede the Venerable. 1985. *Commentary on the Seven Catholic Epistles.* Translated by David Hurst. Cistercian Studies Series 82. Kalamazoo, MI: Cistercian Publications.

Beker, J. Christiaan. 1980. *Paul the Apostle: The Triumph of God in Life and Thought.* Philadelphia: Fortress Press.

Bigg, Charles. 1901. *A Critical and Exegetical Commentary on the Epistles of St. Peter and St. Jude.* The International Critical Commentary. New York: Charles Scribner's Sons.

Billings, J. Todd. 2010. *The Word of God for the People of God: An Entryway to the Theological Interpretation of Scripture*. Grand Rapids: Eerdmans.

Blomberg, Craig L. 2016. *The Historical Reliability of the New Testament: Countering the Challenges to Evangelical Christian Beliefs*. B&H Studies in Christian Apologetics. Nashville: B&H Academic.

Blomberg, Craig L., and Mariam J. Kamell. 2008. *James*. Zondervan Exegetical Commentary on the New Testament 16. Grand Rapids: Zondervan.

Boring, M. Eugene. 2009. "Seven, Seventh, Seventy." Pages 197-99 in vol. 5 of *The New Interpreter's Dictionary of the Bible*. Nashville: Abingdon Press.

Bray, Gerald, ed. 2000. *James, 1–2 Peter, 1–3 John, Jude*. Ancient Christian Commentary on Scripture, New Testament 11. Downers Grove, IL: InterVarsity Press.

Brosend, William F., II. 2004. *James and Jude*. The New Cambridge Bible Commentary. Cambridge, UK: Cambridge University Press.

Brown, Jeannine K. 2021. *Scripture as Communication: Introducing Biblical Hermeneutics*. 2nd ed. Grand Rapids: Baker Academic.

Brown, Raymond E. 1979. *The Community of the Beloved Disciple: The Life, Loves, and Hates of an Individual Church in New Testament Times*. Mahwah, NJ: Paulist Press.

———. 1982. *The Epistles of John: A New Translation with Introduction and Commentary*. Anchor Bible 30. Garden City, NY: Doubleday.

Bruce, F. F. 1979. *The Epistles of John: Introduction, Exposition, and Notes*. Glasgow: Pickering and Inglis, 1970. Reprint, Grand Rapids: Eerdmans.

———. 1988. *The Canon of Scripture*. Downers Grove, IL: InterVarsity Press.

———. 1990. *The Epistle to the Hebrews*. New International Commentary on the New Testament. Rev. ed. Grand Rapids: Eerdmans.

Bultmann, Rudolf. 1973. *The Johannine Epistles*. Hermeneia. Philadelphia: Fortress Press.

Burge, Gary M. 2013. *Interpreting the Gospel of John: A Practical Guide*. 2nd ed. Grand Rapids: Baker Academic.

Chadwick, Henry. 1961. "Justification by Faith and Hospitality." *Studia Patristica* 4 (2): 281-85.

Chapman, John. 1908. *Notes on the Early History of the Vulgate Gospels*. Oxford, UK: Clarendon Press.

Charlesworth, James H., ed. 1983-85. *The Old Testament Pseudepigrapha*. 2 vols. Garden City, NY: Doubleday.

Chase, Frederic H. 1902. "The History of the Canon of the New Testament." Pages 96-144 in *Criticism of the New Testament: St. Margaret's Lectures 1902*. New York: Charles Scribner's Sons.

Childs, Brevard S. 1994. *The New Testament as Canon: An Introduction*. Valley Forge, PA: Trinity Press International.

Cockerill, Gareth Lee. 2012. *The Epistle to the Hebrews*. New International Commentary on the New Testament. Grand Rapids: Eerdmans.

Crowe, Brandon D. 2015. *The Message of the General Epistles in the History of Redemption: Wisdom from James, Peter, John, and Jude.* Phillipsburg, NJ: P&R.

Culpepper, R. Alan. 1998. *The Gospel and Letters of John.* Interpreting Biblical Texts. Nashville: Abingdon Press.

Dahl, Nils A. 1962. "The Particularity of the Pauline Epistles as a Problem in the Ancient Church." Pages 261-71 in *Neotestamentica et Patristica: Eine Freundesgabe, Herrn Professor Dr. Oscar Cullmann zu seinem 60. Geburtstag überreicht.* Leiden, NL: Brill.

Danker, Frederick W., Walter Bauer, William F. Arndt, and F. Wilbur Gingrich. 2000. *A Greek-English Lexicon of the New Testament and Other Early Christian Literature.* 3rd ed. Chicago: University of Chicago Press.

Davids, Peter H. 1982. *The Epistle of James.* The New International Greek Testament Commentary. Grand Rapids: Eerdmans.

———. 2006. *The Letters of 2 Peter and Jude.* The Pillar New Testament Commentary. Grand Rapids: Eerdmans.

de Boer, E. A. 2014. "Tertullian on 'Barnabas' Letter to the Hebrews' in *De Pudicitia* 20.1-5." *Vigiliae Christianae* 68 (3): 243-63.

de la Potterie, Ignace. 1971a. "'Sin Is Iniquity' (I Jn 3, 4)." Pages 37-55 in Ignace de la Potterie and Stanislaus Lyonnet. *The Christian Lives by the Spirit.* Staten Island, NY: Alba House.

———. 1971b. "The Impeccability of the Christian according to I Jn 3, 6-9." Pages 175-96 in Ignace de la Potterie and Stanislaus Lyonnet. *The Christian Lives by the Spirit.* Staten Island, NY: Alba House.

Denzey, Nicola. 2001. "What Did the Montanists Read?" *Harvard Theological Review* 94 (4): 427-48.

deSilva, David A. 2000. *Perseverance in Gratitude: A Socio-Rhetorical Commentary on the Epistle "to the Hebrews."* Grand Rapids: Eerdmans.

———. 2018. *An Introduction to the New Testament: Contexts, Methods and Ministry Formation.* 2nd ed. Downers Grove, IL: InterVarsity Press.

Dowd, Sharyn. 2000. "Faith that Works: James 2:14-26." *Review and Expositor* 97 (2): 195-205.

du Preez, J. 1975. "'*Sperma autou*' in 1 John 3:9." *Neotestamentica* 9:105-12.

Ebrard, John H. A. 1860. *Biblical Commentary on the Epistles of St. John, in Continuation of the Work of Olshausen, with an Appendix on the Catholic Epistles and an Introductory Essay on the Life and Writings of St. John.* Translated by W. B. Pope. Clark's Foreign Theological Library, 3rd Series, vol. 8. Edinburgh: T. and T. Clark.

Ehrman, Bart D. 1983. "The New Testament Canon of Didymus the Blind." *Vigiliae Christianae* 37 (1): 1-21.

Ellingworth, Paul. 1993. *The Epistle to the Hebrews: A Commentary on the Greek Text.* The New International Greek Testament Commentary. Grand Rapids: Eerdmans.

Emerson, Matthew Y. 2013. *Christ and the New Creation: A Canonical Approach to the Theology of the New Testament.* Eugene, OR: Wipf and Stock.

Epiphanius. 2009. *The* Panarion *of Epiphanius of Salamis. Book I (Sects 1-46)*. Translated by Frank Williams. 2nd ed. Nag Hammadi and Manichaean Studies 63. Leiden, NL: Brill.

———. 2013. *The* Panarion *of Epiphanius of Salamis, Books II and III. De Fide*. Translated by Frank Williams. 2nd rev. ed. Nag Hammadi and Manichaean Studies 79. Leiden, NL: Brill.

Eusebius. 1926, 1932. *The Ecclesiastical History*. Translated by Kirsopp Lake, J. E. L. Oulton, and Hugh Jackson Lawlor. 2 vols. Loeb Classical Library. Cambridge, MA: Harvard University Press.

———. 1927-28. *The Ecclesiastical History and the Martyrs of Palestine*. Translated with introduction and notes by Hugh Jackson Lawlor and John Ernest Leonard Oulton. 2 vols. London: SPCK.

———. 2007. *Eusebius: The Church History*. Translated by Paul L. Maier. Grand Rapids: Kregel.

Fee, Gordon D., and Douglas Stuart. 2014. *How to Read the Bible for All Its Worth*. 4th ed. Grand Rapids: Zondervan.

Flemming, Dean. 2009. *Philippians: A Commentary in the Wesleyan Tradition*. New Beacon Bible Commentary. Kansas City: Beacon Hill Press of Kansas City.

Flew, R. Newton. 1934. *The Idea of Perfection in Christian Theology*. London: Oxford University Press.

Gamble, Harry Y. 1985. *The New Testament Canon: Its Making and Meaning*. Philadelphia: Fortress Press.

Gloag, Paton J. 1887. *Introduction to the Catholic Epistles*. Edinburgh: T. and T. Clark.

Gorman, Michael J. 2020. *Elements of Biblical Exegesis: A Basic Guide for Students and Ministers*. 3rd. ed. Grand Rapids: Baker Academic.

Goswell, Greg. 2010. "The Order of the Books of the New Testament." *Journal of the Evangelical Theological Society* 53 (2): 225-41.

———. 2013. "Two Testaments in Parallel: The Influence of the Old Testament on the Structuring of the New Testament Canon." *Journal of the Evangelical Theological Society* 56 (3): 459-74.

———. 2016a. "The Place of the Book of Acts in Reading the NT." *Journal of the Evangelical Theological Society* 59 (1): 67-82.

———. 2016b. "Finding a Home for the Letter to the Hebrews." *Journal of the Evangelical Theological Society* 59 (4): 747-60.

———. 2017. "The Early Readership of the Catholic Epistles." *Journal of Greco-Roman Christianity and Judaism* 13 (5): 129-51.

Grecu, V. 1966. *Georgios Sphrantzes. Memorii 1401-1477*. Scriptores Byzantini 5. Bucharest, RO: Academia Republicae Romanicae, 150-448, 456-590. Retrieved from http://stephanus.tlg .uci.edu.ezproxy.asburyseminary.edu/Iris/Cite?3176:001:672795.

Green, Joel B. 2007. *Seized by Truth: Reading the Bible as Scripture*. Nashville: Abingdon Press.

Gregory of Nyssa. 1967. *Ascetical Works*. Translated by Virginia Woods Callahan. Fathers of the Church 58. Washington, DC: Catholic University of America Press.

———. 1978. *The Life of Moses*. Translated by Abraham J. Malherbe and Everett Ferguson. Classics of Western Spirituality (Cistercian Studies 31). Mahwah, NJ: Paulist Press.

———. 2012. *Homilies on the Song of Songs*. Translated by Richard A. Norris Jr. Society of Biblical Literature: Writings from the Greco-Roman World 13. Atlanta: Society of Biblical Literature.

Grünstäudl, Wolfgang. 2013. *Petrus Alexandrinus: Studien zum historischen und theologischen Ort des zweiten Petrusbriefes*. Wissenschaftliche Untersuchungen zum Neuen Testament 2.353. Tübingen, DEU: Mohr Siebeck.

Gunter, W. Stephen, Scott J. Jones, Ted A. Campbell, Rebekah L. Miles, and Randy L. Maddox. 1997. *Wesley and the Quadrilateral: Renewing the Conversation*. Nashville: Abingdon Press.

Guthrie, Donald. 1990. *New Testament Introduction*. 4th ed. Downers Grove, IL: InterVarsity Press.

———. 2009. "Catholic Epistles." Pages 796-97 in vol. 1 of *The Zondervan Encyclopedia of the Bible*. Rev. ed. Edited by Merrill C. Tenney and Moisés Silva. Grand Rapids: Zondervan.

Guthrie, George H. 1998. *The Structure of Hebrews: A Text-Linguistic Analysis*. Grand Rapids: Baker.

———. 2006. "James." Pages 197-273 in vol. 13 of *The Expositor's Bible Commentary*. Rev. ed. Edited by Tremper Longman III and David E. Garland. Grand Rapids: Zondervan.

Hagner, Donald A. 2012. *The New Testament: A Historical and Theological Introduction*. Grand Rapids: Baker Academic.

———. 2018. *How New Is the New Testament? First-Century Judaism and the Emergence of Christianity*. Grand Rapids: Baker Academic.

Hanson, A. T. 1978. "Rahab the Harlot in Early Christian Tradition." *Journal for the Study of the New Testament* 1:53-60.

Harnack, Adolf von. 1889. *Das Neue Testament um das Jahr 200*. Freiberg: J. C. B. Mohr (Paul Siebeck).

Harrison, Nonna Verna. 2010. "Gregory of Nyssa (c. 335-c. 395), *The Life of Moses*." Pages 25-36 in *Christian Spirituality: The Classics*. Edited by Arthur Holder. London: Routledge.

Hatch, William H. P. 1936. "The Position of Hebrews in the Canon of the New Testament." *Harvard Theological Review* 29 (2): 133-51.

Herron, Thomas J. 1989. "The Most Probable Date of the First Epistle of Clement to the Corinthians." Studia patristica 21 (Louvain, BE: Peeters), 106-21.

———. 2008. *Clement and the Early Church of Rome: On the Dating of Clement's First Epistle to the Corinthians*. Steubenville, OH: Emmaus Road.

Hirsch, Emil G., and M. Seligsohn. 1906. "Rahab." Page 309 in vol. 10 of *The Jewish Encyclopedia*. New York: Funk and Wagnalls. http://jewishencyclopedia.com/articles/12535-rahab.

Hockey, Katherine M., Madison N. Pierce, and Francis Watson. 2017. *Muted Voices of the New Testament: Readings in the Catholic Epistles and Hebrews.* Library of New Testament Studies 565. London: Bloomsbury T. and T. Clark.

Hoppin, Ruth. 2009. *Priscilla's Letter: Finding the Author of the Epistle to the Hebrews.* Fort Bragg, CA: Lost Coast Press.

Hug, Johann Leonhard. 1836. *Introduction to the New Testament.* Translated by David Fosdick Jr. Andover, MA: Gould and Newman.

Hurst, L. D. 1990. *The Epistle to the Hebrews: Its Background of Thought.* Cambridge, UK: Cambridge University Press.

Jefford, Clayton N. 2006. *The Apostolic Fathers and the New Testament.* Peabody, MA: Hendrickson.

Jobes, Karen H. 2011. *Letters to the Church: A Survey of Hebrews and the General Epistles.* Grand Rapids: Zondervan Academic.

Johnson, Luke Timothy. 1995. *The Letter of James.* Anchor Bible 37A. New York: Doubleday.

———. 2006. *Hebrews: A Commentary.* The New Testament Library. Louisville, KY: Westminster John Knox Press.

———. 2010. *The Writings of the New Testament: An Interpretation.* 3rd ed. Minneapolis: Fortress Press.

Johnson, Thomas F. 1993. *1, 2, and 3 John.* Understanding the Bible Commentary Series. Grand Rapids: Baker Books.

Jongkind, Dirk, and Peter J. Williams. 2017. *The Greek New Testament.* Produced at Tyndale House, Cambridge. Wheaton, IL: Crossway.

Just, Felix. 2005. "New Testament Statistics." http://catholic-resources.org/Bible/NT -Statistics-Greek.htm.

Käsemann, Ernst. 1964. "An Apologia for Primitive Christian Eschatology." Pages 169-95 in *Essays on New Testament Themes.* Translated by W. J. Montague. Studies in Biblical Theology 41. London: SCM Press.

Katz, Peter. 1957. "The Johannine Epistles in the Muratorian Canon." *Journal of Theological Studies.* 8 (2): 273-74.

Keener, Craig S. 2014. *The IVP Bible Background Commentary: New Testament.* 2nd ed. Downers Grove, IL: IVP Academic.

———. 2016. *Spirit Hermeneutics: Reading Scripture in Light of Pentecost.* Grand Rapids: Eerdmans.

Kistemaker, Simon J. 1986. *James and 1–3 John.* New Testament Commentary 16. Grand Rapids: Baker Academic.

Klauck, Hans-Josef. 1988. "Internal Opponents: The Treatment of the Secessionists in the First Epistle of John." *Concilium* 200:55-65.

Klink, Edward W., III, and Darian R. Lockett. 2012. *Understanding Biblical Theology: A Comparison of Theory and Practice.* Grand Rapids: Zondervan.

Koester, Craig R. 2001. *Hebrews: A New Translation with Introduction and Commentary.* Anchor Bible 36. New York: Doubleday.

Kruse, Colin G. 2000. *The Letters of John.* The Pillar New Testament Commentary. Grand Rapids: Eerdmans.

Ladd, George Eldon. 1993. *A Theology of the New Testament.* Edited by Donald Hagner. Rev. ed. Grand Rapids: Eerdmans.

Lane, William L. 1985a. *Call to Commitment: Responding to the Message of Hebrews.* Nashville: Thomas Nelson.

———. 1985b. "Hebrews: A Sermon in Search of a Setting." *Southwestern Journal of Theology* 28 (1): 13-18.

———. 1991. *Hebrews.* Word Biblical Commentary 47A-B. Dallas: Word Books.

Law, Robert. 1968. *The Tests of Life: A Study of the First Epistle of St. John.* 3rd ed. Edinburgh: T. and T. Clark, 1913. Reprint, Grand Rapids: Baker Book House.

Lehne, Susanne. 1990. *The New Covenant in Hebrews.* Journal for the Study of the New Testament Supplement Series 44. Sheffield, UK: Sheffield Academic Press.

Lenski, Gerhard E. 1966. *Power and Privilege: A Theory of Social Stratification.* Chapel Hill, NC: University of North Carolina Press, 1966.

Lightfoot, J. B. 1904. *Biblical Essays.* 2nd ed. London: Macmillan.

Lincoln, Andrew. 2006. *Hebrews: A Guide.* London: T. and T. Clark.

Lockett, Darian R. 2008. *Purity and Worldview in the Epistle of James.* Library of New Testament Studies 366. London: T. and T. Clark.

———. 2017. *Letters from the Pillar Apostles: The Formation of the Catholic Epistles as a Canonical Collection.* Eugene, OR: Pickwick.

Lohse, Eduard. 1981. *The Formation of the New Testament.* Translated by M. Eugene Boring. Nashville: Abingdon Press.

Long, D. Stephen. 2011. *Hebrews.* Belief: A Theological Commentary on the Bible. Louisville, KY: Westminster John Knox Press.

Luther's Works. 1955-86. American Edition. 55 vols. Edited by Jaroslav Pelikan and Helmut T. Lehman. Philadelphia: Muehlenberg Press and Fortress Press; St. Louis: Concordia.

Lyons, William L. "Rahab through the Ages: A Study of Christian Interpretation of Rahab." SBL Forum. Accessed February 24, 2023. https://www.sbl-site.org/publications/article.aspx?ArticleId=786.

Macarius. 1921. *Fifty Spiritual Homilies of St. Macarius the Egyptian.* Translated by A. J. Mason. Translations of Christian Literature. London: SPCK.

MacMullen, Ramsay. 1974. *Roman Social Relations 50 B.C. to A.D. 284.* New Haven, CT: Yale University Press.

Manson, T. W. 1947. "Entry into Membership of the Early Church. Additional Note: The Johannine Epistles and the Canon of the New Testament." *Journal of Theological Studies.* 48:25-33.

Manson, William. 1951. *The Epistle to the Hebrews: An Historical and Theological Reconsideration*. London: Hodder and Stoughton.

Marrou, H. I. 1982. *A History of Education in Antiquity*. Madison, WI: University of Wisconsin Press. Reprint of *A History of Education in Antiquity*. Translated by George Lamb. New York: Sheed and Ward, 1956. Translation of *Histoire de l'Education dans l'Antiquité*. 3rd ed. Paris: Editions du Seuil, 1948.

Marshall, I. Howard. 1978. *The Epistles of John*. The New International Commentary on the New Testament. Grand Rapids: Eerdmans.

Marshall, I. Howard, Stephen Travis, and Ian Paul. 2016. *Exploring the New Testament: A Guide to the Letters and Revelation*. 2nd ed. Downers Grove, IL: IVP Academic.

Martin, Ralph P. 1978. *New Testament Foundations: A Guide for Christian Students*. 2 vols. Rev. ed. Grand Rapids: Eerdmans.

———. 1988. *James*. Word Biblical Commentary 88. Waco, TX: Word Books.

Mason, Elliott J. 1968. "The Position of Hebrews in the Pauline Corpus in the Light of Chester Beatty Papyrus II." PhD diss., University of Southern California.

Mayor, Joseph B. 1907. *The Epistle of St. Jude and the Second Epistle of St. Peter: Greek Text with Introduction Notes and Comments*. London: Macmillan.

———. 1910. *The Epistle of St. James: The Greek Text with Introduction, Notes, and Comments*. 3rd ed. London: Macmillan.

McCruden, Kevin B. 2013. *A Body You Have Prepared for Me: The Spirituality of the Letter to the Hebrews*. Collegeville, MN: Liturgical Press.

McDonald, Lee Martin. 2017. *The Formation of the Biblical Canon*. 2 vols. London: Bloomsbury T. and T. Clark.

McLuhan, Marshall. 2001. *Understanding Media: The Extensions of Man*. Abingdon, UK: Routledge, 1964. Reprint, London: Routledge.

McNeile, A. H. 1953. *An Introduction to the Study of the New Testament*. 2nd ed. Revised by C. S. C. Williams. Oxford, UK: Clarendon Press.

Merritt, John G. 1987. "'Dialogue' within a Tradition: John Wesley and Gregory of Nyssa Discuss Christian Perfection." *Wesleyan Theological Journal* 22 (2): 92-116.

Metzger, Bruce M. 1963. *Chapters in the History of New Testament Textual Criticism*. New Testament Tools and Studies 4. Grand Rapids: Eerdmans.

———. 1987. *The Canon of the New Testament: Its Origin, Development, and Significance*. Oxford, UK: Clarendon Press.

———. 1994. *A Textual Commentary on the Greek New Testament*. 2nd ed. New York: United Bible Societies.

Michaelis, John David. 1802. *Introduction to the New Testament*. Translated by Herbert Marsh from the 4th German ed. 2nd English ed. London: Luke Hanford.

Michaels, J. Ramsey. 1988. *1 Peter*. Word Biblical Commentary 49. Nashville: Thomas Nelson.

Mitchell, Margaret M. 2010. "The Continuing Problem of Particularity and Universality within the *corpus Paulinum*: Chrysostom on Romans 16:3." *Studia Theologica* 64 (2): 121-37.

Moffatt, James. 1918. *An Introduction to the Literature of the New Testament*. 3rd ed. International Theological Library. Edinburgh: T. and T. Clark.

Moo, Douglas J. 2000. *The Letter of James*. The Pillar New Testament Commentary. Grand Rapids: Eerdmans.

Nienhuis, David R. 2007. *Not by Paul Alone: The Formation of the Catholic Epistle Collection and the Christian Canon*. Waco, TX: Baylor University Press.

Nienhuis, David R., and Robert W. Wall. 2013. *Reading the Epistles of James, Peter, John, and Jude as Scripture: The Shaping and Shape of a Canonical Collection*. Grand Rapids: Eerdmans.

NIV Cultural Backgrounds Study Bible. 2016. Edited by John H. Walton and Craig S. Keener. Grand Rapids: Zondervan.

Nystrom, David P. 1997. *James*. NIV Application Commentary. Grand Rapids: Zondervan.

Orthodox Study Bible. 2008. Edited by Jack Norman Sparks et al. Nashville: Thomas Nelson.

Osborne, Grant R. 2011. "James, 1 Peter, Jude." Pages 3-398 in *James, 1–2 Peter, Jude, and Revelation*. Vol. 18 of *Cornerstone Biblical Commentary*. Edited by Philip W. Comfort. Carol Stream, IL: Tyndale House.

Painter, John. 2002. *1, 2, and 3 John*. Sacra pagina 18. Collegeville, MN: Liturgical Press.

———. 2009. "The Johannine Epistles as Catholic Epistles." Pages 239-305 in *The Catholic Epistles and Apostolic Tradition: A New Perspective on James to Jude*. Edited by Karl-Wilhelm Niebuhr and Robert W. Wall. Waco, TX: Baylor University Press.

Painter, John, and David A. deSilva. 2012. *James and Jude*. Paideia: Commentaries on the New Testament. Grand Rapids: Baker Academic.

Parker, D. C. 2008. *An Introduction of the New Testament Manuscripts and Their Texts*. Cambridge, UK: Cambridge University Press.

Pate, C. Marvin. 2011. *The Writings of John: A Survey of the Gospel, Epistles, and Apocalypse*. Grand Rapids: Zondervan Academic.

Perkins, Pheme. 1979. *The Johannine Epistles*. New Testament Message 21. Wilmington, DE: Michael Glazier.

Peterson, David. 1982. *Hebrews and Perfection: An Examination of the Concept of Perfection in the "Epistle to the Hebrews."* Society for New Testament Studies Monograph Series 47. Cambridge, UK: Cambridge University Press.

Picirilli, Robert E. 1988. "Allusions to 2 Peter in the Apostolic Fathers." *Journal for the Study of the New Testament* 33:57-83.

Plummer, Alfred. 1907. *The General Epistles of St. James and St. Jude*. 6th ed. London: Hodder and Stoughton. http://www.ccel.org/ccel/plummer/expositorjamesjude.

Rainbow, Paul A. 2014. *Johannine Theology: The Gospel, the Epistles, and the Apocalypse*. Downers Grove, IL: IVP Academic.

Reuss, Eduard. 1884. *History of the Sacred Scriptures of the New Testament*. Translated by Edward L. Houlton. 2 vols. Boston: Houghton, Mifflin, and Company.

Ropes, James H. 1916. *A Critical and Exegetical Commentary on the Epistle of St. James*. The International Critical Commentary. Edinburgh: T. and T. Clark.

Rothschild, Clare K. 2009. *Hebrews as Pseudepigraphon: The History and Significance of the Pauline Attribution of Hebrews.* Wissenschaftliche Untersuchungen zum Neuen Testament 235. Tübingen, DEU: Mohr Siebeck.

Salmon, George. 1999. "Dionysius (3), bp. of Corinth." Pages 430-32 in *A Dictionary of Early Christian Biography and Literature to the End of the Sixth Century A.D., with an Account of the Principal Sects and Heresies.* Edited by Henry Wace and William C. Piercy. London: John Murray, 1911. Reprint, Peabody, MA: Hendrickson.

Salmond, S. D. F. 1901. "Catholic Epistles." Pages 359-62 in vol. 1 of *A Dictionary of the Bible.* Edited by James Hastings. 4 vols. New York: Charles Scriber's Sons, 1901-2.

Scherbenske, Eric W. 2013. *Canonizing Paul: Ancient Editorial Practice and the* Corpus Paulinum. Oxford, UK: Oxford University Press.

Schlosser, J. 2004. "Le corpus des Épîtres catholiques." Pages 3-41 in *The Catholic Epistles and the Tradition.* Edited by J. Schlosser. Bibliotheca ephemeridum theologicarum lovaniensium 176. Leuven: Leuven University Press.

Simisi, Seth M. 2016. *Pursuit of Perfection: Significance of the Perfection Motif in the Epistle to the Hebrews.* Eugene, OR: Wipf and Stock.

Skeat, Theodore. 1999. "The Codex Sinaiticus, the Codex Vaticanus, and Constantine." *Journal of Theological Studies* 50 (2): 583-625.

Smalley, Stephen S. 2015. *1, 2, and 3 John.* Rev. ed. Word Biblical Commentary 51. Grand Rapids: Zondervan Academic.

Souter, Alexander. 1913. *The Text and Canon of the New Testament.* London: Duckworth.

Stanley, Andy P., ed. 2013. *Four Views on the Role of Works at the Final Judgment.* Grand Rapids: Zondervan.

Stendahl, Krister. 1962. "The Apocalypse of John and the Epistles of Paul in the Muratorian Fragment." Pages 239-45 in *Current Issues in New Testament Interpretation, Essays in Honour of Otto Piper.* Edited by W. Klassen and G. F. Snyder. New York: Harper and Brothers.

Stott, John R. W. 2009. *The Letters of John.* 2nd ed. Tyndale New Testament Commentaries 19. Downers Grove, IL: IVP Academic. Reprint of Grand Rapids: Eerdmans, 1988.

Tabbernee, William. 2007. *Fake Prophecy and Polluted Sacraments: Ecclesiastical and Imperial Reactions to Montanism.* Supplements to Vigiliae Christianae. Leiden, NL: Brill.

Thompson, James W. 2008. *Hebrews.* Paideia Commentaries on the New Testament. Grand Rapids: Baker Academic.

Thorsen, Don. 2005. *The Wesleyan Quadrilateral: Scripture, Tradition, Reason and Experience as a Model of Evangelical Theology.* Lexington, KY: Emeth Press.

———. 2018. *The Wesleyan Quadrilateral: An Introduction.* Lexington, KY: Emeth Press.

Treier, Daniel. 2008. *Introducing Theological Interpretation of Scripture: Recovering a Christian Practice.* Grand Rapids: Baker Academic.

Trobisch, David. 1994. *Paul's Letter Collection: Tracing the Origins.* Minneapolis: Augsburg Fortress.

———. 2000. *The First Edition of the New Testament.* Oxford, UK: Oxford University Press.

Vanhoozer, Kevin J., ed. 2005. *Dictionary for Theological Interpretation of the Bible.* Grand Rapids: Baker Academic.

Varughese, Alex, ed. 2005. *Discovering the New Testament: Community and Faith.* Kansas City: Beacon Hill Press of Kansas City.

Wall, Robert W., and Eugene E. Lemcio. 1992. *The New Testament as Canon: A Reader in Canonical Criticism.* Journal for the Study of the New Testament Supplement Series 76. Sheffield, UK: Sheffield Academic Press.

Walls, A. F. 1964. "The Montanist 'Catholic Epistle' and Its New Testament Prototype." *Studia Evangelica* 3 (2): 437-46.

Walters, John R. 1995. *Perfection in New Testament Theology: Ethics and Eschatology in Relational Dynamic.* Mellen Biblical Press Series 25. Lewiston, NY: Mellen Biblical Press.

Walton, John H., Victor H. Matthews, and Mark W. Chavalas. 2000. *The IVP Bible Background Commentary: Old Testament.* Downers Grove, IL: IVP Academic.

Webb, Robert L. 1992. "Catholic Epistles." Pages 569-60 in vol. 2 of *The Anchor Bible Dictionary.* New York: Doubleday.

Wesley, John. 1984. *The Works of John Wesley.* 3rd ed. Edited by Thomas Jackson. 14 vols. London: Wesleyan Methodist Book Room, 1872. Reprint, Peabody, MA: Hendrickson.

———. 2015. *A Plain Account of Christian Perfection.* Edited and annotated by Randy L. Maddox and Paul W. Chilcote. Kansas City: Beacon Hill Press of Kansas City.

Westcott, B. F. 1864. *The Bible in the Church: A Popular Account of the Collection and Reception of the Holy Scriptures in the Christian Churches.* London: Macmillan.

———. 1896. *A General Survey of the History of the Canon of the New Testament.* 7th ed. London: Macmillan.

Williamson, Rick. 2010. *1, 2, and 3 John: A Commentary in the Wesleyan Tradition.* New Beacon Bible Commentary. Kansas City: Beacon Hill Press of Kansas City.

Witherington, Ben, III. 2007. *Letters and Homilies for Jewish Christians: A Socio-Rhetorical Commentary on Hebrews, James and Jude.* Downers Grove, IL: InterVarsity Press.

Wood, Charles M. 1993. *The Formation of Christian Understanding: Theological Hermeneutics.* 2nd ed. Eugene, OR: Wipf and Stock.

Wright, David F. 1976. "Why Were the Montanists Condemned?" *Themelios* 2, no. 1 (September): 15-22.

Wright, N. T. 2012. *How God Became King: The Forgotten Story of the Gospels.* New York: HarperCollins.

Yates, Jonathan P. 2004. "The Reception of the Epistles of James in the Latin West: Did Athanasius Play a Role?" Pages 273-88 in *The Catholic Epistles and the Tradition.* Edited by J. Schlosser. Bibliotheca ephemeridum theologicarum lovaniensium 176. Leuven: Leuven University Press.

Zahn, Theodor. 1888-89. *Geschichte des Neutestamentlichen Kanons.* 3 vols. (vol. 3 was never published). Erlangen, DEU: Andreas Deichert.

www.ingramcontent.com/pod-product-compliance
Lightning Source LLC
Chambersburg PA
CBHW070038100426
42740CB00013B/2724